Immigrating to Canada:
A Realistic Path to Success

For New Canadians, Immigrants,
Business And Government

Terry Sawh

MILL CITY PRESS

Minneapolis

Mill City Press, Inc.
212 3rd Avenue North, Suite 290
Minneapolis, MN 55401
612.455.2294
www.millcitypublishing.com

ISBN - 978-1-936107-14-8
ISBN - 1-936107-14-7
LCCN - 2009937044

Cover Design and Typeset by Kristeen Wegner

Graph statistics courtesy of Statistics Canada
Cover Photo and Portraits by Joe Lavee
Landscape Photos by istockphoto

Printed in the United States of America

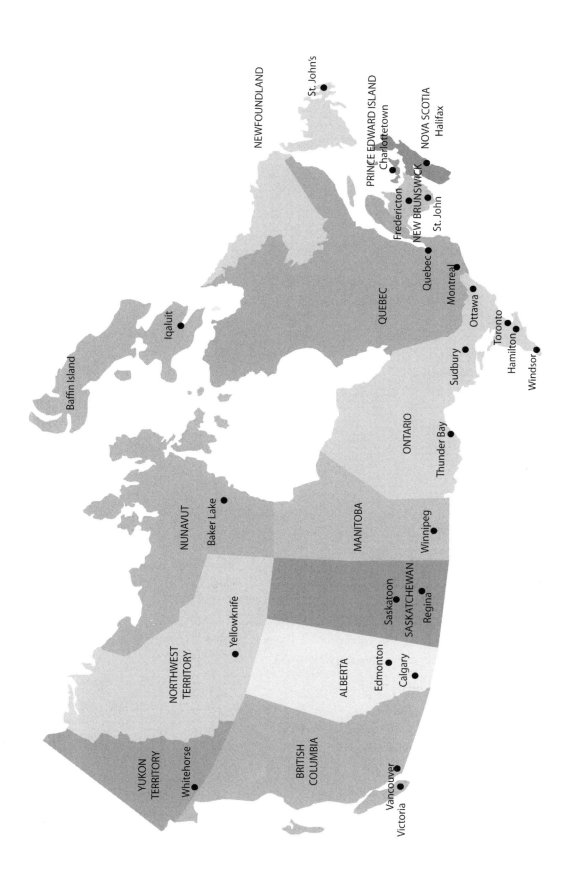

Table of Contents

Chapter Five

Chapter Six

Chapter Seven

Chapter Eight

Chapter Fifteen

Chapter Sixteen

Chapter Seventeen

Chapter Eighteen

Chapter One

An Immigrant's Story

I arrived in Canada on August 1st 1976 with two things: $24 in my pocket (all that I was legally allowed to take when I left my country) and a tremendous amount of enthusiasm and hope for a better future.

During the early years I achieved my first goal by completing my college education. Next, I sought employment, as most graduates do.

The reality of the barriers and challenges faced by new immigrants and visible minorities in particular quickly hit home. It wasn't easy. Eventually my efforts paid off and I landed a full-time job. The struggles that I endured were something I never forgot and prepared me for the future. The lessons that I learned can be passed onto recently arrived immigrants or young minorities who are starting off in their career path.

A few years later I entered the business world with my first company. Subsequently, I used my past experience to establish Topnotch Employment Services Inc. in order to pave the way for others who face the same kind of job search difficulties that I did.

During my 25 years of business experience I have helped thousands of people secure employment in both temporary and full time positions. It gives me a great deal of satisfaction when I look back at how many fellow Canadians that I've been able to assist over the years.

I decided to write this book with the same intention of helping people in their dream of finding a career and starting a new life in Canada and the ever changing challenge of accomplishing that objective.

Much of the material in current books and government documentation is related to the point system, filling out documents and work permits, etc. All of which could be best serviced by your own diligent research and hard work or with the help of a capable immigration advisor. I feel that it is necessary to provide coverage and documentation of all of the major areas necessary to immigrating, working and living in Canada, and that's what I've endeavored to do here.

One major problem from the immigrant's viewpoint is not the documentation but knowing where the jobs are located, where the jobs are not located, where and in what fields future jobs will be found, the growth areas geographically of the country, the resources available to immigrants, the culture and politics in your new community and how to guide themselves to that new community.

My Purpose In Writing This Book

This book is a heartfelt effort written for anyone considering immigrating to Canada and all New Canadians.

Perhaps in your situation, establishing a new life in Canada is just a thought in its earliest stages... or a lifelong, distant dream. Maybe Canada is only one of several potential destinations you're pondering.

Wherever you are on the immigration scale, this book is for you.

You'll find it to be an invaluable guide, loaded with practical, up-to-date information. It's a one-stop source of the most relevant details you need to know about coming to Canada as an immigrant, finding meaningful employment, and establishing roots in this peaceful, thriving and evolving country.

New arrivals in Canada will also discover that this book can be of immense value in adjusting to life here and making it a satisfying and enriching experience overall.

Whether you're just beginning to map out a life-altering move, or you've already landed -- this book can be of great assistance. It can save you years of trial and error learning. You'll discover practical, helpful information you can apply and benefit from right away. And you'll have a much clearer idea of what you can expect in the near future.

It is my sincerest intention to provide important information every prospective and new immigrant to Canada needs to know. While trying to do so, I will:
• Explode widespread myths and replace them with facts
• Demystify, clarify, and simplify your understanding of the processes involved in immigration and...
• Present an objective view of the realities of working and living in Canada

To choose to pack everything you own and relocate in another country is a major life decision. It's not something to be taken lightly. So it's my aim within these pages to provide you with a fair and realistic appraisal of Canada. This way you can base your decisions and actions on accurate information and the experiences of others who've blazed a path to Canada before you.

Now allow me to set the record straight.

Misinformation and half-truths about Canada abound. But misinformation serves no one. Undoubtedly your best protection against such deception is accurate, objective information. That's what this book is all about.

In the following pages I present the facts as I've come to know them from my 30+ years here as a citizen and business executive in the human resources and employment industry.

What you have in your hands is an easy to read, informative guide. I offer practical advice and action steps in a systematic, step-by-step format. Collectively, it's everything you need to know about Canada and the immigration process to succeed with your application in the quickest possible way and to thrive in this great country once you arrive here.

Keep reading and you'll discover:
- 16 popular myths... and the real truths about Canada...
- Various ways you could gain legal entry into Canada...
- Important basic information about Canada, its people and what it has to offer...
- Key details about Canada's regional economies and where today's best opportunities exist...
- How to best prepare for employment opportunities and Canada's workplace environment...
- Specific professions, trades, and industries that are most in need of qualified people to fill vacant positions...
- Valuable resources that are available to help you and your family settle in and adjust to your new life in Canada...
- Various perspectives on immigration (both positive and negative) from those who've actually experienced it...
- Suggestions to help you overcome challenges... suggestions for employers... and suggestions for the government to better serve the needs of immigrants and the country at large...

Why Bother Writing This Book?

An informed immigrant is in a much better position to make key decisions and to take the necessary actions. My goal is to provide high-value, practical, and accurate information to prospective new arrivals.

Unfortunately, many new immigrants are badly misinformed about the realities if Canada. These unfortunate souls have been sold a pipe dream. They've been led blindfolded down an unknown river in an open raft. They've been told that Canada is the land of unlimited opportunity and all you have to do is show up.

What happens next is that invariably these new immigrants struggle to find their way. Some are forced to take menial jobs, far below their level of education and experience. Others choose to leave Canada entirely and return to their homeland, disappointed and disillusioned, taking with them the sour taste of bitter experience.

Clearly nobody wins when this happens.

The immigrant, who has often invested years and several hundred (or thousands) of dollars into the experience, loses it all and may be quick to spread the word about their dismal Canadian experience. Potential employers lose out on capable and qualified labour. And Canada loses not just one contributor, but potentially dozens more who shy after hearing their friend's tale of woe.

Immigration is crucial to sustain Canada's economy and to continue its path of strong growth. The immigrant population already represents a significant portion of Canada's workforce. But this portion can only grow larger over the next 15-20 years as Canada's domestic population ages and retires, while at the same time the birth rate continues to decline.

It's my intention to make each and every immigrant who reads this book to feel welcome in Canada. The more informed you are, the better you're equipped to make the important decisions and take the appropriate actions based on current realities. Improved actions invariably lead to improved results.

Knowing what to expect when you get here makes it much easier to adjust. You won't feel blindsided by any situation having first 'previewed' what life is really like in Canada through the information and perspectives presented in this volume.

Every Available Advantage Is Yours

Reading this book gives you a decided edge over other immigrants. With the information, knowledge, experience, and variety of perspectives presented here, you'll gain the insights and important details you need to create a successful outcome for you and your family.

You'll learn about the processes and what's required of you. You'll find out where today's most abundant opportunities exist. You'll gain an understanding of Canada – its economy, social programs and what it's actually like to live here. And you'll find contact information for hundreds of different government services, agencies, and community support groups who can offer you further assistance.

Leaving one's home country is rarely an easy decision. But if you do decide to leave it's my sincerest desire that this book will serve you well in the weeks, months, and years ahead.

The Importance of Immigration

Canada is facing an upcoming labour shortage: 40% of employers surveyed globally by Monster say that they are having a hard time filling many positions. Alberta faces a shortage of 100,000 workers in the next 10 years. By 2025 Ontario could face a shortfall of 364,000 workers and Quebec could face similar challenges with a shortfall of 292,000 workers.

Much has been written in this book about the importance of immigration to Canada. Immigrants are the key to Canada's continued growth and prosperity. We know what you can do for Canada now what can we do for you. What do you need?
You are our future. You will become Canada. You are valuable and important.

In the next twenty years the face of Canada will be changed by your presence.
You will provide us with new ideas and better ways of looking at life. We have to make it easier for you to enter into our country, find employment and prosper.

You will provide the skills that will propel Canada to world leadership. We have to welcome you and receive your skills and culture into our communities and places of employment. We have to make changes also otherwise your path will be more difficult.

You will develop new domestic and international markets for Canada's goods and services. We have to listen to you in order to service these markets.

You will participate in our democratic process and run for political office and have your influence in the governments of our country.

You will pay taxes and enjoy the high standard of living that Canada is known around the world.

Canada needs you. We should be doing more to help you come to this country.

In a Toronto Daily Star article published on Saturday, October 26th, 2008 titled," Economy will need more immigrants" it was stated that immigration levels in the country will have to go up significantly for future economic growth, the Conference Board of Canada reports.

The report includes measures to allow the growing number of temporary foreign workers with options to become permanent citizens and also suggests increasing refugee intakes to maintain a well-balanced immigration system. The report praises the government's new initiatives including the provincial nominee program, relaxation of work restrictions' for foreign students and the newly created Canadian Experience Class that allows immigrants here temporarily to apply for permanent status with-out leaving the country.

Chapter Two

The Top 16 Myths About Immigrating To Canada

Myth Number One: You need the services of an immigration consultant or lawyer.

The fact is that all required documentation to apply for permanent or temporary residency and employment in Canada is freely and readily available to anyone at any time on the government of Canada website. You can find it here: http://cic.gc.ca

You can download the necessary documents and fill in the required fields on your own. In most cases, the entire process can be handled by the individual applicant. You'll save yourself a lot of money in the process, just as thousands have done. The actual savings in most cases is similar to what you'd save by preparing your own income tax return versus hiring a professional accountant to do it for you. The simpler and more basic the requirements the lower the fee tends to be. The more complicated it gets, the greater the need may be for professional assistance. But you would be well-advised to consider all options before spending any money.

It has been brought to my attention numerous times over the years that some new immigrants to Canada have had bad experiences with some immigrations advisors. To avoid this potential problem it is highly recommended that you seek firms in Canada which are reputable. The way to determine the reputation of a firm is to ask for and check out numerous references of people who have successfully used their services. Any firm that provides quality services will have no problem in providing references and allowing you to search out comments on the firm's performance.

Hiring an immigration lawyer or consultant is totally optional. But, if you are considering this option please bear the following advice in mind and ensure that the lawyer is a member of the law society for their province and that the consultant is registered with CSIC (Canadian Society of Immigration Consultants).

Immigration lawyers in Canada are regulated and licensed by the respective bar associations in each province. This means there's a code of professional conduct that all lawyers are expected to adhere to. Any immigration lawyer could lose the right to practice law if it was determined that fraud or corruption was involved in providing information and services to clients, in or outside of Canada.

Should a problem ever arise in your dealings with the legal profession, there's a system in place for registering a complaint and having it taken seriously. Immigration lawyers and consultants do provide a legitimate and useful service but in our opinion should only be retained if the merits of the particular application warrant it. Should you need the services of an immigration lawyer, hiring one based on sound recommendations makes good sense.

Please remember that no immigration advisor can offer or guarantee you a job in Canada whether they are in your home country or in Canada. You must not pay an advisor to provide you with a job because jobs in Canada are assigned by employers and employees do not pay for being hired. If you are fortunate enough to find a job with a Canadian employer you should validate the position with the company's Human Resource Department before leaving your home country. There have been some examples of foreign skilled workers coming to Canada on temporary work permits with promises of high paying jobs and finding that things are not as promised when they arrive. Also remember that even when you are a temporary worker in Canada your rights are protected.

Myth Number Two: Immigration documentation can be "fast-tracked".

Another reason some prospective immigrants turn to immigration service providers is because of the false impression that an individual has "special contacts" at the Canadian embassy or consulate office in their home country. The perception is that someone with friends in high places can use their powers of influence to improve results (usually faster service) on behalf of the client. But the fact is -- there is no way to obtain preferential treatment with Immigration Canada.

The system is designed to be fair to all applicants. And although it's not without its faults, the system does work. All immigrant applicants are treated in an equal manner by the Government of Canada and there's simply no way any immigration consultant or lawyer can shortcut the process, arrange special treatment, or magically move you to the front of the line. If anyone makes such a claim, I urge you to take your money and run in the opposite direction.

There are several different categories of immigration available and we'll discuss these later in the book. Each has its own timeline, although the range is wide. Under the Federal Skilled Workers program, for example, the time required to finalize Canadian Permanent Resident applications is as indicated:
  • Candidates from the Americas (16 months to 65 months, depending on the specific country of origin)
  • Candidates from Africa and the Middle East (25 months to 68 months)
  • Candidates from Asia and the Pacific Rim (28 to 69 months)
  • Candidates from Europe (22 to 73 months)

Wait times are dependent on the immigration category, your country of origin and its security background, as well as other factors. But no one -- lawyers and consultants included -- can expedite your application to speed up the process. It cannot happen that way, so if anyone suggests to you that your application can be fast-tracked, they're simply not a credible advisor and should be avoided.

Myth Number Three: Most of the available jobs within Canada exist within the 3 major cities of Toronto, Montreal and Vancouver.

This statement would have been more accurate years ago, but it simply doesn't reflect current market conditions. Major changes have taken place and the reality now is that some smaller cities and communities in Ontario, British Columbia, Alberta and Saskatchewan are experiencing more job growth than the major urban centres.

Historically, a large percentage of immigrants were attracted to the big cities. The three biggest cities in Canada attracted the vast majority of immigrants who were drawn to the same areas where family and their native communities had already established roots. Each urban centre experienced economic and multicultural growth, with Montreal the overwhelming choice of those with a French language background or preference.

While these larger cities continue to attract immigrants for family, cultural and community reasons, their dominance as economic drivers has dwindled. As the flow of immigrants to the major cities continues, competition increases, resulting in fewer available jobs and a slower economic growth rate.

Today, it's the smaller cities and towns that are experiencing higher growth rates than the major urban areas. What this means to prospective immigrants is this: there are now greater employment opportunities outside of the traditional areas of Toronto, Montreal and Vancouver. Look towards the west and you'll find the most plentiful job opportunities. Cities like Calgary and Edmonton are growing, as are other smaller cities in Alberta, British Columbia and Ontario. If you widen your search and are flexible in choosing a location in which to settle, you increase your employment opportunities considerably.

Myth Number Four: You should wait until you arrive to find a job.

Technology changes everything. Do not wait until you get to Canada to start your job search. Now all it takes is a computer and internet connection and the world is at the virtual fingertips of anyone, anywhere, at any time. Today's prospective immigrant has almost the same capability and advantages in researching job possibilities in Canada, as the people who live here. Your search for employment should actually begin well in advance of your anticipated arrival. You can use Canadian Search engines such as: Yahoo:Canada. You can begin a preliminary job search at sites like http://Workopolis.com and http://Monster.ca. Those are two of the more popular directories, among several others that you can access around the clock, from any location in the world.

Employment agencies are another valuable resource of information on jobs in specific geographic locations and in various industries and areas of specialization. Begin to develop a relationship with an agency in your chosen area and you'll have a clear advantage over those who arrive and then must begin their job search from a standing start.

Preparation is one of the keys to success in finding employment in your new country. Those who begin planting the seeds of their job search well in advance of their arrival, place themselves in the best possible position to reap the rewards.

Language is another important factor. To maximize your opportunities, you must be able to communicate clearly and effectively. Any language training you can take to improve your speaking, reading, writing, and listening skills beforehand will serve you well from the moment you arrive. Language is a core skill and a necessary requirement to land a job or to gain a promotion.

Research indicates that the first five years are the toughest on new immigrants and their families. Getting settled in a new country is a major life change that brings with it various unique challenges. But the more prepared you are, the less those challenges become major issues. If you do your job search work in advance… if you are at least aware of the available employment opportunities… and if you elevate your language skills, you and your family will have a much more positive experience when you come to Canada.

If any-one tells you that job offers will only come to you after your arrival in Canada they are incorrect in that you can start networking and researching long before you leave your home country. One of the key pieces of information in the book is advance preparation and anything that gives you a headstart will benefit you once you land in Canada.

Myth Number Five: Canada is relatively similar in economic growth patterns.

Canada is a vast country with many different pockets of populated areas scattered across a mass of largely undeveloped land. Its economy is diversified and the major eastern cities of Southern Ontario are now experiencing slower growth rates, while smaller cities in Alberta are expanding rapidly.

Ontario has long been a major driving force in the Canadian economy, but its manufacturing base in the South has stalled somewhat, leading to job losses in recent years. But southern Ontario remains a magnet for immigration, which in turn creates a competitive market for any available jobs. At the same time, the entire region is experiencing problems in creating new jobs.

Currently, the best prospects for employment exist in Western Canada although things have slowed down with the recent world economic problems. It should also be realized that our biggest trading partner is the U.S. and any slowing down of the American economy has a significant impact on Canada. The growth rates in Western Canada will rise and fall with the world economic needs for oil, natural gas and fertilizer. Edmonton and Calgary are experiencing good growth levels, as are many smaller cities throughout Canada including the East coast provinces. This kind of rapid growth creates employment opportunities. But at the same time, housing and other costs in these hot markets are rapidly increasing as well. So the growing Western economy is also a candidate for higher inflation. Saskatchewan, another Western province, is also experiencing a strong economy and growth. Of course, Quebec, is the main destination of immigrants with French language skills and immigrants from the colonial empire of France.

Myth Number Six: It is easier to find work and housing in an area where there is a base of immigrants from your home country -- and family members in particular.

Again, this may have been true in the past, but it's no longer the case. Many industrious immigrants settled in places like Toronto with a desire to find meaningful work. Many did find happiness here while contributing to the growth of Toronto into one of the most ethnically diverse cities in the world.

Many unique communities have emerged. Having family members nearby who are already established and a community that makes you feel at home is comforting. But it might not be the right move for you financially.

In an expanding economy, it's much easier to find employment. But if you choose to settle in an area based on comfort and familiarity alone, you'll find lots of people competing for the same jobs. And those jobs in slow-moving economic areas are fewer in number to begin with. That's not to say there are no available jobs there. It's just that those positions are not as plentiful as they once were. So choosing to locate in traditional areas may cause you unnecessary economic hardship and stress. It's challenging enough to uproot your family to completely change your environment and way of life to start anew in Canada. Don't add to the burden by assuming conditions are the same in the big cities as they always were. Toronto, Montreal and Vancouver already have a higher concentration of people and they continue to attract even more people. For some, staying with relatives or friends within a familiar community provides suitable short term housing. But a longer term housing solution is more challenging when employment opportunities in general are in shorter supply. Family and friends can provide short term support, but it's unlikely that they can offer employment or shelter in the long run.

Myth Number Seven: The country of Canada is multicultural across all provinces and cities.

Canada is in fact one of the most multicultural nations in the world, but the degree of multiculturalism is not uniform across the country. The level of multiculturalism present in any particular area is based on that region's ability to attract people of diverse nationalities. It's the 3 major cities that have traditionally drawn the majority of immigrants, but each city has attracted its own unique mosaic of people from various other countries. Atlantic Canada (New Brunswick, Nova Scotia, Prince Edward Island and Newfoundland/Labrador) has not typically attracted as diverse a group as Ontario because there have traditionally been fewer job opportunities in this region. Earlier immigrants laid the foundation for communities where jobs existed and those communities continue to flourish.

Most immigrants to Quebec settle in the two largest cities: Montreal and Quebec City. Principally, this area attracts immigrants who can speak French and easily fit into the French culture, such as those from former French colonies.

Toronto and the surrounding area known as the GTA (Greater Toronto Area) continue to attract a diverse group of immigrants of various cultures and language. This is due in large measure to the immigrant communities that have already established themselves there. Although it's often viewed as good thing for the newly arrived immigrant, it presents housing and employment challenges.

      Northern Ontario hasn't attracted the numbers or the diversity of immigrants that Southern Ontario has. This is due primarily to its smaller population, resource-based economy and fewer job prospects for anyone relocating there.

      The Southern Alberta cities of Edmonton and Calgary are enjoying a strong and growing economy. But they lack the multicultural base of Toronto or Vancouver. Numerous agencies exist in many communities across the nation to help new immigrants integrate and adjust to life in Canada. But not all areas have the same degree of new Canadians among its populations. Those numbers vary considerably. Western Canada in general lacks the diversity of Toronto, Montreal and Vancouver, though it was initially populated primarily by European immigrants in the early 1900's.

Myth Number Eight: You don't need any language training at home before coming to Canada.

The truth is that language is a major key to your ability to work in Canada. You've got to be able to communicate in order to find a job. If you cannot speak the language effectively, you severely limit your employment and advancement opportunities. Advancement opportunity is an extremely important issue because language and communication skills stick with you for your whole life and form the basis of your career path. But that's not all there is to language skills. Not being able to understand the language prevents you from fully experiencing and enjoying all that Canada has to offer. When you're comfortable about your ability to speak English, you increase your options in terms of location. Few areas would be off-limits with a solid grasp of the English language. English is the international language of commerce so it greatly expands your options not only in Canada but around the world

      If you prefer to learn Canada's other official language, French, you would probably want to locate in Quebec – or perhaps parts of Northern Ontario or New Brunswick, where there are considerable numbers of French speaking inhabitants.

      Being able to speak both English and French gives you an added advantage of admissibility, as well as employment opportunities within the government or customer service areas over time. But if you choose to not learn either language before coming to Canada, you'll have a difficult time integrating.

      The less comfortable you are in speaking English (or French) the more likely it is that you'll want to locate within your particular ethnic community. It would likely be a comfortable environment – one that feels more like home to you – but it may not offer suitable employment opportunities for you.

      Any language training you can take prior to your arrival in Canada will significantly improve your prospects in your new country and accelerate you adaptability and advancement throughout your career. It is also important to note that many young people who come to Canada as students or visitors have advanced English or French language skills because of the excellent educational institutions in Europe and Asia and the Middle East for teaching the English language.

      In some ways these educational institutions are doing a better job than North American educational institutions in teaching correct English conversation and grammar.

A fairly high degree of English proficiency is required to simply complete the various forms required of new immigrants. You'll find it equally difficult to read the material from various web sites (including official Government of Canada sites) books and general information about Canada if you don't understand English at a fairly high level.

Another valid reason to learn the language is to be able to distinguish between fact and fabrication. When you can read, write and speak English, you're far less vulnerable to those who knowingly misinform, in order to take money from you. Education equals preparation. And there's no more fundamental education to prepare you for life in your new country than to learn the native language. This one skill will do more to enhance your experience and improve your chances of success than any other. You will also find that your future ability to be promoted will depend on your language and communication skills.

Myth Number Nine: The "Points System" for skilled worker applicants is an effective way to fill open positions in Canada.

Currently there are six factors in the assessment of skilled workers: education, language, experience, age, arranged employment, and spouse and family. But how these answers relate to actual job shortages within Canada is somewhat questionable, considering that the federal government routinely issues a "Jobs Under Pressure" list. If the qualifications for skilled workers were more reflective of current job shortages, the system would likely be of greater benefit to all – the country, the employer, and the prospective immigrant.

The points system has been around for long time. But there are several considerations with the points system. "Points system" problems include:

1. Qualifying doesn't necessarily mean there are any jobs for you in your chosen field. Candidates can score well on the qualifying questions and receive a passing grade as a skilled worker. But they could find that few jobs are available in their area of expertise.

2. Occupation lists created by the federal government may not be available on a region to region basis. So you could qualify for admission and your skills may be in high demand somewhere in Canada, but perhaps not in the area in which you want to settle.

3. The system may not reflect all of the current needs of the marketplace. There's a shortage of general labour in many areas of Canada. But the system that's in place doesn't recognize general labour as a suitable category of skilled or unskilled labour in which to apply for work in Canada. Even though there is a demand for immigrants who want to work general labour jobs, they wouldn't qualify under the points system. Some immigrants with higher education and skills end up working general labour jobs because they can't find work in their specific field.

The skilled worker application process has been revised recently in that you make a brief application to hold your place in line and then, it could be several years, you are asked for more documentation to complete the application process.

Myth Number Ten: Canada is an expensive country in which to live.

Fact is, in comparison to the other G7 countries (United States, Britain, France, Germany, Italy and Japan) Canada is one of the least expensive places to live among these leading nations. But everything is relative. In relation to your native country, Canada could very well seem expensive by comparison.

Costs vary across the land. Rents and mortgages could easily average $1000 to $2000 per month, if you plan to live in the large urban centres of British Columbia, Alberta, or Ontario. But the further you move away from these more heavily-populated areas, the costs of shelter decreases accordingly. Living outside of the costlier cities and commuting back and forth might seem appealing at first, but any cost savings can quickly be absorbed by additional travel expenses.

Food costs in Canada are among the lowest in the industrialized world. Taxes are lower than in some of the Scandinavian countries, but higher than in the United States. However, universal health care system can make those higher taxes less of an issue for most Canadians.

Those areas of Canada that are now experiencing a growing economy are also experiencing spiraling housing costs too. It's these dramatic increases that can be quite shocking to the uninitiated. Immigrants are best advised to investigate the cost of living in their chosen region before arriving in Canada.

Recently fuel costs have risen substantially in response to the growing price of oil on world markets, however, those rising prices have dropped dramatically in the last month due to the economic slowdown. Canadians are still only paying about half the price for gasoline as people in the UK are paying.

Myth Number Eleven: Canada's health care system is plagued with problems, doesn't adequately serve Canadians, and the country regularly loses its best doctors to the United States.

In reality there are many more positives than negatives when it comes to assessing Canada's health care system. While the system isn't perfect, it is one of the best health care systems in the world.

Canada's universal health care provides one level of care to all Canadians. It's not based on your ability to pay, or the length of time that you've paid taxes in Canada. There are no user fees required in order to receive professional care. It's accessible to every Canadian citizen and most new arrivals right away or with-in a short waiting period. In some provinces however, you will need private health insurance for your first three months in Canada in order to then qualify for universal health care.

The system is not flawless however. Balancing costs, service and accessibility is a constant challenge for Canadian health care. Some of the smaller communities are having trouble attracting doctors. Emergency room wait periods could be up to six hours, or more. Non-emergency surgeries could take several months. Patients with the most immediate needs get the most immediate care, while the rest simply have to wait their turn. This seems like a reasonable approach that most Canadians accept, and does not neglect someone in serious need of urgent attention. It would be so easy to give health on the basis of ability to pay but this would violate one of Canada's guiding principles which is the universality of health care which in itself will present challenges.

Doctors are free to practice wherever they want in Canada. No one is forced to work in a community that they don't want to, simply because there's a need. Canadian-trained doctors and nurses can freely relocate to the United States, even when their education and training has been subsidized by Canadian taxpayers. In the United States, health care is a profit-driven industry.

Myth Number Twelve: Canada is a country of very high taxes.

When you look at the actual numbers, it does appear that taxes in Canada are high, in comparison to the United States, for example. But when you look at the bigger picture, it becomes a question of overall value and quality of life.

Canada has many social programs and with programs such as universal health care and quality education for all, come high taxes in order to foot those bills. There are various levels of taxes that each level of government collects. Both the federal government and provincial governments (with the exception of Alberta) also collect a tax on the purchase of most goods and services. Additionally, there are "sin" taxes on such luxuries as gasoline, alcohol and tobacco products.

While the United States does have a lower tax rate than Canada, life in the U.S. tends to favour those who have money over those who don't.

The United Nations rated Canada as one of the best places to live in the world. So while taxes seem high, they also contribute to a standard of living that is among the best of any nation on the planet.

Myth Number Thirteen: The goal of Canadian immigration is to bring people with money into Canada to stimulate the Canadian economy.

A high level of education and a minimum cash reserve are two crucial components of the qualifying process. Yet neither improves one's chances of landing a job within their field in Canada. It only helps you overcome the first hurdle of qualification. It's easy to see how those immigrants who find themselves doing work of a lesser value, where they're not applying specific skills they trained for, feel somewhat jaded. It's easy to see how an immigrant in this situation could view the process of immigrating to Canada as nothing more than cash grab by the government, or a terribly misleading lie that eventually drives them back to their native land.

The simple truth is that Canada's population is aging. The need for people in various categories and industries outpaces the country's ability to fill those positions from with-in. At the same time, we face increasing competition for talent from other countries eager to woo skilled workers.

Canada needs a steady supply of immigrants to continue to grow economically and sustain its standard of living and leading-edge position as one of the best countries in which to live. But we need to take a good hard look at the process to make it more efficient, effective and user-friendly.

Myth Number Fourteen: Canada has no culture.

Canadian culture does exist -- it's just difficult to define due to our rich and vibrant diversity. Canada's culture is a combination of the cultures of its two founding nations, Britain and France, its First Nation Aboriginals plus the various cultures of immigrants to this country over the past 100 years or so.

What makes Canada unique is that it does not try to assimilate the cultures of immigrants into a giant melting pot of uniformity. Instead multiculturalism is encouraged as a way to incorporate the richness of diversity and understanding into our society.

Immigrants feel comfortable knowing that they can practice their own culture and engage in their own traditions while at the same time, enjoy the attributes of living as Canadians. Many immigrants enjoy this aspect of the Canadian experience and share their stories and experience with family and friends back home in their native countries. Is it not a defining goal of a free and democratic society to join in your new country's nationalism while at the same time maintaining a strong link to your traditional culture?

Myth Number Fifteen: The weather conditions in Canada are difficult.

Canada has four distinct seasons. Many Canadians enjoy each season for all it has to offer and appreciate the renewal that seasonal changes bring about.

Spring in Canada begins in late March and lasts until mid-June. Temperatures vary throughout this transitional season with near freezing weather in April to summer temperatures by June. The average spring time temperature in Canada is 12 degrees C and spring weather usually includes more rain than at any other time of year.

The Canadian summer officially begins June 21st of each calendar year and lasts through September 21st. Warm temperatures have usually set in well in advance of the start of summer. Temperatures extend into the mid 30's C through July and August and are similar to the temperatures found in more southern climates. Temperatures on the East and West coasts tend to be more moderate and receive more rain then the interior of Canada.

Autumn (Fall) begins in September and lasts through mid-December. Some Canadians prefer this season to the others with its cooling temperatures (October through November) and the changing colours of the leaves. This season can be rainy at times, with some parts of the country receiving early winter snow. With December comes the Christmas season , although some cultures don't celebrate it.

The official Canadian winter is the three month period from January through March. It can be bitterly cold for weeks at a time with lots of snow. Some winters are milder, while others more extreme. This is the one season that could be most uncomfortable for immigrants coming from warmer climates.

Canadian winters do take some getting used to. Adequate preparation before venturing out is important. Canadians dress for winter and that includes boots, proper gloves, long coats, hats and scarves. The six most important pieces of clothing in a Canadian winter are insulated, waterproof boots for walking on snow or ice, thick socks to keep your feet warm and dry, a hat or toque to keep your head and ears warm, while containing your body heat, insulated gloves to keep your hands warm, a heavy overcoat that could be waterproof and a scarf to cover your neck and face in case of a cold wind. If you dress for it, you can take on any Canadian winter.

Be prepared and you'll be just fine. Protect yourself from the winter weather. Sometimes older people or people in poor physical condition take it upon themselves to shovel their sidewalks and driveways. Be warned that this is exhausting and you should find some help when this happens so that you do not exert yourself. Snow is light when falling but can be very heavy on the ground. Some Canadians have had back problems or heart attacks from over exerting themselves shoveling snow.

Throughout the winter months, most people spend more time indoors at home, shopping malls, movie theatres, restaurants, and sporting events. Some actively participate in outdoor winter sports like skiing, skating, or snowmobiling.

Many Canadians prepare their vehicles for winter driving with snow tires, tune-ups, booster cables, gas line anti-freeze, additional wiper blades, lock de-icer, bags of salt, flares, and blankets – just to be prepared should any problem arise on the roads. Make sure that your car is properly winterized with anti-freeze and a strong car battery.

When you know what to expect and you take the necessary precautions, anyone can learn to adjust to winter. Some Canadians enjoy the winter months by participating in downhill skiing and cross country skiing, snowboarding, hockey and skating, snowmobiling and ice fishing. Allow yourself to experience the natural beauty of the season and you might even come to enjoy it.

Myth Number Sixteen: Canada is a racist country.

It's hard to believe that anyone could accuse Canada of being a racist nation, with its immigrant origins, history of multiculturalism, the diverse background of its citizens, and Canada's Charter of Rights.

Even though Canada has all the elements of democracy and fair play in place, examples of racism could surface now and then – as it could anywhere. The vast majority of Canadians understand and appreciate what this country is all about and are open and welcoming to people of all nationalities and cultures. But this openness is not often outwardly displayed. Canadians tend to be somewhat reserved. So don't make the mistake of perceiving this tendency as a lack of acceptance, or as a bias against any particular race or nationality.

Racism could however exist at an individual level. Everyone should receive equal treatment and people of all nationalities should be given equal opportunity when searching for housing and employment. Unfortunately, that's not always the case. But to claim that Canada is a racist country is completely inaccurate.

Chapter Summary

Myth: You need the services of an immigration consultant or lawyer.
Fact: If you understand the language, you can complete the immigration application process entirely on your own.

Myth: Immigration documentation can be "fast-tracked".
Fact: No one can expedite the immigration process for you. There are several approaches, but no short-cuts through Immigration Canada.

Myth: Most of the available jobs within Canada exist within the 3 major cities of Toronto, Montreal and Vancouver.
Fact: More jobs exist today in other regions of the country such as Alberta and Saskatchewan and the smaller cities of Ontario, British Columbia and the Maritime Provinces.

Myth: You should wait until you arrive to find a job.
Fact: The best results are usually obtained through preparation and action well in advance of your arrival in Canada.

Myth: Canada is relatively similar in economic growth patterns.
Fact: Geographically, Canada is a large country. But each region's economy is unique and is affected by different circumstances.

Myth: It is easier to find work and housing in an area where there is a base of immigrants from your home country -- and family members in particular.
Fact: Temporary housing might be easier to find with family and friends. But to increase your chances of employment, you're better off to locate where jobs in your field are plentiful.

Myth: The country of Canada is multicultural across all provinces and cities.
Fact: The most multicultural cities for English speaking New Canadians are Toronto and Vancouver and Montreal for French speaking New Canadians. They have long been destinations of choice for new immigrants arriving in Canada. But smaller communities could be less multicultural in nature.

Myth: You don't need any language training at home before coming to Canada.
Fact: Language is the number one skill you need to successfully settle in Canada. The better your skills before you land, the more natural and comfortable will be your experience.

Myth: The "points system" for skilled worker applicants is an effective way to fill open positions in Canada.
Fact: It is the oldest and most established route into Canada but other methods such as the Temporary Workers Program, Provincial Nomination or Canadian Experience Class could be looked at.

Myth: Canada is an expensive country in which to live.
Fact: It's really a matter of perspective and location. Housing costs more in the big cities than in does elsewhere. Fuel costs are roughly half what they are in the U.K. Food prices are generally quite affordable.

Myth: Canada's health care system is plagued with problems, doesn't adequately serve Canadians, and the country regularly loses its best doctors to the United States.
Fact: The universal health care offered in Canada makes quality health care accessible to all, regardless of income or origin.

Myth: Canada is a country of very high taxes.
Fact: Taxes are high, though not as high as some other industrialized nations of the world. But those taxes support our universal health care and quality education system.

Myth: The goal of Canadian immigration is to bring people with money into Canada to stimulate the Canadian economy.
Fact: It's easy to make such a conclusion when one applies through the points system, is accepted into Canada and then can't find a job for which they are trained. Thankfully, better options do exist, and I'll share those details throughout this book.

Myth: Canada has no culture.
Fact: Canada does have a culture, but it's one that's not easily defined. Essentially, it's a culture of diversity where we come together as one nation and yet are free to maintain the cultural traditions of our individual heritage.

Myth: The weather conditions in Canada are terrible.
Fact: Canada is a land of changing seasons. Temperatures and conditions vary considerably throughout each year. Winter can be cold and summer hot. Spring and fall are transitional seasons between these two extremes. Let us be honest in that the Canadian winter takes some getting used to and can be a challenge for many New Canadians. Dress properly for the winter and it is easier to endure.

Myth number sixteen: Canada is a racist country.
Fact: Canada is in essence, a collection of diverse people and cultures. Some racism can occur on an individual basis, but Canada could not in any way be considered a racist nation.

Why is Canada a Good Place to Live and Work
Canada has plenty to offer any immigrant who chooses to settle here.

It is a country where freedom and the rights of the individual are a priority. Canada is ranked number one in providing equal opportunity and is among the safest places in the world to live and work. Canadians enjoy the best the world has to offer and the lowest cost of living among the Group of Seven (G7) countries. Canada truly is a wonderful place to call home.

Geographically, Canada is a vast land of wide open spaces, breathtaking natural beauty, and an abundance of precious, natural resources. Canada has large energy and mineral resources along with hydro-electric systems and a plentiful supply of fresh water.

As a member of the G7 nations, Canada is a world leader. Politically, Canada is a democracy that is both politically and economically stable.

In the area of education, Canada spends more dollars as a percentage of GDP (Gross Domestic Product) on education than any other country in the world. And most of our provinces boast high rates of post secondary school enrolment.

Canada is multicultural in nature. It is one of the most ethnically diverse and multilingual societies in the world today. In the city of Toronto alone, more than 100 languages are spoken on a daily basis.

People ask, "What is the Canadian identity or... "What is Canadian culture?" The answer is that Canada's identity and culture are tied to many things.

Our identity and culture is tied to the size and magnificence of the country, its oceans, lakes, forests and mountains. Canada is a country of enormous natural resources which should help ensure and protect its future. Canada's original identity was connected to its two founding nations: English and French and its First Nation people - the Aboriginals. As Canada evolved, it became a nation of immigrants from all over the world. Today, Canada is a multicultural giant that allows and encourages different cultures to grow and recognizes the value of diversity.

Perhaps it's this freedom and flexibility that allow many cultures to grow, while at the same time cherishing our national identity that makes Canada a great country.

There are many perks to living here and one that Canadians value highly is the universal health care system. The Canadian people recognize the need to take care of one another through this program and other social benefit programs like the Canada Pension Plan, Employment Insurance, and Worker's Compensation. The Canadian Charter of Rights ensures the rights and freedoms of all. And there is legislation in place to protect workers that includes the right to a safe working environment. Each province has a Human Rights Code which legislates against discrimination on the basis of race, religion, sex, age and cultural association.

In spite of Canada's many attributes, there are several challenges facing new immigrants. One is that Canada seems to fall short in meeting the expectations of many of the immigrants coming to this country.

Some of these expectations can be tempered by more research on the part of the immigrant before he or she departs their native country. It's important to conduct your own due diligence and separate fact from fiction. Don't take someone else's word for it. It's your future – and the future of your family – that's on the line. Do your own research and you'll know what to expect.

New and prospective immigrants are also advised to adopt a more realistic approach to the true employment opportunities in Canada, as suggested throughout this book.

Most of the other expectations of new arrivals can only be improved through a change to immigration policy. Change will happen... it has to. But changes of this nature take time to develop. This type of change is evolutionary in nature and often the result of long, drawn out discussions by policy makers. The point is, don't wait for it to happen, or you may be waiting for a long time. Take what you've learned from this book and put these ideas into action. That's the best way to produce a successful outcome.

Immigrants to Canada today have a wider range of options available to them than did the immigrants of 20 or 30 years ago. Do your research and then make your decisions based on accurate information and not hearsay.

Chapter Three
Personal Stories of New Canadians
Impressions on Canada- Reflections and Interviews

In order to objectively express and present a realistic picture of immigration to Canada, I chose to provide real life experiences direct from those who've walked the path. The following summaries represent the personal stories of both established immigrants and recent arrivals.

Ahmed Dendar

Ahmed Dendar arrived in Canada as an immigrant in January, 1977. When he couldn't find a job in his chosen profession as a textile technologist, he took a job selling vacuum cleaners and film. This lasted for a few months, as Ahmed continued to look for a job that suited his qualifications.

Most companies asked for Canadian experience, of which Ahmed had none. It's a common problem many new immigrants encounter. It's a lot like finding your first job right out of school. Most people don't have much work experience at that point, yet it's the very thing employers covet most. But how can you get the necessary experience when you don't have it and no one wants to give it to you?

Through persistence Ahmed found a job through Manpower (an employment agency) as a carpet dyer and eventually worked his way up to Plant Superintendent after 10 years on the job. Seeking further growth, Ahmed left that company to work at another carpet mill firm as Plant Superintendent. After another 10 years of service, Ahmed was promoted to the position of VP of Manufacturing. Eventually, he purchased the company with two other partners in 1997.

When Ahmed arrived in Canada, he saw all of the opportunity and none of the negatives about the country, even though his first 3 to 6 months was tough. For today's immigrant, Ahmed strongly recommends learning the English language(or French for Quebec) prior to arriving in Canada because it will affect your entire experience here from settling in to your initial employment and your ability to advance and make more money in the future.

Once you arrive and find work in Canada, there are hundreds of different courses offered to upgrade your general and language skills. When he was in a position to do so, Ahmed helped others who had weak language skills because he believed in their talent and dedication. But even he concedes that not many of today's employers would likely take that chance. Ahmed Dendar credits his success to working hard to achieve his goals and being honest in everything that he does.

Vekaria Bharatkumar

Vekaria Bharatkumar came from Amreli, Gujarat India. He has a Masters in Science in Agroforestry and held positions in India as an Agronomist and did research in soil and water management.

Vekaria's thoughts about Canada before he came were that Canada was a good country to emigrate to and had a multicultural society and a low crime rate. He believed that Canada had a good infrastructure for work, health care, public transportation and education. Although he was concerned about the cold winters, he believed that he could overcome the challenge. Vekaria believed that he had worked hard back home in his chosen profession and that with his determination and hard work that he would succeed in Canada.

Upon his arrival in Canada in May of 2008, Vekaria found the temperature to be very comfortable because back home it would have been up to 40 degrees C. (Canada has mostly pleasant Spring, Summer and a Fall season, with the hottest temperatures seldom surpassing 30 degrees C.)

Vekaria was very impressed with the disciplined drivers in Canada and the fact that drivers obeyed stop signs and lights. (Pedestrians are given the right of way at crosswalks and intersections, though you need to look both ways and be cautious.) Shopping, Vekaria soon discovered, was an easy task in that all goods and services are available at large malls.

Vekaria came to Canada by himself for a short period of time and settled briefly with a friend. He was able to find an apartment and a temporary job within a month of his arrival but he understands that to find a job in his chosen profession will require some additional study in Canada in that field and he is prepared to take more courses.

In addition to helping with housing, his good friend also introduced him to the general area for shopping and services, provided information about Canada's education system as well as helping enroll his child in school. This assistance also made obtaining a Social Insurance Number and opening a bank account quick and easy. He was also introduced to an employment agency where he could find temporary employment.

Based on his experience in Canada, Vekaria offers the following recommendations to new immigrants or people contemplating coming to Canada are:
- Be prepared to accept a job at first even though it may not be in your chosen profession and consider that it is temporary and learn from your experience
- Take night school courses in your chosen profession if it will help market yours skills and experience in Canada

• Improve your English language skills because they will help you learn and understand business and work situations and improve your chances of promotion in the future
• Face any challenges calmly and confidently

Lastly, Vekaria Bharatkumar suggests that others make use of the advantages and benefits available through government-funded offices and agencies. These agencies and people are there to serve and help you and can be of tremendous assistance in your new country.

Jyotsna (Jo) Dhadwal

Jyotsna (Jo) Dhadwal credits her employment success in Canada to her academic achievements in her home country and the introductory Canadian workplace training she completed upon her arrival.

Born in India, Jo received both her Bachelor of Science in Botany and Masters in Business Administration degrees there. Her family encouraged her towards higher education, which in turn helped Jo acquire considerable English language skills. India, as a former British colony, developed its educational programs from the British system, which places a high emphasis on English language, grammatical structure and literature. So a solid foundation was already in place long before Canada as a destination was even on the horizon.

Jo met her husband in India while he was in the process of applying as an immigrant to Canada. She followed him soon after his arrival. Her husband wanted to come to Canada because he saw it as a land of opportunity. But Jo's arrival in Canada was met with culture shock. She was also amazed at the complex of highway transportation systems such as multiple-lane roadways, traffic lights and the "disciplined" approach of Canadian traffic.

Despite Jo Dhadwal's qualifications, seeking employment in Canada came with its share of frustrations. "You speak English well" was an often heard comment. But the stereotypical "You don't look Indian" was not uncommon either. It appeared as though some potential employers had preconceived expectations based on her profile.

But persistence paid off and Jo landed the position of Human Resource Associate with the Toronto and Region Conservation Authority, a position she holds today. Jo recognizes the positive and supportive approach that the Conservation Authority has taken towards diversity and feels that this approach has helped her and others develop personally towards their goals.

Jo Dhadwal recommends that newcomers to Canada enroll in a course like the one offered by COSTI, or other agencies serving immigrants. That particular course is about 4 weeks long and helps new Canadians gain a clearer understanding of Canadian business and corporate culture. Some of the specific details addressed include:
• **Resume review and assessment:** In India, some resumes do not have cover letters, so one needs to be developed. In India, resumes are expected to cover previous jobs in detail. This itemization allows all details to be assessed by prospective employers.
But in Canada, the job experience section of a resume contains only a brief summary, while specific skills related to the job applied for are highlighted.

• **Recast your resume for the Canadian job market:** Focus on what you can do for the company, not just what you've done in the past. Canadian resumes need to be precise in nature, so a resume written for another country's business market may have to be re-shaped.

Often immigrants are advised in their home country to leave items such as educational achievements off their resumes, fearing that it could make them look overqualified for the job. But Jo Dhadwal's advice is to never omit important details from a resume because it could be that specific detail that may in fact get you the job, rather than disqualify you for it.

• **Cold calls and interview skills training:** Interview skills are an important part of the job search process in Canada. New Canadians need to be aware of this. It may be common in your native country to not look people directly in the eye during communication. But Canadian interviewers expect some eye-to-eye contact.

• **How new Canadians can market themselves to gain entry into the Canadian corporate culture:** Once you're successful in landing a job, it is particularly helpful when you get support and encouragement from the organization and management. According to Jo Dhadwal, more Canadian companies could benefit from programs on diversity. It is not only the formal programs which help new Canadians, but also the feeling that you are part of a team and that you have new ideas and valuable input. It's about making the most of an organization's human resources. The hiring of diversified candidates is a two way street, with both the candidate and the organization (management and staff) working towards an optimized outcome.

Jo also feels that immigrants, new Canadians and all Canadians along with government, institutions, and business should form a bond – a bond designed to help each other develop and maximize our full potential. In the end, it would create a better Canada for all. If each person were to make this commitment, the challenges would melt away. Immigrants would feel welcome in their new land, and businesses and the country as a whole would benefit because of the greater contributions of an optimized workforce.

Marcela Herrada

Marcela Herrada came to Canada from Lima Peru in 1991 with her mother Maria and her sister. Marcella's father emigrated to Canada first because he thought that there would be better opportunities here for him and his family. He then sponsored his wife and two daughters. Mother and daughters had no knowledge of the English language and Maria enrolled in a LINC program and the daughters were enrolled in the public school system. The challenges were hard for the mother and daughters learning the English language. Children at school would tease Marcela about her language skills and accent.

Maria took a job in a laundry and dry cleaners in order to help with the family bills. The job was at minimum wage levels. By the year 2000 Maria was working as a machine operator and earning a better salary but she was laid off from work after 5 years. Marcella has recently graduated from school with a diploma in International

Transportation and Customs but has not been able to find employment in that field. Marcella's English skills are now excellent so she has taken a job as a receptionist.

The family believes that life is becoming harder for them in Canada. Costs for the basics of transportation, shelter, taxes and food have gone up more that their earnings. The lack of funds causes stress upon each member of the family. In spite of these difficulties the family believes that Canada is a wonderful country to live in. The country has a universal health care system and good social benefits. Children are offered an excellent education for free up to grade 12 and university costs are reasonable related to other countries in the world. The family's main problem lies with getting jobs which pay enough to cover the rising costs of shelter, food and transportation.

The family's recommendation to immigrants thinking of coming to Canada is to master the English language first. The importance of having gainful employment waiting for you or at least having a skill set that is immediately in demand also makes life better for the immigrant.

Brian Gouveia

Brian Gouveia was born in Georgetown, Guyana. He came to Canada in 1970 when he was 13 years old. Brian's parents came to Canada to experience better opportunities and used their business knowledge to start up a café in Canada. Brian's English language skills and education made it an easier transition into the Canadian education system and Brian went on to perform jobs in the credit industry and as a manager of information systems.

When Brian's parents arrived in Canada in the 70's they had to rely on friends and families for support because there was not a large infrastructure of government agencies to help immigrants as there is to-day. Brian's recommendations involve using the resources that are provided by the government agencies. Brian wants to alert immigrants that life in Canada can be challenging particularly at the beginning and that hard work is the only route to success. Brian also says that an immigrant may have to take a job that is not necessarily with-in his skill group in order to earn a living and support his family and gain some experience and contacts. Brian also advises that individuals have to weigh the risks and opportunities and make a decision to go for it.

Chapter Four

The Various Types of Immigration to Canada

Annual flow of Temporary Residents by Primary Status

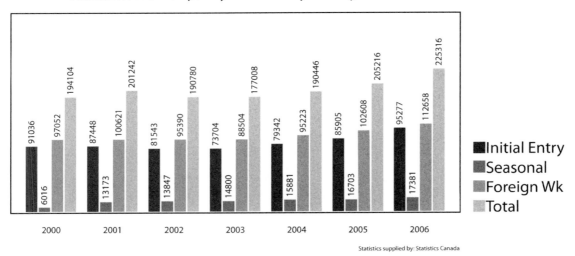

Statistics supplied by: Statistics Canada

Temporary Worker Visas and Work Permits

In order to issue a work permit, a HRSDC (Human Resources Development Canada) Labour Market Opinion is required. The HRSDC Labour Market Opinion basically certifies that no Canadian worker could perform the function of a foreign worker. In this case HRSDC is protecting the Canadian worker. It must be understood that these work permits or visas are temporary in nature and only apply for a specific function and a specific period of time. When the permit expires the individual is required to leave the country or re-apply before the expiration of the permit.

Work Permits allow foreign workers to come and work in Canada for a specific period of time, while a resident visa allows people from other nations to live in Canada for a stated amount of time. A temporary resident visa may also be required (in addition to a Work Permit)

27

depending on the source country of the immigrant. Check the list of countries and territories whose citizens need a visa. The list of countries is too long to publish here but it is available at this web site: http://www.cic.gc.ca/english/visit/visas.asp (CIC stands for Citizenship and Immigration Canada)

Immigrants need to understand that the government wants to maintain some control on people entering and residing in this country and in some cases requires more documentation.

Note the use of the word "temporary". This is not an application for immigration or permanent residency, but a temporary Work Permit in which the employee would have to return to their native country upon completion of the term.

The federal government's Temporary Foreign Worker Program allows eligible foreign workers to work in Canada for an authorized period of time if employers can demonstrate that they are unable to find suitable Canadian/permanent residents to fill the jobs and that the entry of these workers will not have a negative impact of the Canadian labour market.

If an international company wishes to send an individual to Canada to live and work for a period of time a work permit is usually required. The work permit is derived from the fact that the individual is actively involved in the everyday business of their organization and is therefore a participant in the Canadian workforce.

Working Temporarily in Canada: Who Can Apply?

Some temporary workers require a Work Permit and others do not. Some categories of jobs have permits granted quicker than other categories. Even if you don't need a permit you will still be required to provide other types of documentation. All of the information you need to know can be found in the "Working Temporarily in Canada" section on the www.cic.gc.ca web site.

Working temporarily in Canada depends to some degree on the employer because they may need a Labour Market Opinion in order to bring you into the country. A Labour Market Opinion through the HRSDC confirms that a foreign worker can fill the job requested. The individual would also require a temporary resident visa in order to stay in Canada during their work period.

In order to apply for a work permit from outside of Canada requires the following:

1. A job offer from a Canadian employer.
2. The employer must get a written confirmation from HRSDC that a foreign worker can fill the job.
3. A completed application.
4. Any other requirements related to health, financial ability, the willingness to leave at the end of your work assignment, and no criminal record.

There is a list of jobs on the web site that do not require Work Permits if working temporarily in Canada.

Special Category – Information Technology workers
Canada has a simplified entry process for workers whose skills are high in demand such as IT people. A letter of confirmation from HRSDC would not be necessary.

It is up to the employer to ensure that the jobs fall under the NOC categories:

    Senior Animation Effects Editor (NOC 9990.1)
    Embedded Systems Software Designer (NOC 9990.2)
    MIS Software Designer (NOC 9990.3)
    Multimedia Software Developer (NOC 9990.4)
    Software Developer- Services (NOC 9990.5)
    Software Product Developer (NOC 9990.6)
    Telecommunications Software Designer (NOC 9990.7)

Processing Times for Temporary Work Permits

Following is some general information on the time typically required for the processing of Temporary Work Permits:

    Processing percentages of all applications in 28 days or less
    Percentage of Cases Processed at Visa Offices in all regions -- 66%
    Percentage of Cases Processed at Africa and the Middle East Visa Offices -- 48%
    Percentage of Cases Processed at Asia and Pacific Offices -- 49%
    Percentage of Cases Processed at European Visa Offices -- 80%
    Percentage of Cases Processed in the Americas -- 82%

Live-In Caregiver Program

Live-In caregivers are individuals who are qualified to provide care for children, elderly persons or persons with disabilities. The term live-in means that the caregiver must live in the private home where they work in Canada. The details of the program are contained at the following web-site: www.cic.gc.ca/english/work/caregiver/index.asp

Both the employer and the employee must follow the required steps to meet the requirements of the live-in caregiver program. If you are successful you will receive a temporary work permit lasting three years and three months. Applicants are screened by immigration staff at the Canadian Embassies & Mission abroad. When a caregiver has completed 24 months of legal employment, within 36 months of arrival in Canada they are able to apply for Landed Immigrant Status. It appears that this program could be a gateway for providing people to the Personal Support Workers program and the large number of caregivers that will be needed to provide home health care to the aged in the next two decades. Having a source of personal support workers will also be cost effective in that seniors will be able to stay in their homes longer. Unfortunately, there have been some cases concerning live-in care givers where the job responsibilities and re-numeration were not as originally agreed upon by the caregiver. Although most employers are honest and accurate in their terms of employment it is highly encouraged that caregivers come to a contractual agreement on responsibilities, working hours and overtime compensation.

The application for Quebec is slightly different because of the Quebec/Canada Accord agreement. Application forms are available at Quebec Immigration offices:

285 Notre Dame West, Ground Floor, Room G-15,
Montreal, Quebec
14-864-9191 www.immigration-quebec.gouv.qc.ca

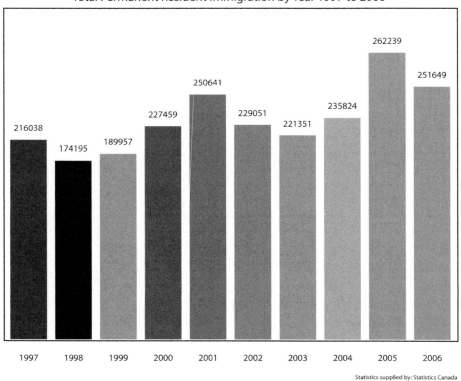

Permanent Residents Immigration Trends

Total Permanent Resident Immigration by Year 1997 to 2006

Statistics supplied by: Statistics Canada

Avenues of Admission: The Various Pathways of Immigration in Canada

There are several routes or categories of immigration leading to permanent residency available to prospective immigrants. Each has its own set of procedures and qualifications. It's best to gain an overview of each available option, before you chose your path of preference. Once you've made your choice, you must see it through and cannot change your application one it's in process.

Working in Canada Tool

This tool is available on the Immigration menu of the Canada Citizenship and Immigration Website (www.cic.gc). This tool provides immigrants with help in finding out what their occupation is called in Canada which may be different to their home country. It tells them what jobs are open across the country. It gives detailed labour market reports on specific areas. It gives information on wages and job opportunities for your occupation and city where you would like to live and work. This site may not give you every single piece of information on job opportunities and should be

supplemented by information from local job agencies, etc but a well informed immigrant is one who is fully knowledgeable about his/her opportunities in Canada.

Skilled Worker Program

The Skilled Worker Program is the most established admission process into Canada, so it's no surprise that the vast majority of immigrants and their families have arrived via this path. This program -- also known as the "Points System" -- requires a passing grade of 67 out of a maximum 90 points. Those points are accumulated based on the following qualifying categories:

Category	Maximum Available Points
Education	25
Official Languages Understanding	24
Job Experience	21
Age	10
Adaptability	10
Total	**90**
(Minimum Required Score)	**67**

We'll look at each category in more detail in a moment, but let me first give you an overview of the Skilled Worker Program.

Skilled Worker applicants have the opportunity to become permanent residents of Canada. Meeting the government's qualifying standards indicates the ability of an immigrant to get established economically by finding work in Canada. Successful applicants qualify with a score of 67 or higher. But they also need to demonstrate that they have the minimum required financial resources.

What The Skilled Worker Program Is

Basically, the Skilled Worker Program is an assessment method available to prospective immigrants who in most cases, seek to establish permanent residency and subsequently become Canadian citizens. Assessments are based on 5 categories of qualification as determined by Citizenship and Immigration Canada, plus the immigrant's financial capability to relocate and adjust to life in Canada. It's a system that allows the country to be somewhat selective in its approach to immigration. Clearly the emphasis is on education, work experience and having the necessary funds to see you through the transitional period of adjusting to life in Canada.

What The Skilled Worker Program Is Not

Perhaps the greatest misunderstanding of the points-based system is that once you qualify, you're all set. But a passing grade that qualifies you for immigrant status does not necessarily mean you'll be able to find a job in your particular field. Meeting the minimum requirements only indicates the capability to do the job as described on your application. But being qualified and landing a position are two different things. You may be accepted, only to later discover that employment opportunities for which you trained are few and far between. *Be forewarned: if anyone promises you employment, request the specific information from them including the company, location, and the name of a contact person in the Human Resources Department at the firm. Only companies can offer genuine employment, not consultants, advisors, or immigration agencies.

The Skilled Worker Program is not a ticket to certain employment. There may or may not be jobs in Canada related to your education, skills and experience. That's why you should begin your job search from your home country before coming to Canada – well in advance of your anticipated arrival here. This means assuming the responsibility of finding suitable employment and taking the necessary actions yourself. Search online. Refer to the resources section of this book for contact information. Begin to establish communication with employment agencies in Canada, so you can get more accurate and up-to-date information about the positions most in demand in Canada.

The Skilled Worker Program is not an endorsement or certification of your education and qualifications. All this system does is to confirm that you meet the criteria for admission. You will still have to certify your education and qualifications through applicable institutions and agencies in Canada before your arrival. Many organizations in Canada will not accept duplicate copies of degrees, certificates, or transcripts. You must send originals only. Some government-sponsored agencies will handle this function for you at no cost to you. Please refer to the resources section of this book for more information. Ensure that your educational qualifications are assessed by a firm such as World Education Services (WES) and translated into the English language.

The Skilled Worker Program is not the most efficient or expedient route for new prospective immigrants. Yes, the points system has been around for a long time and most immigrants have been funneled in though this process. But there's a noticeable backlog in the system, so applicants choosing this method could expect to wait 3-4 years before attaining official immigrant status.

How To Proceed

You can find the application forms for the Skilled Worker Program at the Citizenship and Immigration Canada web site:
http://www.cic.gc.ca/english/information/applications/index.asp

It's crucial for the immigrant to fully understand the Skilled Worker Program if he or she is applying via this method. Most, if not all of the forms you need, can be found on this site. All are provided in PDF format -- which can be read easily on any computer, with any operating system, using Adobe Acrobat Reader®. See www.adobe.com for a free download.

It's a good idea to print out two copies of each form. This way you can use one copy as a draft and the other as the final version submitted to Citizenship and Immigration Canada. It also gives you a clearer idea of the information required, should you eventually decide to apply through a representative.

If you need preprinted forms instead, those can be obtained by contacting any Canadian embassy, high commission, or consulate office abroad, or through Citizenship and Immigration Canada directly.

With most required applications, preparation guides are also available to help clarify and simplify the completion process for you. Read through each guide before filling out the corresponding form.

Completing a draft of the actual application on your own actually helps you several ways, including:

1. It makes you familiar with the kind of information required. Use this to help   prepare you for immigration and job interviews. Get comfortable talking about yourself and your skills. Think like a marketer. Position yourself as a valuable asset to your prospective employer and new country.

2. It improves your English skills. You'll need to read, write and enter specific data about yourself. You are entering a period of your life where you'll be asked to fill out form after form. That's just the way it is. But you can look at each form as another opportunity to practice your English skills.

3. It helps you refine your information, so you provide quality responses. Share your information with friends, relatives, teachers, or clergy – anyone who can assist you. Show them what you have and ask for their input.

4. It could potentially save you thousands of dollars. You can always outsource the task of completing application forms to a representative. But you'll save yourself lots of money and you'll gain an understanding of the entire process to a greater degree by forcing yourself to read, respond and complete the application yourself. Just take your time and refer to the appropriate guide whenever you need assistance.

Simplified Skilled Worker Application Process

In 2006, Citizenship and Immigration Canada introduced a simplified application process for those prospective immigrants opting to apply through the Skilled Worker Program.

With this newly revised process, you submit a basic application form along with the required fee. When the Visa office in your home country is ready to assess your application, they will then request all supporting documentation from you.

This simplified approach reserves your place in the processing line and ensures that your application will be evaluated according to the rules and regulations in effect at the time of your submission. So you can begin to gather all the background information and documentation while you're already in the queue, awaiting the next step.

Below is a brief summary of the revised Skilled Worker application procedure.

Stage One:

1. Application for Permanent Residence in Canada (form number: IMM 0008SW) This application includes the following details: your personal information, information on all members of your family, assessment details relating to your skills and qualifications.

2. Use of a Representative form (if applicable) (form number: IMM 5476)
3. Processing Fee
Stage Two:
1. File all supporting documents

Details Concerning the Points System of Assessment

The first category is Education. Education is worth a maximum of 25 points, which is more than any other single category. Clearly the level of education of applicants is a top priority of Citizenship and Immigration Canada.

25 points are awarded to any applicant with a PhD or Masters degree, with at least 17 years of study in total. 22 points are awarded to applicants with skilled trade certification or apprenticeships, with at least 15 years of study. A two-year university degree and 14 years of study will earn you 20 points. A two-year college diploma, trade certificate and 14 years of total study will also rate a 20 point score. 15 points are assigned to graduates of one-year college programs.

Understanding Canada's official languages is next. This category offers a maximum of 24 points, but all 24 are only awarded to those with fluency in both English and French. The candidate decides whether French or English is their first language of communication and whether English or French is their second official language.

A maximum of 16 points is offered for proficiency in English and 8 points for French, if you are applying for residency outside of Quebec or the reverse if applying for residency in Quebec. Strangely, the overwhelming majority of jobs in Canada don't require you to be bilingual but applicants are deprived of those eight points because they don't know both English and French. Yet to attain a score higher than 16 in the language category of the Skilled Workers Program, requires proficiency in English and at least some understanding of French. If you had a moderate proficiency in one of the official languages you would receive a score of 8 out of 24, thus making it difficult to gain the required 67 points to qualify.

It seems unfair that we demand more from our immigrants than we would from most Canadian citizens who do not work in bilingual government or customer service jobs where two languages are a distinct advantage. Perhaps this is one reason other countries might have a competitive advantage in attracting highly-qualified immigrants from around the world. We should also realize that some of the bilingual government jobs in Canada are not available to people who are not yet Canadian citizens because they are in Federal government departments. In spite of all of the efforts to make Canada a bilingual country the end result is that Canada is basically unilingual French or English in each province, except perhaps New Brunswick, with Federal government services across the country in both official languages. Are we really gaining anything as a country which is looking for skilled immigrants and tradespeople to promote proficiency in two official languages rather than one or the other? Bilingualism in the major cities of Toronto and Vancouver will eventually become proficiency in Cantonese or Mandarin or Punjabi. Is the English language a valuable asset in obtaining employment in Quebec City outside of some jobs in the federal government or service?

Perhaps the government could look at the eight point second language assessment as a general bonus for any second language, a skill that is highly demanded, relevant work experience, a spouse with relevant work experience or any other factor regarded as economically valuable to Canada.

Language grading takes into account the four areas of Speaking, Reading, Writing and Listening. Since you cannot evaluate your own language performance, the best way to accurately measure your current level of skill is through testing. Refer to the Resources Section for more information on standard language testing. At the time of this writing the government was considering using IELTS as the standard for the language testing into Canada.

Job Experience is another key category. Through the Skilled Worker Program, on the job experience is worth a maximum of 21 points. Work experience recognized by Citizenship and Immigration Canada has to meet the following criteria:

1. Must have taken place within the last ten years.
2. Must not include a restricted occupation. (*Note: at the time of this writing, no occupations were listed as restricted.)
3. Must be listed as an eligible occupation on the National Occupation Code (NOC)

*The NOC is a classification system of occupations in Canada. It describes the duties, skills, aptitudes and work settings typical of jobs in Canada. See the web site here: http://www.cic.gc.ca/skilled for more information.

Four years of full-time work experience in your field of specialization will earn you the maximum of 21 points. Three years of on the job experience qualifies you for 19 points, while two years of work gives you 17 points and one year, 15 points.

The following minimum requirements are necessary to apply as a Skilled Worker:
• You have at least one continuous year of full-time, paid work experience or the equivalent in part-time continuous work
• Your work experience must be Skill Type 0 (managerial occupations) of Skill Level A (professional occupations) or B (technical occupations and skilled trades) on the Canadian National Occupational Classification (NOC)
• You have gained this experience within the last 10 years

Next is the category of age and here a maximum of 10 points is available. 10 points are awarded to applicants between the ages of 21 and 49. But 2 points are subtracted for every year over 49 and every year under 21. So if you're 52, for example, you'd lose 6 points and score only 4 in the age category. If you fit into the range of the ideal candidate (according to CIC) you automatically score the maximum number of 10 points. Again, the same parameters of limitation would not apply to a Canadian citizen because it would look very similar to age discrimination.

Adaptability is the final category and again, a maximum of 10 points are available. Points awarded for adaptability are based on your experience and that of your spouse. Up to 5 points are awarded if you or your spouse has a relative living in Canada as a permanent resident or citizen. Another 5 points are awarded based on your spouse's level of education.

Arranged employment is important. To show how valuable a prearranged job with an employer is to the new immigrant or to the temporary worker, consider the following. Ten points are awarded to a skilled worker for arranged employment in Canada in an occupation

that is listed in Skill type 0, Management occupations, or skill Level A or B according to the National Occupational Classification matrix. The following conditions also apply:
   a. The skilled worker is in Canada and holds a Work Permit
   b. There would be a neutral or positive effect on the labour market in Canada
   c. The Work Permit is valid

The above 5 categories account for the total number of 90 available points. Remember, you must score at least 67 to successfully qualify using the "Points System".

Supporting Income Requirements

In addition to the points program, there are important financial considerations you need to be aware of. You are required to pay any application processing fees in addition to having adequate financing in place to help you become established in Canada.

Current processing fees for the Skilled Worker Program are as follows:

Individual	$550
Spouse	$550
Dependents over 22	$550
Family Members under 22	$150

It's also important to note that the government of Canada provides no financial assistance to new skilled worker immigrants. To qualify for admission, you must prove that you have the required level of funds to provide for yourself and your family upon your arrival in Canada. Citizenship and Immigration Canada has set the following amounts as minimum requirements for new immigrants:

Individual applicant	$10,168
2 family members	$12,659
3 family members	$15,563
4 family members	$18,895

These figures change yearly on the 1st of January. The attached low income cut-off indicates the minimum income required to qualify as a new immigrant, as of December 31, 2008. New immigrants should have one half of the low income cut-off to attain the minimum level for entry.

Size of family unit	Minimum necessary income	Half of Minimum Income
1 person(sponsor)	$21,202	$10,601
2 persons	$26,396	$13,198
3 persons	$32,460	$16,230
4 persons	$39,399	$19,700

Again, please note that these figures are minimum levels and make no consideration for delays that you might receive in certification, training, or finding a job. You should have a financial plan in place which takes any problems into consideration and protects you and your family. You also need to be in a position of showing these amounts in bank draft form to a Canada Customs officer when you arrive at a Canadian Airport terminal.

Business Immigrants

There are three categories of business related immigration to Canada. These are Investors, Entrepreneurs, and Self-Employed individuals. The objective of the Business Immigration Program is to attract capable, experienced businesspeople who will contribute to a strong and expanding Canadian economy.

Each applicant may only pursue one particular category and that category cannot be changed once the application has been submitted. Consider your options and then decide which category best suits you.

Investors

Investors are required to turn over a $400,000 loan to Citizenship and Immigration Canada. CIC manages these funds over a five year period. After five years, your $400,000 investment in returned to you, without any interest. Over the five year duration, your principle investment is guaranteed by whatever province you choose as your new home. Canada benefits from any interest accumulated over the same timeframe. With this option, you literally "invest" in Canada but your investment is managed entirely by government.

To qualify as an Investor applicant, you need:
1. A minimum two years of business experience.
2. A minimum net worth of $800,000 CDN.
3. To be willing to make an investment in Canada of $400,000 – for a five year term.
4. To score a minimum of 35 points on a selection grid similar to the Skilled Worker points system. Successful investor candidates are also able to prove that they have enough money to support themselves and their dependents after they arrive in Canada.

Entrepreneurs

Citizenship and Immigration Canada considers an "entrepreneur" to be an experienced businessperson who will run a business and create jobs in Canada. To qualify as an entrepreneur, you must:
1. Have a minimum net worth of $300,000 CDN.
2. Possess various business-related skills, indicating the capability to run a business successfully.
3. Have previously managed a qualifying business in your native country.
4. Have contributed a percentage of the equity in that business for at least two years within the five years preceding the submission of your application.

*Note: Your proposed business in Canada must be an active enterprise and not solely an operation created to derive interest or dividends.

Self Employed Individuals

The self employed candidate has the ability to create his/her own job. According to the government, this individual would support the various cultural, artistic or athletic programs in Canada by making a significant contribution to those aspects of life. Another area of qualification for self employment status is farm management. If you have experience in managing a farm and have the intention of starting and operating one in Canada, you could qualify under the Self Employed category.

If the self employed individual is interested in small business management courses there are a large number of these courses offered through community college courses in each province. Various Chambers of Commerce can also provide guidance in the selection of courses and training for self employed individuals. Such organizations as CAMSC have business training and development programs. The provincial governments have Small Business Enterprise centres which are listed in the diversity is good for business section. There is also information available from the Canadian Council for Small Business and Entrepreneurship(CCSBE) web-site.

Provincial Nomination Program

This is the newest avenue of immigration available and it has numerous advantages. Yet surprisingly, only a small percentage of immigrants and businesses have so far pursued this opportunity. It's available in every province and territory across Canada. The Provincial Nomination Program is designed to fill vacant positions more efficiently than traditional methods.

Ultimately, Canada's goal through its immigration policy is to provide skilled people to fill specific jobs. Anyone with the skills, education, and work experience to make an immediate contribution, can qualify under the Provincial Nomination Program. It's a process that gives the individual provinces a direct hand in matching new immigrants to the demands of the marketplace. This makes perfect sense since the Canadian economy is a collection of diverse regional economies.

The Provincial Nomination Program is suitable for immigrants wanting to establish themselves as permanent residents of Canada. With proper clearance, a nominated applicant could have a Permanent Resident Card in hand within a few short months, instead of the three to four years it typically takes.

It also allows prospective immigrants to take a more proactive approach to immigration. They can first establish contact with prospective employers and agencies from home and then apply to the specific province of their choice for nomination.

Each province and territory in Canada has its own evaluation criteria. But the Provincial Nomination Program does not use the same selection factors that apply through the Skilled Workers application process.

Instead, the individual province assesses each applicant based on a combination of skills, experience, and provincial and corporate needs, in order to determine acceptability. Those who qualify are nominated by the province or territory and their names are forwarded to Citizenship and Immigration Canada, which issues approval pending final security and health checks. At the same time, the applicant must also apply for permanent resident status.

It looks like the Provincial Nomination Program has plenty of potential. After all, it's a win-win solution. It helps solve a region's individual labour requirements, while meeting the immigrant's need for employment.

The program was designed to address the chronic needs of business that are not being adequately fulfilled by the Federal Skilled Worker Program. Prospective immigrants can seek employment in Canada before filing their documentation. Employers with available positions can nominate suitable candidates. The province then screens nominees, with an eye toward its regional labour market needs. Next, the names of those who qualify are then forwarded to Citizenship and Immigration Canada.

The Provincial Nominee Program is an expedited process that's of benefit to all. It accelerates the immigrant's arrival and integration in Canada. It provides much needed skilled labour to business, which in turn helps to fuel local economies. And a growing economy benefits everyone right across the country by contributing to our high standard of living.

Could the Provincial Nominee Program be the ultimate solution?

Obviously it's an effective method and a more direct route to Canada for qualified applicants. When the demands of the market are matched by the skills and qualifications of new immigrants, this program can become an efficient service to new immigrants. Unfortunately, it's been slow to develop. Though launched in the year 2000, it still only accounts for approximately 10% of all economic immigrants across the country.

Here is the step-by-step process for applying for Provincial Nomination:

1. Obtain a Certificate of Provincial Nomination for your chosen province. (Each province has its own set of procedures – see link below)

http://www.cic.gc.ca/engish/immigrate/provincial/apply-how.asp

2. If successful, you will receive a copy of the Certificate of Provincial Nomination. One copy will also be sent directly to the visa office in your home country.

3. Locate, print and complete the application kit.

4. Submit your application to the correct visa office in your home country.

5. Obtain instructions from the visa office on such items as medical examinations, criminal and security checks.

6. Calculate your fees.

7. Check your application and send it along with the required fee.

Canada Experience Class (CEC)

The Canada Experience Class is a new class of immigration expected to be introduced in the summer of 2008. It will cater to applicants with educational and job experiences in Canada.

This process would appeal to immigrants because it would be much quicker to get a Work Permit than to obtain entry through the Skilled Worker Program. It takes 30 to 60 days to process a work permit application for temporary employment. Part of the goal of the Canada Experience Class is to utilize temporary work permits as a transition to move immigrants into permanent residency and provide them with a vehicle to get Canadian business experience and training, which would address the critical shortages to Canada's labour force.

Some critics say that this emphasis would take away from family reunification efforts but there is an urgent need to speed the process and backlog of economic immigrant workers into Canada.

The highlights of the Canadian Experience Class category were revealed in a Citizenship and Immigration announcement on August of 2008.

Eligibility- Temporary foreign workers employed in management, professional or technical occupations, or skilled trades (type O, A and B of national classification) and international students who have completed a two-year university program in Canada.

Work Experience- One year for the international student category and two for temporary workers.

Start-up of program-October 2008.

Family Class

Immigration to Canada has a section called Family Class. This section is different from spouses and dependents arriving with economic immigrants and refugees. Family Class includes spouses and partners, children and parents and grandparents sponsored by an immigrant who has attained Canadian citizenship or permanent residency.

The sponsor must meet certain requirements including the essential needs for a prescribed period of time. Canadian Immigration and Refugee Law is the law regulating the admission of immigrants into Canada. The main law on this subject is in the Immigration and Refugee Protection Act which covers economic growth, family reunification and the acceptance of refugees and humanitarian concerns.

The Family Class portion of the Act allows permanent residents or citizens to sponsor a family member's entrance into the country. In order to get family reunification in Canada you must have a sponsor who is a Canadian citizen or permanent resident and be 18 years of age. You may sponsor:

- Your spouse
- Parents and grandparents
- Dependent children including adopted children
- Brothers, sisters, etc. who are orphans and under 18 years of age
- You must also agree as a sponsor to take care of your relative's essential needs for a period of up to 10 years

There is a misconception among Canadians that these Family Class members are affecting the level of economic immigration and its effectiveness on the Canadian economy. In the year 2006 the number of Family Class immigrants outside of economic immigrants and refugees was 16,531. This number included 6,846 spouses and 10,417 parents and grandparents. Out of a total of 251,649 permanent immigrants, the percentage of those entering Canada via the Family Class category was just 7%.

Canada recognizes that we attract immigrants and investors to this country if we allow their families to come with them. Otherwise they will take their skills and money and go elsewhere.

These immigrants end up paying taxes just like every other Canadian and support our benefit system and standard of living. They will become an integral part in building our social systems and leading Canada in the global economy. We also have an opportunity as a country to use the skills brought to Canada by family members including spouses, children graduating from educational institutions, as well as the skills and investments from parents and grandparents.

Refugees

The basis of Canada's refugee program is that everyone is entitled to protection from persecution. To be granted refugee status in Canada a person must be outside his or her host country and have a fear that they will be persecuted or that harm will come to them if they go back to their home country.

There are two types of refugees: a convention refugee who could be persecuted in his/her home country based on race, gender, nationality, being a member of a particular social group or have a differing political opinion. The other category is a person in need of protection who fears that they would be a recipient of torture or harassment if they returned to their home country.

Because of the complex nature of coming to Canada as a refugee it is advisable to seek advice from a Canadian attorney based upon references of that attorney's performance. Processing time for refuges vary according to their country of origin so it is advisable to get that information from a web site on the refugee system before coming to Canada. More information is available from these two web sites:
www.citizenshipandimmigrationcanada.com
www.canadavisa.com

Sometimes immigrants are advised to seek refugee status when they visit Canada without first reviewing the various types and qualifications for refugee status that Canada has as a requirement. You are advised to thoroughly review the government web site and ensure that you qualify for refuge status in Canada otherwise there is the potential that you will spend some time in Canada while your application is reviewed and then eventually be sent back to your country of origin. More information on this subject is available at the following web sites:
www.en.wikpedia.org/wiki/Canadian_immigration_and-refugee_law
www.canada-law.com/familyclass.com

We may be missing an important economic component of admitting refugees into Canada in that the various immigration programs focus on skills, language and job experience and may not admit people with lower level skills and language ability. Our economy needs people who may have lower level skills but they can be trained and become skilled for the many jobs in manufacturing, distribution, retail and construction. Many of these jobs can be unappealing to Canadians and skilled immigrants but may be perfectly acceptable to a person seeking refugee status and a new start in Canada. These refugees could help to address the long term need for semi to unskilled workers in the Canadian economy.

Jobs Under Pressure

The federal and provincial governments of Ontario, Alberta and British Columbia have collaborated to develop a list of "Jobs Under Pressure." Its purpose is to provide an updated list of occupations in which the current demand exceeds supply. Shortages in the Canadian workforce present entry opportunities for prospective immigrants. Anyone interested in immigrating to Canada would be well-advised to stay current with the employment needs of their province of preference. A note of caution should be used when reviewing the "Jobs Under Pressure" lists in that the economic situations have become very dynamic and the list could change from one week to the next so confirm this information with other employment sites and employment agencies in the geographical area that you want to locate.

You significantly increase your chances of success when your skills can be applied to a job under pressure. It's self-marketing. You find a need and fill it. When the demand is already there, you increase your odds by having the skills and experience to fill the vacancy. The "Jobs Under Pressure" listing is available online at the following web sites:

http://www.immigration.ca/jobs-under-pressure.asp
www.hrsdc.gc.ca/en/workplaceskills/foreign_workers/oup/onouplist.shtml
www.ontarioimmigration.ca/english/how_work_market.asp
www.hrsdc.gc.ca/en/workplaceskills/foreign_workers/occunderpres.shtml

Processing Times

In a recent article in the Toronto Daily Star on February 11th titled "Immigration Wait-Time Surge Angers Liberals" the opposition party Liberals blame the Conservative party for the long wait times in processing applications for immigrants. The Liberals accuse the Conservatives of not providing enough resources for the processing of applications and increasing the wait times by up to 20 per cent. They claim that there is a large disparity in processing times between countries of origin of the immigrants.

The Conservatives, in their defense, blame the Liberals for handing them an 800,000 application file backlog when they took over from the previous Liberal government. In any case this points to another problem in the welcoming and processing of immigrants to Canada and does not help in the worldwide competition for talented immigrants. Each immigrant should research the various government web sites and Canadian Immigration lawyer services for an estimate of their own countries' processing times.

Key Point Summary

- There are several ways to apply to Citizenship and Immigration Canada
- Each method has its own set of requirements and procedures, but all require health and security clearance and adequate financial resources
- The Skilled Worker Program assesses immigrants through a points system:
  - Points are awarded in each of the following 5 areas: Education, Official Language Understanding, Job Experience, Age and Adaptability
  - Emphasis is on Education and Work Experience
  - Admission through the Skilled Worker process does not necessarily mean that you will be able to find employment in your field of expertise
  - Acceptance is not an endorsement of your qualifications, nor a certification of your

education

- The entire process from beginning to official acceptance into Canada can take 3-4 years
- Recent changes mean immigrants get placed into the queue sooner, but how this affects overall wait times is yet to be seen

- Financial requirements include set fees of $550 per adult over 21, plus a minimum cash reserve of $10, 168 for a single applicant
• Business Immigrants are classified into three distinct groups: Investors, Entrepreneurs, and Self Employed individuals

   Investors are required to put up a $400,000 investment in Canada for years, have a net worth of at least $800,000, and score at least 35 points on their assessment evaluation

   Entrepreneurs are required to have a net worth of at least $300,000, possess various business skills, and have at least 2 years of managerial experience in a similar business

   Self Employed people need to have the capability to create their own jobs
• The Provincial Nomination Program is the quickest way to gain entry into Canada and secure suitable employment

   This program matches marketplace needs to the skills and experience of prospective immigrants
• Enables candidates to become more proactive in the immigration process
• Based more on specific skills and work experience in relation to market needs, rather than on education
• The "Jobs Under Pressure" list indicates current needs of the job market on a regional basis
• Prospective immigrants can use this list to discover suitable opportunities in various regions of the country

Other Elements of Permanent Residency, Medical, Security and Other Requirements

Medical Requirements

Security Checks

Under all classifications of permanent residency you and your family must pass a medical examination and security and criminal checks. You can find more information on these subjects in the Quick find section of the web site. www.cic.gc.ca

Permanent Resident Card

The Permanent Resident Card is a wallet sized plastic ID card. If a person has obtained Permanent Resident status but are not yet Canadian Citizens they will receive this card as a proof of permanent residency status. On October 14th, 2007, the Toronto Daily Star published an article on so called phantom residents of Canada. These residents received permanent resident cards but did not spend the required amount of time in Canada to qualify for renewal of their permanent residency. Individuals with a permanent resident card are required to spend 730 days out of five years residing in Canada. A large number of these individuals received their visas from the Abu Dhabi office. Those individuals who do not meet the residency requirements can have landed status withdrawn.

Canadian Citizenship

You can apply for Canadian Citizenship if you are: eighteen years of age, have been a permanent resident for three out of the previous four years, can communicate in English or French, have knowledge of Canada including the rights and responsibilities of citizenship.

If you meet these requirements for Canadian citizenship then you can get an application form from the call centre or download an application at http://www.cic.gc.ca

Special Information for African Immigrants

A study that was outlined in the National Post of February 14th, 2008 by Charles Lewis states that recent immigrants from Africa have the hardest time integrating into the Canadian workforce. Contributing factors to this situation are:

• Up to 20% of African immigrants are refugees and refugees have the hardest time adjusting to the Canadian workforce because of their particular circumstances and lack of opportunity to prepare for their migration with training, education and job experience

• Many African communities and social agencies have been developed much more recently than other established communities and social agencies.

• It is obvious that immigrants from Africa will need more direct support in the future in order to provide them with the tools necessary to integrate into the Canadian workforce.

Immigration Consultants and Lawyers

You should be aware that Immigration Consultants are private business people who make their living by charging for their services. Let's differentiate between Immigration Consultants in your native country and Immigration Consultants in Canada. An Immigration consultant in your country is not regulated by any Canadian agency or government. They are for-profit enterprises and will charge you for their services. Immigration consultants or lawyers do not have any leverage with foreign embassies or visa offices. They cannot improve waiting times or guarantee that your application will pass.

Canadian Immigration consultants who live in Canada may or may not be a member of the Canadian Society of Immigration Consultants. This society is a self-regulated body that promotes professionalism in the field of consulting.

Immigration lawyers in Canada are regulated by their respective law societies. Lawyers will obviously charge for their services. While there is a complaint mechanism run by the law society, it's always a good idea to check for your lawyer's law authorization and standing, qualifications, references and recommendations.

Negotiate a written agreement listing services and fees so there are no hidden costs or surprises. Ask for receipts and copies and ensure that everything is signed by both parties. Also ensure that you are the one holding the original documents.

Job search fees would not be a normal charge by a consultant or lawyer and recognize that there are free services available, such as, your own internet search, Human Resources

Canada, Workopolis, a myriad of social agencies in the community providing job searches, and local employment agencies.

Before any immigrant considers an immigration consultant or lawyer they should seriously peruse the sites below to gain an understanding of immigrating to Canada.

www.cic.gc.ca/english or French
This web site is loaded with all of the relevant information, guides, forms and questions and answers. If the immigrant masters this information they can certainly fill out their own forms and save money.

Housing once you get to Canada
Housing becomes a critical issue for all New Canadians because it is so fundamental to starting life. A first step is to contact friends and family in Canada and see if they can accommodate you for a period of time until you get settled in your new country. Another step is for those friends and family to explore the various housing opportunities in Canada for you looking at neighbourhoods, costs, schools, services and shopping and transportation accessibility. Many families could use the extra money as long as you commit to a time period and do not stay with them indefinitely. Some New Canadians might say that they do not have any friends or family so they should determine a settlement service from the social agency list in the geographic that they are settling in. Start the process before you leave your host country and develop a relationship with one of the advisors at the settlement service or social agency by email. Also remember that all apartment dwellings require first and last month's rent before you can move in.

Chapter Five
Immigration Law

Robin Seligman

This book would not be complete without a section on Immigration Law. We are fortunate to have one of the preeminent lawyers in Canadian Immigration law provide the expertise for this section.

Robin Seligman is a Canadian Barrister and Solicitor certified as a specialist in immigration law by the law Society of Upper Canada. Robin obtained her law degree from the University of Western Ontario and was called to the Bar in 1985. She has been certified as a specialist in Immigration Law by the Law society of Upper Canada since 1995. Robin has spoken extensively on the subject of Canadian immigration law.

Robin's areas of expertise include: skilled workers, independent immigration, work permits, business immigration, family reunification, humanitarian applications, citizenship applications, immigration appeal division and federal court litigation.

If you want to get in touch with Robin, her email is robin@seligmanlaw.com and her phone number is 416-967-7878. Robin's office is located at 30 St. Clair Avenue West, 10th floor,

Toronto, Ontario M4V 3A1.

At the time of writing this book the Conservative Party of Canada had introduced changes to Canada's Immigration Laws Bill C-50 which they wanted to pass along with a budget bill. The opposition parties didn't agree with this process and wanted the changes debated in Parliament and presented as a separate piece of legislation. Many immigration lawyers and immigration lobby groups felt the same way that the changes were too important not to have full and open parliamentary debate. Refer to the following web site for more information: www.newimmigrantstoCanada.com Some of the concerns that Robin has involve changes to the Immigration Act.

As previously mentioned, the legislation was introduced along with the Federal Budget. This action is seen as parliamentary undemocratic, in Robin's view and intended to limit debate on the proposed changes. Typically such legislation would be submitted as an amendment to the Immigration and Refugee Act with full debate by all of the parties at the Citizenship and Immigration Parliamentary Committee.

These changes would give the Minister of Immigration power to issue instructions such as which applications get processed and ultimately which applications don't get processed. In the wording of the legislation the instruction "not to process" an application is not legally a refusal and therefore the right of the immigrant to pursue an appeal would not be granted against a *not to process* application. By using the term "not to process" much of the jurisdiction of the Federal Court over immigration matters is eliminated, causing a significant removal of proper checks and balances in the system.

The "Points System" established objective criteria for immigration into Canada and while there has been much criticism of this system, it is more equitable than ministerial instructions which may become very political in nature.

In section 11, the new provision says that the immigration officer "may" issue a visa if the person meets the requirements. The old provision says that the immigration officer "shall" issue a visa. The difference between "may" and "shall" are readily apparent. One means a mandatory provision of a visa while the other indicates that a visa could be refused even if the immigrant qualifies with all of the requirements.

Another change affects humanitarian and compassionate applications in section 25.

The third provision is that set out in section 87, which deals with the issuing of instructions. The minister can issue instructions allowing the establishing of categories of applications to which those instructions might apply. The only applications exempt would be refugees and sponsored applicants. In essence, what these provisions do is give the Minister the power to determine how many applications are processed or to dictate which applications get processed and which ones don't get processed, regardless of the objective criteria. In addition, the minister could determine that a specific application should not be processed.

Another area that Robin expressed concern about and we have discussed in the book is the lack of an immigration program for skilled tradespeople or blue collar workers.

Follow-Up To Changes to Canada's Immigration Law Bill C-50 and English Language Testing

In April of 2008, the Conservative Party of Canada and the Prime Minister introduced a budget that included changes to Canada's Immigration laws Bill C-50. The changes as outlined by the Prime Minister were to streamline the large backlog of immigration applications and address Canada's urgent need for skilled immigrants. The opposition parties accused the government of attaching the immigration changes to a budget in order to bypass the usual parliamentary process, with the goal of focusing only on Canada's economic needs or goals of political expediency.

Typically I applaud measures that speed up the application process and reduce the current backlog of applications. However, I believe that much of this correction could have been done within the existing immigration framework and by adding resources.

Unfortunately, the current backlog of immigration applications will not be affected by the changes because the backlog is grandfathered back from February 27th, 2008.

During the writing of this book on Monday, June 2, 2008, the budget bill containing the immigration reforms passed a confidence vote in Parliament and looked certain to get final approval and go to the Senate. Defeating the changes would have meant an election for Canada and the opposition parties were not prepared to force an election on the immigration reform issues.

One of the problems in the accumulation of the backlog is that by law Citizenship and Immigration Canada has been obliged to process every application in the order it was received. Because of the huge backlog that has developed over the years, Canada is losing out on the competition for immigrants. The Canadian average for a visa require 33 months on average. Canada is simply not competitive in processing times and unfortunately, is losing out to several other leading countries. The new law is intended to contain the backlog of applicants so that ultimately people who want to come to Canada receive a decision within 6 to 12 months. The new law also more closely aligns Canada's immigration system with labour shortages so that immigrants who come to Canada will have more opportunities to find employment in their chosen field.

A news release titled "Government of Canada Announces Consultations on Immigration Priorities" was issued in Ottawa on July 3rd, 2008 by Citizenship and Immigration Canada. In it Diane Finley, Minister of Citizenship and Immigration, released details of consultation on Canada's immigration priorities following the passage of changes to Canada's immigration legislation under Bill C-50. The new immigration law gives the minister the authority to issue instructions on which categories of applications are prioritized, returned with a refund, or held for future consideration.

The skilled worker points program rewards people with high language and educational skills but tradespeople may not have enough language skills to qualify. We should remember that the skilled tradespeople who came to this country over the last 100 years may not have had high language skills but were proficient in their trades and learned the language over the years. Canada needs to reassess it's priorities to better reflect current realities. Do we want the trade or do we want language fluency? That's essentially what it comes to.

The list of "Jobs Under Pressure" for each province is full of jobs for skilled tradespeople. The Skilled Labour Program should be modified to accommodate the language skills of blue collar workers otherwise we perpetuate the very shortages we're trying to correct. We may be as a country disqualifying the very talent that we need to grow and prosper in the new world economy.

These labour shortages were also noted in a recent Toronto Sun article of April 26th, 2008. The article titled "Employment Gaps" indicated the highest vacancy rates existed in the following jobs in Canada: construction, hospitality, mining, forestry, agriculture, retail, manufacturing and transportation.

In a follow-up story in the Toronto Daily Star on June 4th, 2008 titled, "Ottawa Drops English Exam", Diane Finley, Minister of Immigration stated that the Immigration Department was dropping their plans to have a rigorous IELTS English language test for all immigrants. The Canadian Bar Association along with others were part of a series in the Star requesting that Canada not go the route of rigorous language testing which might exclude many immigrants and skilled workers from entering Canada.

Chapter Six
Canada: A Brief Introduction To The Country,
Its People and Programs

Population of Provinces and Territories

YUKON TERRITORY 31,247
Whitehorse

NORTHWEST TERRITORY 42,594
Yellowknife

NUNAVUT 31,142
Baker Lake

Baffin Island

Iqaluit

NEWFOUNDLAND 508,099
St. John's

BRITISH COLUMBIA 4,413,973
Vancouver
Victoria

ALBERTA 3,497,881
Edmonton
Calgary

SASKATCHEWAN 1,006,644
Saskatoon
Regina

MANITOBA 1,193,566
Winnipeg

ONTARIO 12,861,940
Thunder Bay
Sudbury

QUEBEC 7,730,612
Quebec City
Montreal
Ottawa
Toronto
Hamilton
Windsor

PRINCE EDWARD ISLAND
Charlottetown
Fredericton
NEW BRUNSWICK
St. John
NOVA SCOTIA
Halifax

New Brunswick	751,250
Prince Edward Island	139,089
Nova Scotia	935,573

General Information About Canada

Canada is the second largest country in the world (only Russia is larger in land mass) -- with a total area of 9,984, 670 square kilometres. The country stretches from the Atlantic Ocean in the East, to the Pacific in the West. Canada's northern region meets the Arctic Ocean, while its southern edge borders the United States, Canada's largest trading partner. At a distance of some 202,080 kilometres, Canada boasts the longest coastline of any nation.

The Trans-Canada Highway connects the East and West coasts of Canada. It stretches from St. Johns, Newfoundland all the way to Victoria, British Columbia -- an expanse of some 7604 kilometres, making it the longest national highway in the world. The Country of Canada consists of 10 provinces and three territories, covering five distinct regions. Starting in the east, the Atlantic region -- also known as the East Coast -- includes the provinces of New Brunswick, Nova Scotia, Newfoundland and Labrador, and Prince Edward Island. Central Canada includes Quebec and Ontario. The prairies are represented by Manitoba, Saskatchewan and Alberta, while the West Coast Region consists exclusively of British Columbia. Northern Canada is divided amongst the three territories of the Yukon, Northwest Territories and Nunavut, a recent addition that was once part of the Northwest Territories.

As of this writing, the total population is estimated at *33.2 million (*Source: Statistics Canada). At an average of only 3 people per square kilometre, Canada has one of the lowest population densities in the world although much of this unpopulated area lies in the northern section of each province. The portion of Canada which lies within 100 miles of the US border is fairly densely populated.

But Canada is essentially a collection of communities spread out over a large land mass. Approximately 80% of Canada's population lives in the southern regions, within one or two hour's drive to the U.S. border. The major urban centres, plus the many smaller cities and towns house an overwhelming majority of Canada's population. Yet these more densely populated areas occupy only a small portion of the total land area that is Canada.

The northernmost 60-75% of Canada is only sparsely populated. Native peoples or Aboriginals (also referred to as First Nations and Inuit) inhabit some areas of the Yukon, Northwest Territories and Nunavut, but they're also located in cities and on reservations. Most provinces including Ontario and Quebec are more heavily-populated to the south versus the northern regions.

Current estimated populations of the 3 largest metropolitan areas of Canada are as follows:

Toronto	5.3 Million people
Montreal	3.6 Million people
Vancouver	2.2 Million people

Total the number of inhabitants in just these three cities and you get 11.1 million -- or approximately one third of the entire Canadian population. That's a huge portion of the total population contained in a relatively tiny area. Geographically, it's a small fraction of the total land area of Canada.

Ottawa is the capital city of Canada. It's located in Eastern Ontario, roughly halfway between Toronto and Quebec City -- the provincial capitals of Ontario and Quebec, respectively.

Origins of Canada

Aboriginals were the first inhabitants in Canada. Early explorers from Western Europe (England and France) settled in Canada as far back as the 1500's. Among them was Jacques Cartier, the man credited with giving Canada its name. The name originates from the word 'Kanata' – which literally means a "settlement" or "village" in the Huron language.

The Dominion of Canada was founded in 1867. Although established as a colony of the British Empire, Canada formally gained its independence in 1982.

There are two official languages in Canada -- English and French, which is reflective of the origin of the majority of its settlers. Both languages have official status in government, institutions and the courts. Outside of the province of Quebec, English is the dominant language. In the larger cities, many other languages are also spoken. And Toronto is one of the most ethnically-diverse cities in the world with as many as 100 different languages are spoken every day. Although English is spoken in the province of Quebec, particularly for tourist services, the working language of the province is French and you need to speak French fluently to live and work in the province of Quebec.

A Wealth of Resources

Canada is the seventh-largest industrial power among nations. It has a high per-capita income and consequently, its standard of living is among the best anywhere. Large natural gas and oil deposits mean that Canada is a net exporter of energy. Alberta's Tar Sands hold one the world's most abundant oil reserves, giving Canada a supply that is second only to Saudi Arabia. Canada ranks among the top five producers of not just oil but natural gas, copper, zinc, nickel, aluminum and gold too. Additionally, Canada holds approximately 25% of all the fresh water available in the world.

Today, the service sector is a driving force of the Canadian economy. Additionally, the resource-based components of mining, processing, logging, and the automotive industry are major economic influences as well.

Immigration To Canada: A Historic and Economic View

Canada is a relatively young country. Though people had come from other destinations for a few hundred years, it wasn't officially considered a country until the year 1867. Aboriginals were the first people here, followed by a wave of new arrivals from France and England. The French settled in Quebec and the Acadia region (now known as Nova Scotia and New Brunswick) while the English established roots in Upper Canada (Ontario).

Prospects of gold drew many to British Columbia and the Yukon. While the promise of free land in the prairies (offered by the government to stimulate the economy) lured many hard-working immigrants who farmed the land and helped build the nation. The building of the national railway continued to spur development as it formed a connecting link between East and West.

As Canada continued to grow, it attracted immigrants from around the world who made significant contributions to the country's development, uniqueness and varied heritage. Today Canada is one of the most ethnically diverse countries in the world.

According to Citizenship and Immigration Canada, the top 10 source countries for immigrants to Canada in 2006 (the latest available statistics) are as follows:

Permanent Residents by Country
2006 Top Ten Source Countries for Permanent Residents

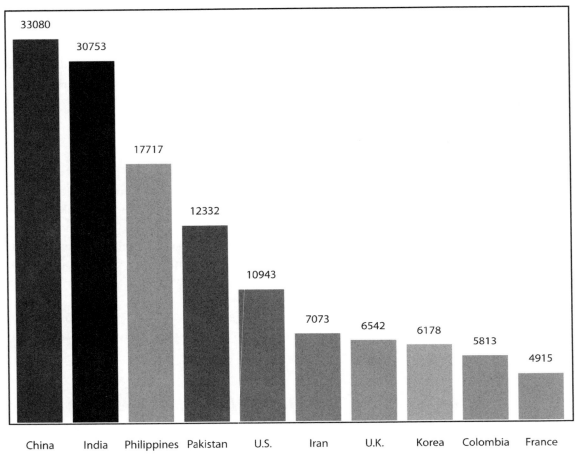

Statistics supplied by: Statistics Canada

1. China
2. India
3. Philippines
4. Pakistan
5. United States
6. Iran
7. United Kingdom
8. Korea
9. Columbia
10. France

Keep in mind that this ranking is countrywide and not necessarily indicative of any specific region in Canada. The actual percentages of new immigrants and their origins will vary widely from region to region.

But there are some interesting trends that have occurred over the last decade. For example, the number of immigrants from the United States has doubled since 1997. In 2006 there were 10, 942 Americans who relocated in Canada. Most of these Americans are well-educated and could find employment in the United States. However, they have chosen to come to Canada for a variety of reasons other than employment. Political issues, health care, social issues -- such as views on abortion or homosexuality, and the strengthening of the Canadian dollar have been cited as reasons for an increasing number of Americans migrating north.

During the same period, the numbers of new immigrants from Taiwan dwindled from 13,324 in 1997 to just 2823 in 2006. In 1997, 22,250 people emigrated from Hong Kong and 18526 from China for a total of 40,776. But in 2006, those numbers were 33,080 from China and just 1489 from Hong Kong.

Meanwhile, the number of immigrants from the United Kingdom and France increased substantially. In 1997 there were 4657 new immigrants from the U.K. But in 2006, those numbers rose by approximately 40%, to 6542 new arrivals. From France, the increase in numbers from 1997 and 2006 was even more substantial, with nearly a 70% boost from 2858 to 4915 people.

From Columbia, the increase was tenfold. In 1997, the number of Columbian immigrants was just 571 and in 2006, it had climbed to 5,813. Immigrants from India also arrived in larger numbers -- from 19,615 in 1997 to 30,753 in 2006 -- a 57% increase.

Where Do Immigrants Go?

Permanent Residents in Urban Areas of B.C.

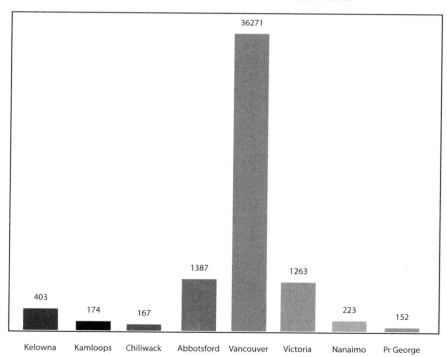

Statistics supplied by: Statistics Canada

Permanent residents in cities of Southern Ontario

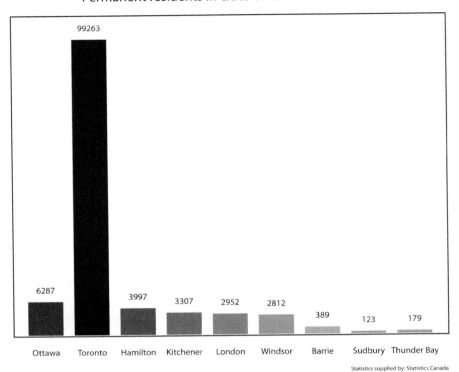

Statistics supplied by: Statistics Canada

Quebec Permanent French Speaking Immigrant Residents by City

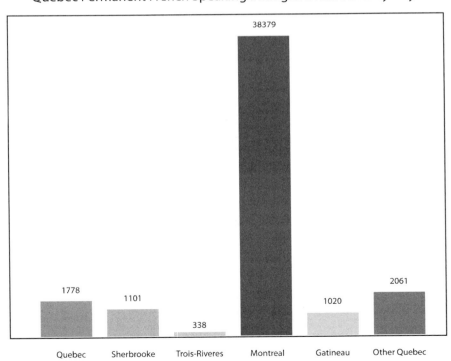

Statistics supplied by: Statistics Canada

Most new immigrants select the major cities as their desired destination. Fully 75% choose Toronto, Montreal or Vancouver as their new home. The majority of those headed to Toronto these days tend to come from China, India, Pakistan, the Philippines and Korea.

Recent Montreal-bound immigrants arrive mostly from China, France, Morocco, Algeria and Haiti. There's an obvious connection to the last four countries on the list, where French is the native language.

Statistics Canada reported that 17% of the 2.5 million people living in the Metropolitan Vancouver area were ethnic Chinese. Other prominent and diverse ethnic groups in Vancouver are the Vietnamese, Filipino, Cambodian, Japanese, Russian and Punjabi communities.

Immigrants want to feel comfortable in their new country. So it's no surprise that they prefer to locate where there are already established communities of the same origin. The number one reason new immigrants gave as a reason for settling in one of the major cities is that they wanted to be close to family and friends. Spouses and children factored heavily in their preferred location decisions.

Between the years of 2001 and 2006, 581,000 international immigrants came to Ontario. By the year 2017 visible minorities will make up 29% of the Ontario population with most of the new Canadians moving to the Greater Toronto Area.

In an article in the National Post on April 3rd 2008 titled "Integration a Challenge, it was noted that combined metropolitan Toronto and metro Vancouver are home to 23% of the Canadian population, but 60% of all Canada's visible minorities.

Canadian Culture

Canadian culture is deep in diversity. The country of Canada is best described as a cultural mosaic, rather than a melting pot.

People from all over the world are welcome to share the common values of Canadians, while at the same time maintaining and celebrating their traditional customs. It's this rich cultural diversity that adds perspective, variety, flare, and uniqueness to the Canadian experience.

Canada's first inhabitants were native Aboriginals and early settlers from two nations: England and France. During the early to mid 1900's, European immigrants came to Canada from such countries as Italy, Portugal, Germany, Scandinavia, Poland, Ireland and the Ukraine. These early immigrants helped build the country and its economy, while establishing a foundation of many different cultures.

During the later years of the twentieth century, Canada attracted immigrants from other regions of the world such as the Caribbean, South America, Africa, Asia and the Middle East. As nations go, Canada is relatively young by comparison, having been established a mere 141 years ago. But it's a growing collaboration of various peoples, languages and customs. As Canada evolves, its cultural makeup continues to diversify.

Chapter Seven

Education In Canada

Education in Canada, from kindergarten or grade one through to grade twelve, is a publicly-funded program. Education is solely the responsibility of each province. Though standards may vary somewhat, Canada does offer a quality education system that's freely available to all. Approximately 7% of Canada's GDP (Gross Domestic Product) is spent on education.

Let's take a closer look at education in Ontario, as an example.

In addition to the standard system of education, Ontario also offers a pre-school program called "Best Start". It's an added program designed to:

- Help give Ontario's children a solid foundation for learning in the years ahead
- Provide child care services in a quality learning environment
- Initiate healthy mental, physical and emotional development during the early years
- Numerous organizations offer helpful advice to new immigrant families and parents of children starting school in Canada. There's a helpful 'tips sheet' found on the *People For Education* web site here: www.peopleforeducation.com
- Questions answered here include:
  - What will my child learn in Junior and Senior Kindergarten?
  - How can I help my child settle in?
  - Where can I go if I need help?
  - A full range of services are available to support the healthy growth and development of children from before their birth up to the age of six. Another avenue of assistance is provided through the infant hearing program. There's also a speech and language therapy program for children who need extra help. Numerous options and opportunities exist for high quality, affordable early learning and child care.

Primary (Elementary) and Secondary Education

Primary and Secondary Education is also referred to as K-12 (Kindergarten through grade twelve). Children stay in primary school through to grade eight. They then move on to high school (Also called secondary school).

In Ontario there is both a junior and senior kindergarten level. The complete K-12 program is offered through public, separate (Catholic), and private school systems. Both public and separate (Catholic) schools are fully funded by taxpayers and administered by the province. But private schools receive no government funding, relying on tuition fees instead.

Some private schools also provide residence facilities. Costs can vary from thousands of dollars to tens of thousands, if the student lives on campus.

A private school should be selected based on the recommendations of personal friends, other students, and interviews with the school's administrative staff. Most private schools have excellent records of achievement in education. But it's always wise to fully investigate all available options before settling on any one in particular.

Public schools are open to every child and do provide for a well-rounded, quality education. Separate schools offer a comparable education to the public school system, with the addition of the teachings of the Catholic religion. Both systems are fully funded from K-12. No other religious-based educational institutions receive financial support from any level of government. For more information, visit the Ontario Government's web site at:
http://www.edu.gov.on.ca

A pilot program has been instituted in some Ontario high schools called Newcomer Orientation week which was created to help newly arrived immigrant youth get a head start in high school. It was created from a partnership among the Toronto District School Board, Citizenship and Immigration Canada and settlement agencies. The concept brings New Canadian students into school a week early so that they can meet their teachers, settlement workers and fellow students and particularly other New Canadian students.

Apprenticeships

An apprenticeship program is hands-on training for those entering skilled trade fields. It's usually a combination of on-the-job training and study. An established set of guidelines and specific course of action is laid out in each area of specialty and trainees are required to meet minimum standards. Among the occupations offering apprenticeship programs are auto mechanics, carpenters, plumbers, electricians, and several others.

Apprentices are paid while they learn their trade. The amount an apprentice earns increases as their experience and skill level rises, until they become a certified tradesperson, where they are at virtually the same pay level as every other qualified specialist. It's a great way to learn a trade and earn income at the same time. Apprenticeships are best-suited to young people who are not interested in pursuing their academic studies at college or university. Completion of the program usually places you at the higher end of the pay scale in the trade of your choice.

There is a shortage of skilled labour across Canada. The Jobs Under Pressure Lists show this and the problem is particularly acute in the province of Alberta. Skilled labour licenses are regulated by each province and you should refer to your province and trade for information on accreditation. Ensure that your credentials are assessed and translated into English and that you have adequate English language skills in order to receive direction and know the rule of safety.

Apprentices work with licensed tradespeople while they are on-the-job and must be employed by a company.

Colleges

Currently there are 24 colleges of applied arts and technology in Ontario. They provide academic training programs covering a wide range of fields.

Here's a short list of just some of the programs available through Ontario's colleges:

Early Childhood Education, Fashion Arts, Business Administration, Child and Youth Worker, Paramedic, Computer and Network Support Technician, Radio Broadcasting, Graphic Design, Print Journalism, Public Relations

College programs vary in length and scope. Options include:[insert bullet points here}

- Certificate programs (one year or less)
- Diploma programs (two year and three year programs)
- Apprenticeship programs
- Programs that lead to a bachelor degree
- Programs offered in conjunction with a university

You can find a list of community and technical colleges in Ontario and throughout Canada by going to the following web site: www.cset.sp.utoledo.edu.canctool.html. These colleges offer courses identical to the ones listed for Ontario and give students career focused programs in the format of a one, two or three year program.

Private Career Colleges

Another option to further your education is available through one of several career colleges. These privately-operated organizations offer specialized training to prepare students for today's employment opportunities.

Currently available courses in the Toronto area include copywriting, pharmacy technician, paralegal, network systems technology, 3D animation, travel and tourism and many more. These private career colleges can offer a quality education. However, the buyer should be aware that there have been some problems with some private career colleges. Parents and students should check the cost of the college and the quality of education along with job prospects in the field and the success rate of placement. Parents and students should also interview some of the college's current students and graduates and be completely comfortable with the school, prior to enrollment. Costs should be itemized and provided to you in writing.

If the goal of the student is to learn English, the candidate should explore the opportunities and training available through the government agencies and immigration centres. Some of this training can be made available at no cost to you. Discuss the various options available with counselors at the immigration centres or government sponsored social agencies. If a private career college is the only option available, try the following path:

- Get a reference on the college from a government-run agency
- Find out the number of years that the college has been in business. Get references and discuss the college performance with current students
- Payment plans should offer flexibility. Some colleges have asked for the full tuition payment of over $5,000 upfront and then ran into difficulty and did not refund any money to students. There should be various payment options along with a written statement on refunds, in order to protect consumers.

Universities

Using Ontario as an example it currently has 18 universities, offering a wide array of options at the highest levels of academic achievement. Programs offered through the universities include:
- Undergraduate programs leading to a bachelor degree
- Graduate programs leading to a master's and/or doctorate degree
- Continuing Education classes and certificate programs
- Part-time programs
- Programs offered in partnership with colleges – allowing students to earn a university degree and a college diploma at the same time

For information on all Canadian universities including locations, programs, etc., is located at the Association of Universities and Colleges of Canada web site: www.aucc.ca/can_uni/our_universities/index_e.html

Maclean's Magazine in Canada does a yearly review of Canadian universities where it rates the various programs and ranks the professional schools and fields of study right across the country. MacLean's also does an annual assessment of what the students think of their current university on various topics.Refer to this web site for more information: www.macleans.ca/education/universities/article

Private Schools Located in the GTA

A complete list of Private Schools in the GTA is available here: www.privateschool.about.com

Private Schools in Other Parts of Canada

Information on private schools in Quebec, Alberta and British Columbia can be obtained at the following web sites:

Montreal, Quebec - www.highschool.suite101.com/article.cfm/montreals_best_high_schools www.montrealfamilies.ca/edfair.htm

Alberta - www.education.alberta.ca/parents/coice/private.aspx

British Columbia - www.bceducation.com privateschool.about.com/od/topschlbc/The_Best_Schools_in_British_Columbia.htm

Number of Foreign Students attending Canadian Schools

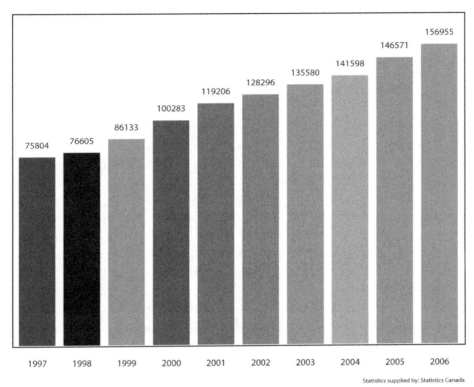

Statistics supplied by: Statistics Canada

Costs of Education For a Foreign Student

The average tuition cost in 2006-2007 for a Canadian student who is a Canadian citizen was $4,347. These fees applied to fulltime students. Foreign students can expect to pay up to 3 times the average Canadian student rate.

Contact each individual university you're considering for a quote on the exact tuition rate for foreign students. Fees vary according to the program in which the student wishes to enroll.

Community College costs for a Canadian citizen are between $1800 and $3300 -- depending on the program. Foreign students can expect to pay a higher fee, but it's a good idea to confirm fees with the specific college you have in mind.

In spite of these higher fees for foreign students, the costs of post secondary education covered by tuition only represents 11% of the total education costs to the province. Not included in tuition costs are the cost of books, athletic fees, student associations and health service fees outside of private health insurance paid by the student. These extra costs could add up to another $1500 annually.

Room and board is also another consideration and rates are dependent on the various accommodation and meal plans that the student chooses. Foreign students are not entitled to student loans unless they have obtained Canadian Citizenship or landed immigrant status first.

More information on this subject is available form the specific university and the Statistics Canada web site: www.statcan.ca/Daily/English/d060901a.htm. Permanent resident students and those who become Canadian citizens are entitled to pay the same tuition fees as some-one born in Canada would pay. International students who come to Canada for their education pay a much higher tuition fee and the exact amount should be checked out by college and university. Professional schools will also cost more than a standard education and this should be taken into consideration also. Check out all costs before enrolling and plan out the entire cost of the education including any professional school cost.

Foreign Students Studying in Canada

Canada has plenty to offer incoming students from around the world. In a UNICEF world survey on education, Canada ranked in the top four countries in terms of quality of education. The countries that ranked higher than Canada were non-English speaking countries – namely, South Korea, Japan, and Finland.

On average, more than 130,000 foreign students are enrolled in Canadian schools in a typical school year. Students from around the world come to Canada to pursue their studies in our educational institutions and to learn or improve their English or French language skills.

To study in Canada, you need either or both of these documents -- a *Study Permit* and/or a *Temporary Resident Visa*. Before applying for a study permit, you must be accepted for enrolment at a recognized school, college, or university in Canada.
Following is a series of steps you should follow in order to acquire a study permit:
1. Check the appropriate processing times so you know how long it will take so you don't miss any classes
2. Download the study permit kit found here: <insert URL> and print it out
3. Identify the location to which your completed application should be sent
4. Ensure that you have all required documentation
5. If you're planning to study in Quebec, additional information is required
6. Complete the application
7. Include the appropriate fee
8. Check to see that you've filled out the application form correctly and completely and then send it along
9. Be prepared to forward any additional information requested

Once approved, you'll receive a letter of introduction and a Temporary Resident Visa, if your home country is one that temporary resident visas have been designated.

*Please note: a Temporary Resident Visa is not your actual study permit, but it is part of the documentation needed for admittance to Canada as a foreign student.

Your next step is to make your way to Canada and begin your studies. Upon arrival, you will be channeled through Canada Customs and Immigration. This is standard operating procedure for everyone entering the country from abroad.

As a foreign student, you'll be asked to show the following documentation:
• Your passport
• Your letter of introduction

- A valid temporary resident visa (if required based on your country of origin)
- A letter of acceptance from the school that you'll be attending
- Any letters of reference requested by the visa office

With everything in order, you'll be issued a study permit on the spot. Before proceeding, check the permit to make sure the dates accurately reflect your study time in Canada and are not indicative of when you have to leave.

Be prepared in advance. This includes having your own medical insurance coverage for the duration of your stay in Canada. Foreign students are not covered by Canada's health care program.

Make the most of your stay here as a student. Those who derive maximum value from their experience not only excel academically, they prepare themselves for life beyond school. It's a great opportunity to scout the job market in your field of interest. Research the various employment opportunities that exist in Canada by using the resources available to all students. Establish contact with employment agencies and companies that hire people with your qualifications.

Companies and immigrant students should take the opportunity to do recruiting and research on job possibilities while the student is enrolled at a Canadian university or college. This option could be a valuable resource in finding skilled immigrants who are right on our doorstep and are familiar with the country and might be more globally mobile at this stage in their career.

Unfortunately, according to an article in the Toronto Daily Star dated October 30th, 2007 concerning "Work Permit Regulations Prove Costly For Canada" foreign graduates must leave Canada if they can't find a job within 90 days. Since these students are educated in Canada and would be prime candidates to help fill the shortages experienced in the health, energy and computer sectors. The article also states that Canada has dropped to 14th place (from a previous ranking in the top five) in retaining skilled foreign students.

A report examining the problem asks for more time than the current ninety days for the student to find work. It also suggests a work permit of five years, which is longer than the one or two years currently granted. We have an opportunity to become a world class leader in attracting skilled talent because of our first class education system, and yet Canada has not capitalized on this abundant opportunity.

Loan Opportunities (in Ontario) For Immigrant Students With Landed Immigrant Status

The Ontario government has recently changed the residency requirements for immigrants with landed immigrant status to qualify for an Ontario student loan. Currently a landed immigrant does not have to live in the province for 12 months, which was the previous qualification period. Details of the program are available at the following web sites:

www.cfsontrio.ca/english/general.php

www.settlement.org/sys/faqs

www.ogov.newswire.ca/ontario

www.ontarioimmigration.ca/english

Please be aware that student loan re-payment generally starts six months after you stop taking courses as a full-time student. This repayment consists of the principal sum plus an interest charge on that principal. Students should compare the terms and rates of interest of loan with one that would be available to them in their home country.

Students that wish to enter into post graduate studies after graduating from an international educational facility require their education to be assessed and accredited by a firm such as WES.

AIESEC

An important organization for international and foreign students studying in Canada is AIESEC Canada. AIESEC is the world's largest student-run organization and is an international platform for students to optimize their impact on business and society.

The AIESEC development process consists of placing the student in a position where they learn leadership and global business knowledge. The AIESEC Global Internship Program provides companies with a pool of talent on a global basis.

AIESEC Canada Inc. is headquartered in Toronto and is a registered not-for-profit organization with representation at 26 leading Canadian universities. AIESEC is an international global network of students and recent graduates numbering 23,000 and currently are present at 1,100 universities in 103 countries around the world. AIESEC provides 5,000 leadership and global internships around the world where students gain business experience and initiate contact with large and medium sized businesses along with gaining international experience and leadership. AIESEC gives students a chance to network with other students and also an opportunity to work and live abroad and also obtain valuable Canadian business experience.

The AIESEC Canada web site which shows all of the AIESEC university locations in Canada is: www.aisec.ca

Centennial College- International Students

Centennial College, situated in the east end of Toronto, On is Ontario's first government funded college. The campus and area is ethnically diverse providing students with an education that makes them job ready. 75% of the courses have a co-op(study and work experience) or work placement component. All information is on their web site
www.centennialcollege.ca

Key Point Summary

• A high standard of education is available to every child in Canada from Kindergarten or Grade One through to Grade 12, or completion of a high school diploma

• Multiple post-secondary educational opportunities exist for all, including immigrants and foreign students seeking to study in Canada

• Universal health care provides quality and accessible health care to anyone in Canada based on need

• Health Care is publicly-funded, so no user fees apply

• Depending on the province, new immigrants may require private health care insurance for their first 3 months in Canada, before qualifying for Medicare

Chapter Eight

Canada's Economic Opportunities:
A Provincial and Regional Overview
A National Perspective

Canada has a diversified economy composed of numerous regional economies right across the country. But the forces driving the economic performance of one province are usually quite different in another.

Natural resources have long been a major economic factor fuelling Canada's growth and development. But today's regional economies have recognized the importance of diversification by placing less emphasis and dependence on one or two local resources. It's an economic strategy that continues to contribute to Canada's sustainability.

Principle resource-based industries that contribute significant value to the Canadian economy include forestry, mining, oil, natural gas and farming. Although some resources exist in the central region and Atlantic Canada the primary source of our natural resources are the Western provinces.

Forestry continues to be the most dominant in British Columbia. Oil and natural gas are primary exports of Alberta. Saskatchewan with its flatlands and Manitoba have traditionally been strong in agriculture, but now a diversified economy in these provinces lends greater stability and far less dependence on farming.

Canada has also become a world leader in telecommunications, biotechnology, aerospace, pharmaceuticals, service, and information technology and these industries are more concentrated in the major urban centres across the country.

It's difficult for anyone to accurately forecast every area of economic growth, years in advance. But it's the prepared and well-informed immigrants who place themselves in the best possible position to seize suitable opportunities as they arise. Adequate preparation is crucial for the prospective immigrant with an eye toward Canada as their new home. Preparation is vital. It can make a huge difference in the quality of your experience here in Canada.

Recent results indicate positive economic growth for several provinces, while others haven't fared quite so well. The biggest gains were experienced by the Western provinces, while

Growth Rates Total Canada and Province 2007

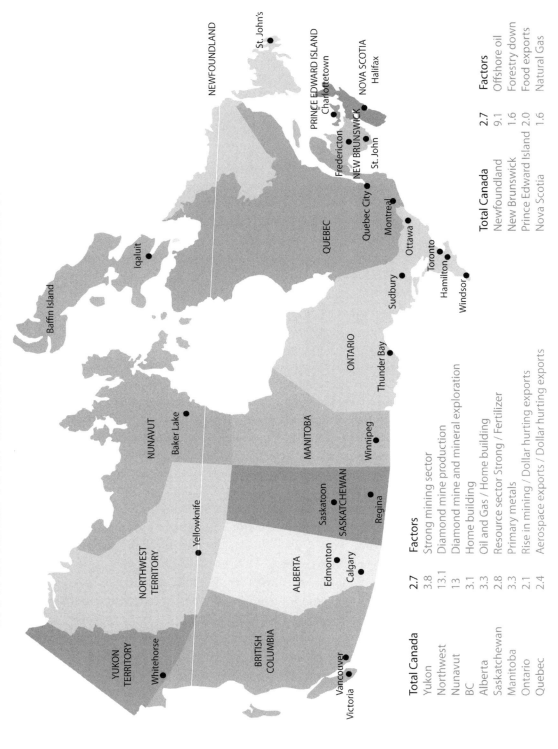

Total Canada	2.7	Factors
Yukon	3.8	Strong mining sector
Northwest	13.1	Diamond mine production
Nunavut	13	Diamond mine and mineral exploration
BC	3.1	Home building
Alberta	3.3	Oil and Gas / Home building
Saskatchewan	2.8	Resource sector Strong / Fertilizer
Manitoba	3.3	Primary metals
Ontario	2.1	Rise in mining / Dollar hurting exports
Quebec	2.4	Aerospace exports / Dollar hurting exports

Total Canada	2.7	Factors
Newfoundland	9.1	Offshore oil
New Brunswick	1.6	Forestry down
Prince Edward Island	2.0	Food exports
Nova Scotia	1.6	Natural Gas

others are not doing as well. The growth rate in Canada's Western provinces, because they are reliant on energy and natural resources, has been tempered somewhat by the decline of the U.S. and world economies. Alberta's economy continues to grow, recording a spectacular growth rate of 7% in 2006. Alberta's economic success is propelled by its wealth of natural resources, with large oil and natural gas deposits in the Athabasca Tar Sands. Exports to Asia from Alberta and British Columbia are triggering current growth rates which are expected to continue for some time to come. Western Canada's resource-based industries continue to supply an emerging China, providing the raw materials that fuel its dynamic growth. The recent economic slowdown may impact provinces that are resource based and lower the growth rate expectations that were present in the last few years. Most job losses in Ontario come from the manufacturing sector, as a soaring Canadian dollar and lower labour costs elsewhere make it more appealing to manufacturers to produce goods outside of Canada. Ontario continues to diversify, but its foundation built on manufacturing is taking a significant hit. Ontario's economy more than any other province, is closely tied to the American economy and for many years, Ontario was the main engine powering the Canadian economy. But as the U.S. sinks into recession, Ontario bears a major portion of the negative spin-off effect in Canada particularly for manufactured goods.

Ontario's rate of economic growth in 2006 was 1.5%. That's approximately one fifth the rate of growth experienced in Alberta. Experts forecast the slowdown in the United States -- triggered by a massive housing and credit crisis -- along with a higher Canadian dollar, could seriously weaken the Ontario economy over several years.

The Western provinces have taken the lead. Collectively, they are the chief economic engine driving Canada today. And it looks as though the West will remain as the principle power for the foreseeable future.

Alberta has experienced record growth but is drawing downward as the world economic slump takes hold. It's also the only province that does not have a provincial sales tax on the purchase of goods and services. But Alberta's expansion has caused a housing shortage, driving prices upward. If you're thinking of locating in Alberta, you need to be aware of the realities of the marketplace. Jobs are a bit more plentiful, but housing is scarce. The shortage has driven house prices and rents to record highs.

British Columbia and Saskatchewan are also experiencing strong growth, charged by the strong Asian demand for resources. BC is a major supplier of pulp, while Saskatchewan is a key source of oil, gas, uranium, and potash.

Economic growth, whether it's in the form of resource-based industries or manufacturing, triggers expansion and creates countless additional jobs that can run the gamut from various services, to information technology, human resources and logistics.

There has also been noticeable activity from provinces with high economic growth rates to advertise for job vacancies in provinces with lower growth rates. This action has shown the competitive nature of each of the provinces in their ongoing search for qualified workers. Now let's take a brief at the economies of the individual provinces of Canada:

An update on the Canadian economy was published by the Conference Board of Canada during the writing of this book. Some of the optimistic growth forecasts from the figures in early 2008 were tempered considerably by the world economic downturn. The Conference Board of Canada

issued a generally gloomy forecast for the Canadian economy in 2009, with a slowing housing market, rising unemployment rate and scarce GDP growth. GDP is expected to grow by only 1.5% in 2009. Exports will continue to suffer this year and next, the board forecasts. Canada's major trading partner is the United States, along with other world nations that use our natural and energy resources. These countries will slow their economies and use less of Canada's resources. A slowdown in the world economy along with a large drop in the price of oil will dramatically affect the growth , in particular, of Canada's Western provinces. The fact that Canada does have some impressive energy resources means that in the longer term these resources will prove to be a valuable factor in Canada's economic recovery which may start in 2010.

British Columbia

British Columbia continues to experience strong domestic growth. But the high Canadian dollar and the housing/credit crunch south of the border has slowed exports of lumber and natural gas. BC is projected to outperform the national average for some time to come, though it does face challenges which will limit its rate of growth over the next several years.

Positive economic indicators in British Columbia such as the volume of exports to China are tempered somewhat by the weakening world economy, higher Canadian dollar, and local labour shortages. British Columbia has moved towards a more diverse economic base that's less dependent on its natural resources.

Alberta

The massive growth Alberta is experiencing far surpasses that of any other province in Canada. Oil and its ever-increasing price on the world markets is the main reason for this unparalleled growth. Oil prices have dropped dramatically in recent months and will slow down Alberta's growth rate.

Future increases could come from further turmoil in the oil-rich Middle East, interruptions in production or flow, greater demand from developing countries like China and India, plus increased processing costs in challenging environments like the Tar Sands or offshore developments. Recent drops in the price of oil are related to the world economic slowdown.

Like its neighbour to the west, Alberta recognizes the need to diversify its economy to spur growth in areas other than resource-based industries. It's striving to match the booming energy sector with a knowledge-based economy that will serve Alberta well into the future. The objective is to use technology to replace resources in the long term. To succeed, Alberta plans to attract more businesses and skilled people, while emphasizing the growth and development of small and medium-sized businesses that will add value to the province's economy.

Alberta's chief growth industries include: Energy Technology and Services, Chemicals and Refined Petroleum Services, Agri-Food (Agriculture and food processing), Building Wood Products, Information Communication Technologies, and Environmental Technologies.

Calgary was recently rated as the number one city in Canada for new immigrants based on 7 different measurements including: the economy, innovation, environment, education, health, society and housing. Of the top 5 selected cities, 4 of them were in Western Canada. The lone exception was the city of Toronto.

Do your research and check out what jobs are short in Alberta before making the big decision to go west. Check with the Jobs Under Pressure list and also check with Provincial Employment Agencies.

Saskatchewan

Saskatchewan's population is nearly one million people. Most residents live in the southern region of the province. Its largest city is Saskatoon, though the capital is Regina. Other notable communities include Prince Albert, Moose Jaw, Swift Current and North Battleford.

Saskatchewan's economy has grown from its predominantly agricultural roots to a more widely-varied and more prosperous base. These days Saskatchewan is emerging as a province of considerable economic power. Its economy is now driven by energy resources, mining, high-tech research, as well as business and personal services. Agriculture still plays an important role, but now the province is better positioned for long term growth and stability.

All indications are that Saskatchewan has a solid foundation for robust economic growth. The future looks bright indeed. What this means is that there should be an abundance opportunities for immigrants who opt to make Saskatchewan their new home. Solid   market prices for oil, agricultural products, potash and uranium translate into a positive and prosperous future for Saskatchewan. A GDP rate of growth of 3.3% in 2007 should continue over the coming years, though labour shortages can limit Saskatchewan's growth.

In a Toronto Daily Star article of Tuesday, September 30th, 2008 entitled "Workers enticed to go west" the Premier of Saskatchewan, Brad Wall said that Saskatchewan has a people shortage. The premier, for his part, admitted that many New Canadians were overqualified for the jobs his province has to fill. What the New Canadian has to do is weigh the factors of a growing economy in Western Canada along with a variety of jobs and a place that is not crowded like a major city against the fact that the jobs may not match his/her skills and there may not be a community of people from his/her home country. Again the historic positive growth rates of the Western provinces will be tempered somewhat by the slowing world economy.

Manitoba

Manitoba has a population of 1,200,000. Half of total population is located in Winnipeg, its capital city. Other communities with more than 10,000 people are Brandon, Thompson, and Portage la Prairie.Major reasons for wanting to work and live in Manitoba include:
• Reasonable housing costs
• Low electricity costs
• Quality educational institutions
• Short commuting distances
• Affordable cottages in beautiful, natural environments

What makes Manitoba particularly appealing to newcomers is the free "settlement services" offered to new arrivals. It's the intention of these services to help new immigrants learn English, find employment, and adjust to life in their new environment. Manitoba has done an excellent job in designing programs for immigrants and proving them with information and resources to ease their transition to life in Canada. Manitoba lays claims to one of the most stable regional economies in Canada. Its diversified approach and sound financial management has helped the province weather economic storms better than other regions. In 2004, its GDP was 2.5%. By 2005, the figure was 2.8%. And by 2006, Manitoba's GDP had climbed to 3.1%.

Surprisingly, due to its location, resources and history, Manitoba's largest industry is manufacturing, which accounts for 12% of its GDP. Other primary industries include mining, forestry, and agriculture.

Additionally, Manitoba's growing service sector makes a significant contribution to the economy. Winnipeg, Manitoba's capital city houses the head offices of Canada's largest insurance company (Great West Life), Canada's largest mutual fund distributor (IGM Financial Inc.), plus one of the largest of Canada's media companies (CanWest Global Communications Corp.). With its centralized location, Manitoba also serves as a major North American transportation hub.

Ontario

One of the recurring challenges facing Canada is simply that what is good for one part of the country could be (and often is) damaging to another. Rising world oil prices means prosperous times for Alberta and to a lesser extent, the other western provinces. But increasing energy costs have negatively impacted Ontario, particularly its manufacturing sector. Sluggish economic conditions in the United States, combined with a surging Canadian dollar have reduced exports south of the border, Ontario's major trading partner. When the American economy sours, typically it's Ontario that pays a hefty price. The recent lowering of oil prices has helped Ontario in one way but the overall economic slowdown particularly in the US will affect Ontario for months into the future.

To-day's market conditions are of great benefit to Western Canada. This in turn means significant tax revenue generation for the federal coffers as long as the price of oil stayed high. In response to its vulnerability brought about by external market conditions, Ontario has moved to diversify its economic base. In 2004, 74% of the jobs in Ontario were in the service sector, with 18% in manufacturing. Market diversification is a step in the right direction that should help stabilize Ontario by improving its ability to endure economic swings.

One of the challenges facing Ontario is whether it can attract immigrants with the necessary skills to grow its service-based economy. Another important consideration is the number of university (Canadian and foreign) students enrolled in Ontario's schools. Out of the approximate 616,000 full-time undergraduate students registered in Canadian universities, 273,000 were based in Ontario. That's a whopping 44% of the total number of university students in Canada living in and attending classes in just one province. And as students graduate, they tend to stay within the urban areas, creating more competition for those available jobs.

Health care related occupations will be among those most in demand in Ontario over the coming years. The need for qualified people in all areas of health care from care givers to doctors is driven by Ontario's changing demographics. It's estimated that seniors will represent a larger segment of the total population in Canada through the year 2025. A larger seniors' base will require more healthcare workers over the next two decades. On average, Ontario spends more than three times as much on health care for seniors as it does on the general population.

In order to meet labour shortages in caring for an aging population, Ontario will have to rely on new immigrants and the skills they bring. But the burden of paying for the added costs of senior care is something all workers in Ontario, including immigrants, will have to share.

It's projected that by the year 2025, Ontario will have a skilled labour shortage of more than 360,000 people. As Ontario's baby-boomers (those born between the years 1946 and 1964 - a period of record numbers of births) age and retire from the workforce, vacancies are created. But today's declining birthrate can't even come close to replacing those retiring workers. Therefore immigration will become even more important to Ontario in the years ahead.

Toronto – Now and in the Future

Toronto continues to be a primary choice for many new immigrants to Canada. As one of the world's most ethnically diverse cities, over 100 different languages and dialects are spoken there. Though English is the most common language, more than one third of all households speak a language other than English in their homes. 43% of Toronto's residents identify themselves as being part of a visible minority and at last count, Toronto had 79 different ethnic publications. For Toronto, recent immigration trends include the following:

• A 16% increase in Chinese immigrants since 1996
• A 13% decline in immigrants of Italian origin
• A 25% increase of East Indian immigrants
• A 5% decline of immigrants from Portugal
• A 31% increase of immigrants from the Philippines

In Toronto, nearly half of the population is composed of visible minorities. Markham, a city that borders Toronto to the north, topped the list of communities in the GTA with just over 65 percent of the total inhabitants identified as visible minorities.

The actual city of Toronto itself is only a part of the urban sprawl that surrounds it. The GTA or Greater Toronto Area includes many other cities too. In the east, there's Oshawa, Whitby, Ajax, and Pickering. To the west, there's Oakville, Guelph, Milton, and Mississauga. North of Toronto you'll find Brampton, Vaughan, Richmond Hill, and Markham. South Asians -- which include immigrants from India, Bangladesh, Pakistan and Sri Lanka -- form 57 percent of Brampton's population, which makes it easier for immigrants from that part of the world to settle there and integrate into the community.

While the city of Toronto itself has recently faced some economic challenges, several areas near and around Toronto are thriving. There are indications of large economic and employment growth in some industry sectors and it's these categories that hold the best employment prospects for new immigrants.

One area just outside of Toronto that is experiencing strong growth is Brampton. Many new immigrants choose Brampton because of its community, area stores and affordable housing. But rapid growth presents new challenges in maintaining an infrastructure of services to accommodate the growing community of new immigrants.

Toronto's city planning officials project significant growth in three specific categories: Business Services, Food and Beverage, and Finance, Insurance and Real Estate. It's important for prospective immigrants to note that all three of these segments are service industries. The most dramatic declines are expected in Primary Industries, Wholesale Trade and Construction.

Wholesale Trade, and Storage and Warehousing are expected to decline in the city but grow in the outlying areas with lower property costs but growing populations.

Quebec

Quebec has posted a solid economic performance over the last few years. Its overall performance is helped by its diversification. Quebec is strong in the areas of research and development and entrepreneurship, and has many successful small and medium-sized businesses.

Quebec is the only province to have its own immigration policy and procedures. French is the official language of the province of Quebec and therefore tends to mostly attract immigrants with a French language background or former colonies of France or France itself.

The Atlantic Region

Each of the provinces in Atlantic Canada is experiencing a different level of growth. But the entire region offers immigrants a lifestyle that is very different to life in the major cities. The maritime location provides plenty of natural beauty, recreation and sports. Additionally, the people of Atlantic Canada are naturally warm and friendly.

Available jobs, though smaller in number, exist in specific industries. Prospective immigrants are urged to do their own preliminary research. Each province has its own Provincial Nominee Program, and it's an avenue that can save substantial time for new applicants seeking to relocate here.

New Brunswick

New Brunswick is the only constitutionally bilingual (English and French) province in Canada. The current population of New Brunswick is 730,000. Proportionally, there are more French-speaking people in New Brunswick than in any other province, with the exception of Quebec.

Fredericton, Moncton, and St. John are the three largest cities in New Brunswick. Fredericton is the capital, while Moncton is the information technology, commercial and retail centre of the province. St. John is one of the largest shipping ports in Canada and a major distribution hub on the east coast.

The economies of New Brunswick's major cities are dominated by health care, education, retail, finance and insurance businesses, government institutions, and transportation and distribution. New Brunswick's rural economy is based on four primary, resource-based industries including forestry, mining, mixed farming, and fishing. The province's largest employers include two well-known names – the Irving Group (Oil) and the McCain Group of Companies (Food Products). Several multi-national forest products companies are also sizable employers in the region.

Prince Edward Island

Prince Edward Island is located in the Gulf of the St. Lawrence, off the coasts of Nova Scotia and New Brunswick. PEI is separated from mainland Canada by the Northumberland Strait.

The island is connected to New Brunswick by the Confederation Bridge, an engineering triumph that spans a distance of some 13 kilometres. Career and business opportunities in Prince Edward Island exist in such high-tech fields as aerospace, bioscience, information and communications technology, as well as the traditional economic forces of agriculture and fisheries.

Nova Scotia

Nova Scotia is a province with plenty of potential for new immigrants. It offers both opportunities and a quality lifestyle. Its present population is approximately 930,000. Halifax, Nova Scotia's capital has a growing population, a thriving economy, affordable housing and cost of living, and quality health care and educational facilities. The city also offers countless historic sites and recreational opportunities, along with short commuter distances, and even the possibilities or walking or cycling to work.

Civilian career opportunities with the Canadian Navy and National Defense are available to Canadian citizens. Opportunities Nova Scotia featured 95 employers across the province with more than 2,300 job postings, indicating an availability of varied positions in Nova Scotia.

Newfoundland and Labrador

Labrador (part of mainland Canada) and Newfoundland are considered one province. Newfoundland is the large island off the east coast of Canada. It is accessible by ferry from the mainland, while access to Labrador is available by road from Quebec, or by ferry from Newfoundland. Total population is 506,000 -- or just over half a million.

Primary industries in Newfoundland include the traditionally dominant industry of fishing, to the more recent, high-potential industries of hydro-electric power, off-shore oil and gas refining and tourism. Mainland Labrador's economy is driven by mining and forestry.

Nunavut, Northwest Territories and the Yukon

These territories' economies are principally affected by mining, forestry, tourism and other natural resources

Key Point Summary

- Canada's economy is based on the performance of individual regional economies
- Canada's natural resources have always played a major role, though some of the specifics have changed
- British Columbia's economy is showing solid gains, due in part to large exports to Asia
- Alberta shows the strongest rate of economic growth in Canada at 7%, mostly due to its oil reserves
- But such massive growth in Alberta has increased housing costs while diminishing availability
- Saskatchewan is thriving from it's abundant resources of oil, agricultural products, potash, and uranium
- Manitoba's economy is strong and growing at a solid rate.

- Manitoba also offers numerous helpful services and resources to immigrants
- Ontario's economy is largely dependent on the economy in the United States been effected somewhat by problems in the US economy
- Today's best opportunities in Ontario exist in the service sector and health care
- Toronto is facing challenging times economically, though some regions nearby are doing better
- Quebec's economy has performed solidly the last several years
- Atlantic Canada offers a wide array of job opportunities, though quantities are more limited than other areas

Chapter Nine

Setting Yourself Up For Success:

Today's Best Employment Opportunities For New Immigrants In Key Regions of Canada

There are some preliminary steps every prospective immigrant should take well in advance of their planned arrival in Canada.

As an immigrant, you need to find work on your own. But your job search should never be postponed until you plant your feet on Canadian soil. Advance planning and taking action towards getting established will help ensure you of the best possible results once you are here.

Job searching is a lot like fishing. But finding a job in a new country is like fishing in a lake you've never seen or ever heard of before. If you simply drop your line in the water, you may get a nibble, a solid bite, or nothing at all. It could be that there isn't any fish in your area of the lake. Or perhaps there are fish, but they just aren't biting. Most people who use this passive "let's wait and see what happens" approach come up empty-handed in both situations. But there's a much more productive way to find the right kind of job for you in Canada and it begins with basic research.

Ideally, you want to cast your line in the most abundant waters. Take a closer look at the areas of Canada that are thriving economically and investigate employment opportunities there that you are #1: Qualified for (or could qualify for with some additional training) and #2: Interested in.

Look first at thriving communities teeming with opportunity. The more job opportunities available in your particular field, the more likely you are to land a position that suits you. Go where the jobs are -- just as you would go wherever the fish were biting. If your intention was to catch fish, you would increase you odds by dropping your line in a freshly-stocked lake. Since most new immigrants don't take these pre-arrival, job search steps, your line may be the only one in the water, giving you a competitive advantage.

Locate specific regions that need people with your skill sets. In other words, find a need in the marketplace and offer to fill it with your expertise.

Next, position yourself to suit the available job. Be the best 'fit' for the position and you stand a much better chance of getting hired. Once again, basic research comes into play. You need to know what employers want, in order to provide it.

Now that you have a basic understanding of the regional nature of the Canadian economy and the areas where growth is greatest, its time to look at the specific jobs that are in high demand.

Positions that are in highest demand, but short in supply of those qualified to do the work, have been labeled '*Jobs Under Pressure*'. On a regular basis, the federal and provincial governments compose lists of occupations where there's an obvious shortage of people. In these industries, the labour needs of the province exceed the currently available supply of workers. These *Jobs Under Pressure* lists are designed to identify problem areas to in turn help connect qualified people to those industries and professions who need them.

A complete list of 'Jobs Under Pressure' is available for each province, and can be accessed quickly by visiting the following web site: www.hrsdc.gc.ca

Regional Lists of Occupations Under Pressure
www.workingincanada.gc.ca for more information

The "Jobs Under Pressure" list for each province is dynamic and ever-changing. Listings change over time based on the economic needs of the province. You are encouraged to refer to web sites on employment in Canada for the 'Jobs Under Pressure' lists at the time you are searching for employment. Don't rely on outdated information.

For a list of jobs by city, visit a job board like Workopolis and use the search guidelines of location like: Toronto and area; Calgary and area: Edmonton and area; Montreal and area; Vancouver and area then use as a keyword your field of interest. Workopolis.com will provide you with a list of open jobs in that area. Many times companies use employment agencies to find candidates for them and the specific company is not mentioned in the job posting. In any case, treat the employment agency as a direct representative of the company because they will be making interview recommendations to the people doing the hiring.

Canadian Employment Agencies

A significant number of jobs which are both permanent and temporary are sourced through Canadian Employment Agencies. This practice offers more advantages to employers and for the worker, these agencies provide avenues to employment.

Although I own a successful service (Topnotch Employment Services Inc. in Toronto, Ontario) I recommend a list of national agencies that can help you find employment, improve your resume and interview skills and perform a job search for you. Besides Topnotch, which operates in the Greater Toronto area, the following are recognized national agencies: Adecco, Manpower, and Kelly Services.

Employment Agencies are required by law to make all of the necessary deductions from an employee's pay including Taxes, Canada Pension and Employment Insurance. Employers are also obligated to pay for the employee's Workers Compensation contribution. Employees are not allowed to be paid in cash and in any way bypass the payment of all taxes and contributions. Employment agencies do not charge the candidate for their services. They charge the employer for the candidate's services by either charging an hourly rate for part-time work, or a fee based on a percentage of the candidate's salary for finding a permanent individual for a company.

Employment agencies find jobs that are full-time, part-time and part-time temporary to permanent. The use of employment agencies allows the immigrant to gain business experience as a part-time employee and move to a full-time position after gaining valuable business experience.

Canadian Jobs with the Highest Vacancy Rates

The Toronto Sun of April 26th 2008, reported that the following jobs in Canada currently had the highest vacancy rates:

1. Construction
2. Hospitality, personal services
3. Primary (mining, forestry)
4. Agriculture
5. Retail
6. Business Services
7. Health, education
8. Manufacturing
9. Transportation

As earlier indicated, many of these jobs are offered by small to medium size businesses and many are semi-skilled trades and service positions. But immigrants considering work in these fields may have difficulty accumulating the necessary points to get into Canada under the Skilled Worker Program. It's a question of whether the current program is serving the country effectively in meeting the demands of an evolving economy, or whether it's time for Canada to make some changes.

It should also be pointed out that all of these jobs may not be available across the country but only in a few areas. This list was also developed before the recent economic decline in the Fall of 2008 and may have changed substantially by the time that the book is printed.

Opportunities In Ontario

The short-term outlook for Ontario is driven primarily by its demographics. Ontario's population is aging and the province's health care program is already feeling the strain. Based on the numbers, the demand for health care professionals in a wide range of specialties will continue for some time to come.

Investment planning is another area that could see substantial growth in the coming years. Again, this will be fueled by aging Ontarians facing retirement and looking for sound financial advice to make the most of it.

Segments of the investment field have already become automated with online accessibility, resulting in some job reductions. But the aging population combined with a longer average lifespan means there's a growing market in need of specialized financial services.

Numerous opportunities are currently available in the construction trades and related fields. It is projected that the building and construction trades will continue strong over the short-term, but may be negatively impacted over the long term. Again, these market changes can be attributed to Ontario's aging population, combined with a declining birth rate. With less need for housing and slower economic time construction of homes, condo and offices will naturally slow down.

A wide variety of skilled trades (including but not limited to the construction industry) will continue to show shortages as positions are not being filled. Fewer Canadians are entering the skilled trades these days and that can only mean that we will become increasingly dependent on the immigrant population to fill labour shortages in the trades now and in the future.

Listed below are those positions currently in need in Ontario, as listed at the 'Jobs Under Pressure' web site. Although it is difficult to forecast the long term needs by job category, the following factors are making an impact in Ontario and can be of assistance to anyone evaluating the Ontario jobs market:

1. An aging population means solid, long term job prospects in the various areas of health care and health care administration.

2. An aging population increases the demand for investment and financial consulting services.

3. Human resources will become an increasingly important field due to the challenges employers face in finding quality people. Attracting and keeping new employees whether they are Canadian-born or immigrants will be crucial in the years ahead. Unfortunately in the short term Human Resources personnel may be required for their expertise in laying off and providing employees with severance benefits.

4. More scientists will be required for research in various areas.

5. An increasing number of engineers and architects will be required to design cost and energy efficient building and structures.

6. Significant slowdowns in apprenticeship enrollments by Canadians will continue to make Ontario businesses increasingly dependent on immigrants to fill vacant jobs such as transportation and equipment operators, auto mechanics, heavy equipment mechanics, and many other skilled occupations.

7. A general lack of unskilled and semi-skilled labour to perform service functions in logistics, manufacturing, and general service jobs. There is a definite learning curve as an individual moves from an unskilled to semi-skilled job and many Canadians went through this learning curve as they apprenticed in road construction, warehousing, or fork-lift operators. Food service and retail management are two areas that require thousands of people in unskilled and semi-skilled positions.

8. Small businesses in Ontario require qualified IT, clerical, accounting, and salespeople to fill available positions.

Ontario's current list of 'Jobs Under Pressure' include the occupations listed below. Visit the 'Jobs Under Pressure' website for up-to-date information. These lists will change constantly reflective of the province's needs and economic circumstances.

Management-Senior Financial, Communications
Purchasing managers
Banking Credit and Investment
Managers in Health Care
Administration
Financial and Investment Analysis
Specialists in Human Resources
Natural and Applied Sciences
Biologists
Civil Engineers
Mechanical engineers
Architects
University Professors

Health Occupations
Specialist Physicians
General Practitioners and Family Physicians
Pharmacists
Audiologists and Speech-Language Pathologists
Physiotherapists
Registered Nurses
Medical Laboratory Technologists and pathologists' Assistants
Medical Radiation Technologist
Dental Hygienists and Dental Therapists
Licensed practical Nurses
Ambulance Attendants and other Paramedical Occupations

Skilled Trades
Transport and Equipment Operators
Heavy Duty Equipment Mechanics
Refrigeration and Air Conditioning Mechanics
Automotive Service Technicians
Truck Mechanics and Mechanical Repairers
Machinists and Machining and Tooling Inspectors
Industrial Electricians
Construction Millwrights
Carpenters, Bricklayers, Cement Finishers and Setters
Drywall Installers and Finishers

To learn all about internationally-trained tradespeople, visit this government web site: www.edu.gov.on.ca/eng/training/foreign.html

For information about apprenticeships and a list of all the trades in Ontario, visit: www.apprenticesearch.com and click on the "About Trades" heading.

Some trades are regulated by the provincial government and you must be licensed in order to work in these businesses. The following is a list of government-regulated trades in Ontario:

Bakers, Carpenters, Cooks, Early Childhood Educators, Electricians, Hairstylists and Barbers, Industrial Electricians, Machinists, Motor Vehicle Mechanics, Plumbers, Refrigeration Mechanics, Tool and Die Makers.

The list is not indicative of job shortages in these areas which may or may not exist.

Following the route of the other provinces, Ontario has also introduced a Provincial Nominee Program. It is designed to address the shortage of qualified workers and expedite the processing of candidate applications at the same time. A more detailed description of the Provincial Nominee Program is available in the section titled "Avenues to Immigration".

Each submitted application is then screened by the province, with an eye towards its own current labour marker needs. Next, the names of all suitable candidates are forwarded to Citizenship and Immigration Canada. Final approval is given to those who meet security and health check requirements.

Given official clearance, an applicant could have a Permanent Resident Card in hand within a few months, instead of the three or four years it typically takes.

Refer to the sections on professional and trade licensing in Canada and the process of evaluation which is supplemental to this section. An occupation on the 'Jobs Under Pressure' list still requires all of the steps required to be licensed for that job in Canada.

Opportunities in Alberta
Jobs Under Pressure In Alberta

The Alberta 'Jobs Under Pressure' list in indicative of the growth rates Alberta is enjoying. Chances are Alberta's economy will continue to perform above that of most other provinces for some time to come. There may be some short term blips in the Alberta economy based on a slowdown of the American and world economies but a province with energy resources will show growth in the long term. Forecasts for the next twenty years are more reflective of an established and growing economy than a resource-based single economy. Success breeds success. Alberta's efforts to diversify it's economy, so it continues to thrive with or without oil, has been made easier through its many years of strong growth. Alberta's 'Jobs Under Pressure' list is accessible at the following web site: www.hrsdc.gc.ca

Regional Lists of Occupations Under Pressure

Management Occupations
    Engineering Managers
    Architecture and Science Managers
    Computer and Information Systems Managers

Sales, Marketing and Advertising Managers
Retail Trade managers
Construction Managers

Business, Finance and Administrative Occupations
Financial Auditors
Securities Agents, Investment Dealers and Brokers
Supervisors, Mail and Message Distribution Occupations
Loan Officers
Assessors, Valuators and Appraisers

Natural and Applied Sciences and Related Occupations
Physicists and Astronomers
Chemists
Geologists
Biologists
Civil Engineers
Mechanical Engineers
Electrical and Electronic Engineers
Chemical Engineers
Industrial and Manufacturing Engineers
Metallurgical and Materials Engineers
* Plus 20 additional occupations

Health Occupations
Specialist Physicians
General Practitioners and Family Physicians
Veterinarians
Pharmacists
Audiologists and Speech-Language Pathologists
Registered Nurses
Medical Laboratory Technologists
Registered Nurses
Medical Laboratory Technologists and Pathologists' Assistants
Veterinary and Animal Health Technologists and Technicians
Medical Radiation Technologists
Medical Sonographers
Dental Technologists, Technicians and Laboratory Bench Workers
Midwives and Practitioners of Natural Healing
Nurse Aides, Orderlies and Patient Service Associates

Occupations in Social Science, Education, Government Service
College and Other Vocational Instructors
Ministers of Religion

Community and Social Service Workers
Early Childhood Educators

Occupations in Art, Culture, Recreation and Sport

Producers, Directors, Choreographers and Related Occupations
Musicians and Singers
Dancers
Actors and Comedians
Film and Video Camera Operators
Graphic Arts Technicians
Audio and Video recording Technicians
Other Technical and Occupations in Motion Pictures, broadcasters
Announcers and Other Broadcasters
Other Performers
Program Leaders and Instructors in Recreation and Sport

Sales and Service Occupations

Retail Trade Supervisors
Food Service Supervisors
Chefs
Cooks
Butchers
Bakers
Hairstylists and Barbers
Sales Reps
Sales Clerks
Hotel Front Desk Clerks
Plus 18 other occupations

Trades, Transport and Equipment Operators and Related Occupations

58 occupations listed including: Contractors and Supervisors, Pipefitting Trades, Tool and Die Makers, Industrial Electricians, Plumbers, Carpenters, Welders, Concrete Finishers, Painters and Decorators, etc.

Occupations Unique To Alberta's Primary Industries

Oil and Gas Well Drillers, Testers and Related Workers
Farm Supervisors and Specialized Livestock workers
Aquaculture Operators and managers
Oil and Gas Well Drilling Workers and Service Operators
General Farm Workers
Nursery and Greenhouse Workers

Occupations unique to Processing, Manufacturing and Utilities include: Labourers, Plastic Processing Machine Operators, Wood Product Assemblers and Inspectors.

Opportunities in British Columbia
Jobs Under Pressure In British Columbia

The available positions in British Columbia that are listed in 'Jobs Under Pressure' are numerous and varied. They include career positions in business, the sciences, health care, construction trades, and more.

Business, Finance and Administration Occupations
  Specialists in Human Resources
  Business Services to Management
  Medical Secretaries

Natural and Applied Sciences and Related Occupations
  Physicists and Astronomers
  Geologists
  Biologists
  Civil Engineers
  Mechanical Engineers
  Electrical Engineers
  Aerospace Engineers
  Architects
  Database Analysts
  Agricultural and Fish Product Inspectors

Health Occupations
  Specialist Physicians
  General Practitioners
  Dentists
  Veterinarians
  Dietitians and Nutritionists
  Head Nurses and Supervisors
  Registered Nursing Assistants

Occupations in Art, Culture, Recreation and Sport
Sales and Service Occupations
  Butchers and Meat Cutters
  Roofers and Shinglers
  Glaziers
  Insulators
  Painters and Decorators
  Floor Covering Installers
  Refrigeration and Air Conditioning Mechanics
  Upholsterers
  Crane Operators
  Aircraft Mechanics and Aircraft Inspectors
  Elevator Constructors and Mechanics

Refer to the sections on professional and trade licensing in Canada and the process of evaluation which is supplemental to this section. A position listed on the 'Jobs Under Pressure' list still requires all of the steps required to be licensed for that job in Canada.

Key Point Summary

• Advance planning is of primary importance for every prospective immigrant to Canada. Planning is crucial to your success.

• Look first towards the regions of Canada where job opportunities are most plentiful.

• That's where you stand the greatest chance of securing employment.

• Position yourself as the best 'fit' for the available job

• Examine the 'Jobs Under Pressure' lists and note any positions that you may qualify for

• Use demographics to locate opportunities presented by trends in the population

• Ontario needs people now in these areas of specialty: medicine, financial and investment planning, senior management, and the sciences

• Alberta, due to its leading economic performance offers the most employment opportunities covering a wide span of industries and professions

• British Columbia's current labour needs include: human resource specialists, scientists, engineers, medical professionals, and skilled trades workers

• Medical Doctors are in demand right across the country, but the current strict restrictions make it difficult for foreign-trained specialists to gain the certification required to practice here

• Nursing is in high demand Canada-wide

• Foreign-trained nurses find it easier than doctors to meet the required criteria for certification, in order to work in Canada

Chapter Ten
Regulated Professions in Canada
Careers in Medicine

Dr. Divi Patel

Dr. Divi Patel is a graduate of the Witwatersrand Medical School of Johannesburg, South Africa. He is a family physician practicing in the Kitchener-Waterloo area of Ontario. Dr. Patel came to Canada and arrived in Vancouver in January of 2002.

Dr. Patel's credentials were recognized through an arrangement with Health Match BC, which is a non-profit recruitment agency with co-operation from the College of Physicians and Surgeons of BC.

South African physicians are well recognized internationally, however, Dr. Patel's credentials were reviewed by both HealthMatch BC and by the Registrar of the College of Physicians and Surgeons of BC. Dr. Patel then wrote the qualifying and LMCC (Licentiate of the Medical Council of Canada) exams in the following two years and the CCFP (Certificate College of Family Practice) exams under the guidance and direction of the college.

Dr. Patel has some suggestions for new immigrant professionals who are looking for work in the medical profession in Canada. Get in touch with the regulatory bodies in the provinces that you are planning to work in. The colleges have a list of all job postings and of regulatory non profit agencies that can assist new physicians. As well, certain provinces like Newfoundland, Saskatchewan and Manitoba may make it easier for foreign trained MD's to acquire licensure depending on the individual circumstances.

Dr. S. Ralh

Dr. Ralh came to Canada in 1978 after graduating as a Doctor in India. At that time he did not prepare for any of the requirements for medical licensing in Canada. Dr. Ralh came to Canada sponsored by his wife, so advance preparation to practice medicine was not planned. The realities of coming to Canada were similar for Dr. Ralh in that Canada, just like his home country of India, requires lots of hard work to succeed and life at times is not easy.

The medical aspects of Canada were somewhat different to those of India in that India's doctors concentrated mainly on infectious diseases, while in Canada the focus was on heart disease, diabetes and cancer. Canada also has more of a "North American approach" to medical liability than does India.

Dr. Ralh recommends the following for foreign-trained doctors wanting to practice in Canada.:

• Get all of your tests done for qualification by arranging visits to Canada rather than packing up the family and moving here. Because of the costs of having your family with you and the possibilities of delays it is advisable to come by yourself to write and prepare for your medical exams. Also by doing this you cut down on the total time taken.

• If you do not have the financial resources to make it through the qualifying and licensing stages, you may have to be prepared to take any type of employment to make ends meet.

• Use all the material resources you can find to prepare for the tests such as old multiple choice tests, etc. which will give you an idea of the type of questions and time limits.

• Dr. Ralh recommends the Kaplan Educational Centres as a good training centre for preparing for medical exams: www.kaptest.com/index.jhtml

Careers in Medicine

All areas of the medical profession in Canada are regulated. The specific requirements in order to practice medicine are determined by the Medical Council of Canada and each Provincial College.

In Ontario, that task is left to the College of Physicians and Surgeons of Ontario. Their job is to monitor and regulate the practise of medicine, issue medical certificates, uphold a standard of practice, and investigate complaints against doctors. There are different requirements for specialists and general practitioners and the requirements should be checked out with each of the medical boards.

If you know where you intend to practice medicine then you can contact the regulatory board concerned. If you want to get further information on the practice of medicine in Canada then visit The Canadian Information Centre for International Medical Graduates (IMGs) web site which is located at: http://www.img-canada.ca/

The above site also includes a chart outlining the steps any applicant needs to follow in order to register to practice medicine in Canada. You should also contact the Medical Council of Canada for additional information at the address and/or web site below.

Medical Council of Canada (MCC)

P.O. Box 8234, Station T

Ottawa ON K1G 3H7 Canada

P: 613) 521-6012 F: (613) 521-9417   http://www.mcc.ca/

For more information on International Medical Graduate programs in Canada, please refer to the following web sites:

Ontario

HealthForceOntario

www.healthforceontario.ca

British Columbia

International Medical graduates of British Columbia

www.imgbc.med.ubc.ca/home.htm

Alberta

Medical Communication Assessment Project (M-CAP)

www.ucalgary.ca/news/may2007/immigrantdocs

Manitoba

Health Employment Manitoba

www.healthemployment.ca/

Saskatchewan

Saskatchewan Immigrant Nominee Program (SINP)

www.immigration.gov.sk.ca/physician/

New Brunswick

College of Physicians and Surgeons of New Brunswick

www.cpsnb.org

Nova Scotia

Association of International Physicians and surgeons

www.capprogram.ca

Prince Edward Island

Government of Prince Edward Island Skilled Worker category

www.gov.pe.ca/immigration/index

Newfoundland

International Medical Graduate

www.nlphysicianjobs.ca

The provincial licensing authorities for medical doctors in the provinces of Ontario, B.C and

Alberta are:

College of Physicians and Surgeons of Alberta (CPSA)
900 Manulife Place, 10180-101 Street
Edmonton AB T5J 4P8 Canada
P: 80 423-4764 F: 780 420-0651
rburns@cpsa.ab.ca   http://www.cpsa.ab.ca

College of Physicians and Surgeons of British Columbia (CPSBC)
400-858 Beatty Street
Vancouver BC V6B 1C1 Canada
P: 604 733-7758   F: 604 733-3503
registration@cpsbc.ca   http://www.cpsbc.ca/cps

College of Physicians and Surgeons of Ontario (CPSO)
80 College Street
Toronto ON M5G 2E2 Canada
P: 416)-967-2603
feedback@cpso.on.ca   http://www.cpso.on.ca/

Any foreign-trained doctor must realize that there's a process they have to complete before they're able to practice medicine in Canada. This process includes the writing of the medical council of Canada's evaluation exam and then the same council's qualifying exam. These exams are built around Canadian standards and the foreign-trained professional should assess how long it will take to prepare for and write the examinations.

It's also important to take into account the financial requirements of candidates and their families while he/she studies and completes the exams. Perhaps this is an area where business and citizens could press the government to make loans available to foreign-trained medical professionals. It seems like an obvious solution, one that would alleviate the shortage of medical professionals in Canada. After all the basic training has already been completed and paid for by the individual and their host country. With the availability of financial aid, everyone would benefit to a greater degree.

Medical candidates should also realize that after passing the exams, they are required to register with CaRMS, which is the Canadian Registry for Postgraduate Residency. Postgraduate residency is required to give the doctor practical and clinical training in their field of specialization -- within a hospital setting.

Another certification test is done after the term of residency has been completed. These residencies are granted in 13 medical schools across Canada and two things should be noted: 1) The term varies with the specialization chosen and 2) There are a very limited number of available spaces. Foreign trained doctors compete for positions after Canadian trained doctors have been placed. As an example in 2003, 625 international graduates competed for 67 open positions. Foreign-trained doctors not successful in receiving a residency position, still have to support themselves and their families, until a residency position is made available to them.

One of our most critical shortages in Canada is the shortage of family doctors, emergency care physicians, and specialists. If we cannot satisfy this shortage with the large number of foreign-trained doctors who are ready to step in and take on this responsibility, then how are we to meet the other needs of our country? Even with the co-ordination of the Federal and Provincial governments and the Medical Associations, Canada has not yet developed a solution to this problem, a problem that is growing ever critical.

The solution lies in Canada's ability to streamline the process of placing foreign-trained medical candidates and providing expanded resources for them to qualify and finance their studies.

During the writing of this book an article was published in the Toronto Daily Star on June 7th, 2008 titled, "Foreign-Trained Doctors To Get a Break in Ontario" in which the Health Minister, George Smitherman, said he will propose legislation that should provide more foreign-trained doctors by cutting red tape.

The legislation contains two provisions 1) Fast tracking of accreditation for doctors already working in Canada, the US and other countries with comparable health-care systems. 2) A new system involving a transitional license, allowing specialists to practice under the supervision of a local specialist in their field for 2 to 5 years before they are fully licensed.

The government is also looking at speedier assessments of foreign trained doctor's abilities and language training. The Ontario Medical Association applauded the moves and said that it supports bringing in more foreign-trained doctors as long as they are properly assessed and trained. The article goes on to state that over 5,000 foreign-trained doctors are now treating patients in Ontario so their value has already proved itself.

Nursing in Canada

Nursing is another medical-related profession that's in high demand. Nursing is also fully regulated in Canada. But at the present time, it's much easier for foreign-trained nurses to ply their trade here, than it is for doctors.

The following 12 registered nursing specialties are those that are most in demand in Canada today:Critical Care
   1. Intensive Care
   2. Cardiac Care
   3. Emergency
   4. Burn Unit and Care
   5. Neonatal Care
   6. Dialysis Care
   7. Neurosciences
   8. High Risk Labour and Delivery/Maternal care
   9. Trauma and Neurotrauma
   10. Operating Room
   11. Oncology

If you're an internationally-trained nurse and have specialization in one of the areas listed above, you stand a very good chance of finding employment in Canada. Following are the precise steps you should take to work in nursing in Canada:

1. Chose the province where you would like to work and then contact the provincial nursing licensing body.

2. Nurses who trained outside the country must complete a program that can be compared to one that exists in the province selected.

3. Provide proof of recent experience in the practice indicated.

4. Candidates must achieve a passing score on a professional examination administered by the provincial licensing board.

5. Candidates need to demonstrate reasonable fluency in English or French.

6. Show proof of Canadian citizenship, or proof of authorization to practice nursing in your chosen province. (This allows you to obtain a temporary registration card for one year. With this card, you can apply for a Work Visa for a longer period of time.)

7. You may apply for permanent residence in Canada for you and your family once you have completed one year of full time employment.

The licensing body for nurses in Ontario is the College of Nurses of Ontario. Each province has a similar licensing body.

The Toronto Star of May 10th, 2008 published an article entitled "York's Retraining Program a Hit With Foreign Nurses". The article suggested that Ontario alone will require 9,000 additional nurses over the next three years. The main reason for this demand is that the majority of nurses are over 50 years of age and beginning to retire just as other baby boomers are doing. The article describes the nursing program at York University which helps foreign-trained nurses to upgrade or retrain based on Canadian qualifications. The foreign-trained nurses are registered nurses in their home country but they require a Bachelor of Science in Nursing degree which takes the student about 20 months to complete. Students pay a tuition fee of $12,000, but scholarships and bursaries are available.

This program is open to nurses who already have landed immigrant status or are Canadian citizens. This means that the student nurses are entitled to apply for the Ontario Student Loan program. Graduates are virtually guaranteed jobs, which pay an estimated starting salary of $45,000 a year. If the York program is full or has too long a waiting list for you there are other schools of nursing which can be applied to and are available from the College of Nurses.

Dentistry

Dr. George Warda

Dr. George Warda was born in Iraq and studied dentistry in that county. There are two dental schools in the country of Iraq. One school is at Baghdad University and the other school is at Mosul University. In the University you require 5 years of study before you graduate. The first two years you study basic science and basic dentistry while the last three years focus on dentistry and clinical practice. All of the study material is in English.

When Dr. Warda arrived in Canada in September of 1997 he asked how to get a licence to practice dentistry. He was told that he had two options: One option was to go through 4 examinations from the National Dental Examining Board of Canada (NDEBC). There were 2 written and 2 clinical exams with each exam held in a different city and a patient had to be found to do the clinical portion. The second option consisted of a 2 year program in any Canadian Faculty of Dentistry after passing the qualification exam and interview.

Dr. Warda chose the NDEBC option and got his certificate. The next step was to get a licence from the province and membership in the Royal College of Dental Surgeons of Ontario.

To-day the process is different in that there is a two year program after you pass the TOFEL exam which is a qualification in English. The program initially requires you to take a qualification exam, a clinical exam and an interview at the university where you applied. There is a great deal of competition for these placements because of the number of foreign trained dentists applying to the program. For a dentist from Iraq it is difficult to get a visitor visa to Canada because of the situation in that country and also the nearest TOFEL testing centre or IELTS centre is in Amman Jordan.

A recommendation that Dr. Warda has for individuals seeking a dental licence in Canada is to contact the NDEBC and get all of the requirements and information and, although it is difficult, try to get as much of the preparation as possible on visitor visas to Canada. Also get as much English training as possible in your home country in preparation for taking English testing.

To work in a regulated profession in Canada you need to be certified by a professional association. So far, we've listed information on three regulated health professions in Ontario: Doctors, Nurses and Dentists. In total there are twenty two regulated, health care professions in Ontario, which are listed on the web site at:
http://www.citizenship.gov.on.ca/English/working/licensed/

Now let's review the regulated profession of dentistry. In order to work in dentistry, you need to be certified by the professional association that regulates dentists in your chosen province. In Ontario, that regulatory body is the...

Royal College of Dental Surgeons of Ontario
5th Floor, 6 Crescent Road
Toronto, Ontario M4W 1T1
T: 416-961-6555 Toll free- 1-800-565-4591

info@rcdso.org   http://www.rcdso.org

If you have a professional designation from your home country, the Royal College of Dental Surgeons of Ontario can provide you with all of the requirements necessary to practice dentistry in the province of Ontario. Be sure to have your certificates translated into English by a reputable translation firm.

For a foreign-trained dentist to obtain the certificate of registration or licence, graduates of dental schools outside of Canada and the United States must first complete and pass a full-time, two-year qualifying program at a Canadian university, before becoming eligible to write the National Dental Examining Board of Canada (NDEB) exam.

Other Regulated Medical Professions in Ontario

The following information is from an Ontario government web site called www.ontarioimmigration.ca/english.

Provinces outside of Ontario regulate their professionals in a similar manner and you should refer to the specific web sites for each province. A list of regulated, non-health and regulated health professionals in Ontario is available at this site.

Health Force Ontario offers a number of services to health professionals, including a recruitment centre and jobs listing service. A full list of regulated professions for the province of Ontario is at the following web site: www.citizenship.gov.on.ca/english/working/licensed

Additional information is available here:
www.img-canada.ca/en/careers/regulated.html

Regulated Non- Medical Professions in Canada
Accounting

Certified General Accountant (CGA)
Certified General Accountants Association of Ontario
240 Eglinton Avenue East
Toronto, On M4P 1K8
416-322-6520   info@cga-ontario.org

For specific information related to working as a CGA in Ontario as a new immigrant, refer to the following web site: www.ontarioimmigration.ca/english/how_work_cga.asp

Certified Management Accountant (CMA)
The Society of Management Accountants of Ontario
Suite 300, 70 University Avenue
Toronto, Ontario M5J 2M4
416-977-7741
info@CMA-Ontario-org   http://www.cma-ontario.org

For specific information related to working as a CMA in Ontario as a new immigrant refer to the following web site: www.ontarioimmigration.ca/english/how_work_cma.asp

Chartered Accountants
The Institute of Chartered Accountants of Ontario
69 Bloor Street East
Toronto, On M4W 1B3
416-962-1841
custserv@icao-on.ca   http://www.icao.om.ca

For specific information related to working as a CA in Ontario as a new immigrant refer to the following web site: www.ontarioimmigration.ca/english/how_work_ca.asp

Engineering

Professional Engineers of Ontario, PEO, is the self-regulated organization that controls, sets standards and licenses the 70,000 professional engineers in Ontario. It has a statutory mandate to protect the public interest where engineering is concerned. PEO consists of 37 chapters, representing the different geographic area in Ontario.

More information on the profession of engineering for new immigrants to Ontario is available on the following web sites:
www.citizenship.gov.on.ca/english/working/career/professions/engineers.shtml
www.peo.on.ca/welcome.html
www.ontarioimmigration.ca/english/how_work-engineer.asp

Please bear in mind that you will receive accurate information on the registration and licensing process for professionals. But what you won't find is a loan or financing options for you and your family. If you need to study for an extensive period in preparation for your license, you need to take care of your financial arrangements in advance. No province provides financial assistance of any kind to foreign professionals preparing for and writing qualifying exams. This preparation might take years. Therefore, the individual needs to recognize that they are solely responsible for their own finances.

*Ontario has recently introduced the "Fair Access To Regulated Professions Act" which attempts to break down the barriers foreign-trained professionals have in finding employment in Ontario. The new bill would provide for the following:
• An appeals process, should an individual want to appeal the decision of the regulatory board.
• Review of all of the regulatory board requirements, in order to remove barriers
• Provide decisions within a reasonable period of time and inform applicants on how their regulatory body process works.

Global Experience Ontario (GEO) is set up to help internationally-trained individuals in regulated, non-health professions. Their purpose is to assist immigrants who trained in their home country to qualify for professional practice of their area of expertise in Ontario.

In the Toronto Daily Star of Thursday, August 14th, in an article titled," Licensing offer draws few takers" it was stated that fewer than 10% of foreign-trained engineers have used a free-licensing assessment program offered by the Professional Engineers Ontario. The fees are a $230 licensing fee and a $70 enrolment fee for an intern training program. The application needs to be filed within six months of arriving in Canada or graduating from a Canadian university.

The Legal Profession in Canada

The legal profession in Canada is governed by the laws, rules and regulations of the law society of which a lawyer is a member. There are 14 law societies in Canada, one for each of the 10 provinces and one for each of the three territories. The province of Quebec has 2 law societies, which respect the civil law tradition from France that governs the province of Quebec, making it different from the other provinces and territories which are based on the common law traditions of England. It should be understood that qualifying for legal practice in Quebec would require civil law training in the French language.

Admission to a Law Society

In order to be admitted as a student in a Canadian Law School the applicant must have a minimum three year Bachelor degree, however, many law schools could set their standards higher and it is advisable to check the admission requirements of each school. If the candidate wishes to apply to a Canadian Law School they would go through an evaluation of their undergraduate marks, a review of their Law School Admission Test (LSAT) and an interview with the Law School of their choosing if they are approved based on their undergraduate marks and LSAT scores. Some bilingual universities offer the common law program in English and French. In order to take the solicitor and barrister exams a student must hold a 3 year L.L.B. degree from a Canadian university. Therefore, the student who applies for membership in a Canadian law society has studied for a minimum of 7 years and obtained 2 university degrees. The civil law faculties of the province of Quebec do not require that the applicant hold an undergraduate degree.

The student will then need to complete an articling period and then will have to pass the Barrister and Solicitor exams in all provinces except Quebec where the exams would consist of a notary or law exam or both depending on the candidate's choosing. Candidates are also required to pass a professional legal training course.

Foreign Trained Lawyers

Foreign lawyers who wish to become members to Canadian Law societies must apply to the National Committee on Accreditation (NCA) for an evaluation of their legal credentials and experience. Entry into the Barreau du Quebec or the Chambre des Notaires du Quebec is done directly through their offices in the province of Quebec.

In the Toronto Daily Star of Thursday, January 15th, 2009 in an article entitled "Foreign-trained lawyers hold their breath for help" by Paul Dalby the article outlines some of the areas to help foreign trained lawyers. First, anyone interested in practicing law in Canada should have their transcripts from their home country for their law degree and their university education. Transcripts should be translated to English and processed by a recognized accreditation service such as WES. References in English from professors and deans would also be helpful. It is easier to do this at home than from Canada. How your credentials are assessed will determine what other exams you will require in order to obtain an articling job. Other projects to help the foreign trained lawyer include an intern-ship program at the law firm Fraser Milner Casgrain which will help foreign- trained lawyers find an articling job. The University of Toronto has submitted a proposal to the Ontario government for bridging program to help internationally trained lawyers into the Canadian system.

A list of the Canadian Law societies is shown below:
    Law Society of British Columbia
    Law Society of Alberta
    Law Society of Saskatchewan
    Law Society of Manitoba
    Law Society of Upper Canada (Ontario)
    Barreau du Quebec
    Chambre des notaries du Quebec
    Nova Scotia Barristers' Society
    Law Society of New Brunswick
    Law Society of Prince Edward Island
    Law Society of Newfoundland and Labrador
    Law Society of Yukon
    Law Society of the Northwest Territories
    Law Society of Nunavut

A helpful web-site for information on this subject is:
www.flsc.ca/en/lawSocieties/lawSocieities.asp
flsc stands for federation of law societies of Canada

To communicate with the Federation:
Federation of Law Societies of Canada
Constitution Square
360 Albert Street, Suite 1700
Ottawa, On K1R 7X7
613-236-7272

For information on: Accreditation of foreign Law Degrees
Fran Russo, Assistant Director
613-562-5204   Fran.Russo@uottawa.ca

National Committee on Accreditation c/o faculty of law, Common Law Section
University of Ottawa
57 Louis Pasteur
Ottawa, On K1N 6N5

Chapter Eleven

Employability
Twenty Ways to Find a Job in Canada

It is my opinion that a major reason that immigrants come to Canada is to take advantage of the opportunities available to them in this country and to find suitable and gainful employment so that they can fulfill their dreams and aspirations and take care of themselves and their family.

This segment is focused on the hurdles that new Canadians could encounter when seeking work in Canada and how to overcome them. This information is provided to help people resolve any difficulties and challenges along the way so they can find succeed in their endeavors.

These tips are not only good advice for those immigrants wishing to come to Canada but will serve you well in any job searches done around the world. Immigrants and new Canadians are always in a much stronger position when they arrive in Canada with some specific job prospects or are fully informed of what and where their job prospects are.

Getting Ready to Work: 20 Ways To Help You Land Your First Job in Canada

Our advice through-out this book has been to start the process of preparing for employment in Canada before you leave your home country. In many cases the time between filing your initial application and a request for more information could be a perfect time to hone the skills mentioned below.

1. Learn English or French. Your language of choice depends on which province you wish to live and work. If you learn the English language early in life it will be more helpful than just assisting in your immigration to Canada. The English language is recognized as the international language of commerce so it will help you to find employment in your home country along with immigration possibilities in other countries. If you do plan on immigrating, you should take some preparatory courses which can be used to certify your proficiency in English. Your ability to communicate in the English language (French for Quebec) before entry into Canada is related to your skills development and your speed of integration into Canadian society. Language skills will also help you to network and improve your ability to be promoted. Your home country culture and language and ideas are still very valuable and Canadians do not expect you to give anything up. But superior language skills will help you to find employment at a quicker pace, making your transition to life in Canada much smoother. It would also be advisable to take some language courses from a Canadian-based language school so that you become familiar with Canadian vocabulary and phrasing. Any courses which help to focus on enunciation and clarification would be advantageous to the job seeking immigrant. Language and communication skills are different and both are very important. Language is mastering the verbal and written elements of the English language along with proper grammar while communication skills relate to using the language to communicate your ideas, your opinions, your presentations, your selling of yourself and your products and services and your coaching skills. Refer to the various language school web sites in the book.

2. Computer skills and communication skills. Improve your computer skills and prepare to be tested on them. Improve your skills on Microsoft Office -- including Word, Excel and PowerPoint. Skills in data base management software such as ACCESS will make you additionally valuable to any organization Also courses which improve your communication on the phone and your customer service and sales skills will reward you in any position that you are trying to obtain.

3. Accreditation. Have your documents translated to English by an accredited service such as World Education Service before you come to Canada. Do this in advance of coming to Canada because it will be difficult for you to do it from Canada. It will streamline the whole process if you have the documents with you when you come to Canada. If you can choose schools in your native country that are highly recognized there and around the world, it will make it easier when employers look at your educational qualifications. Also have references from professors and Deans of Professional Schools who can be contacted by phone and questioned about your qualifications. Refer to the "Accreditation" section. There are different methods for students and immigrants whereby you can gain Canadian experience through mentoring programs offered by such organizations as TRIEC and AIESEC.

4. Internet use to do your research. You are equal in this area to anyone in Canada. **Use a search engine such as Yahoo Canada to help you in your research.** Internet sites on a variety of subjects including documentation, requirements, programs, job and social agencies, tips on resume writing and interview skills, language and computer skills are available to you. A key to your employment success is to do as much as possible before coming to Canada. This book is loaded with Internet sites in Canada which will assist you in coming to and finding a job in Canada. Four important internet sites to help you find a job in Canada are; Workopolis.com., Jobshark.ca, Service Canada's jobbank.gc.ca, Monster.ca. Employment Agency web sites where jobs in Canada are listed, and the list of 'Jobs Under Pressure' provided by the government for each province:

http://servicecanada.gc.ca/en/workplaceskillsforeign_workers/occunderpres.shtml

Also make it a point to learn as much as possible about the company that you are applying to and do some extensive research if you get an interview opportunity. The research that you conduct will show an interest in the firm and can separate you from other candidates. This book contains lists and web-sites for companies that are welcoming to immigrants and diverse cultures along with companies that are in the top hundred performers in Canada. Also under the web-site: www.manta.com. You can learn the top 20 list of companies in various categories by province so this will also help you in your search for employment.

5. Visit Canada first. See the area where you and your family will live and work. Budget for a visit and stay with friends and family. Research the area. Research jobs. Visit employment agencies and government services. If you are being tested for a regulated or non-regulated profession then integrate the visit with the testing so that you do not have to stay for lengthy periods on your own or with your family.

6. Review the requirements of Provincial Nomination and Canadian Experience Class. Keep on top of this because there can be fast tracking for specific individuals with specific skills. Review your skills against the job demands and the exact skills required. Refer to the various government web sites for jobs under pressure and jobs available. As stated in a news release from Citizenship and immigration Canada on changes to Canadian Immigration Law, "The new law also more closely aligns Canada's immigration system with labour shortages so that immigrants who come to Canada will have more opportunities to find employment in their chosen fields."

The provinces will continue to be a driving force in attracting immigrants that fill there specific job skills required to grow that province's economy. Immigrants should match their skills to requirements in the provinces and this process could expedite their move to Canada. Look to the provinces that list your skills as under pressure and use the provincial nomination process. Go where the jobs are located.

Review the options of using a Temporary Work Permit to gain entry into Canada which is quicker than the skilled worker program and utilize your skills and Canadian experience to apply under the Canadian Experience Class. You can also upgrade your English language skills while you are in the country.

7. Check available services. Review the services provided for by government agencies and programs offered in the area where you are planning to live. These services are all free to the immigrant and New Canadian   Develop a relationship with an advisor at an agency. Take some of the courses provided by these agencies because they will help you find employment and help acclimatize you into Canadian business and culture. The book contains reference to all government agencies by city and province.

Working in Canada Tool
This tool is available on the Immigration menu of the Canada Citizenship and Immigration Web-site (www.cic.gc). This tool provides immigrants with help in finding out what their

occupation is called in Canada which may be different to their home country. It tells them what jobs are open across the country. It gives detailed labour market reports on specific areas. It gives information on wages and job opportunities for your occupation and city where you would like to live and work. This site may not give you every single piece of information on job opportunities and should be supplemented by information from local job agencies, etc but a well informed immigrant is one who is fully knowledgeable about his/her opportunities in Canada

8. Upgrade your job search tools. Ensure that your resume and cover letter do not have any spelling mistakes or grammatical errors since this will indicate carelessness to a potential employer and you will not have a chance of making it to the interview pile. Review your resume and make it more job friendly for employment in Canada by stating what you can do for the organization, not what they can do for you. Show your objective as being positive for the company considering hiring you. Canadian resumes do not require extensive detail on your history of jobs or education. But they do want to know how you can make them more profitable, serve their customers better, communicate performance to their employees and motivate them, make them more efficient, make it safer for each employee, make their employees more knowledgeable. Keep track of your accomplishments through the years because that is what companies want you to tell them. They are interested in your teamwork skills, leadership skills, social skills and community skills. Some international resumes carry information that is not relevant in North America such as marital status, horoscope sign and a large amount of personal detail and detailed job descriptions. Again the Canadian employer is interested in what you can do for them. Some cultures are not used to highlighting their own personal achievements while the North American culture puts a value on personal performance as measured by statistics, targets, goals and metrics. Include in your resume references to your performance in categories that the company would consider valuable to the position. Such measurements occur in service, productivity, safety, cost efficiency, sales, profit, return on investment, innovation, training, teamwork, etc. In hard times companies are looking for accomplishments in efficiency and cost reduction. Be realistic and truthful in your performance achievements but you really do have to mention them in order for the company to know what you have to offer. You will also be asked how you achieved those numbers. Most North American resumes are under 2 pages. If your resume is over two pages, you should look over the resume tips in the book for streamlining and making your resume more concise. Usually the extra page consists of personnel information and job duties and should be edited out. Focus on your accomplishments and what they can do for the company and not your previous job duties. The person reviewing the resumes may look at 500 resumes for a position, so a lengthy resume may not make even it through the first pass. There is no problem in having a resume for your host country and a second edition resume designed for North American standards. It's perfectly acceptable to have multiple resumes designed to fit the parameters involved. This is a targeted approach to marketing your skills and experience. Also the ability to do word processing allows you to revise your resume and cover letter to each job and even each time that you send out your resume. Keep fine tuning your resume to the job and talents and achievements that you have that will benefit the company hiring you. North American resumes also require a cover letter at all times. You should customize your resume and cover letter to place you as the best candidate for the job being offered. You are not restricted to one single resume and one single cover letter. Word processing allows quick and easy changes that enable you to customize. A cover letter is mandatory in applying for a job and attached to a resume and it gives you a specific opportunity to market your skills against the job. You are also perfectly entitled to follow up with hiring managers if you have not heard from the with-in a reasonable period of time but beware of being overly persistent. Remember your resume is never finished. It is constantly being updated and made better. Keep recording and revising it because the first job that you get in Canada will not be your last. In a survey of interviewers and resume reviewers prepared by MSN "Quiz: Test your Job Hunting Skills" the following pieces of information were presented: over two-thirds of jobs are filled by word of mouth; hiring managers like to see a chronological resume; take your seat at the interview after your interviewer has offered it; hiring managers consult with receptionists and administrative assistants about candidates; after ability executives liked these skills in job seekers-honesty, enthusiasm and verbal skills; and finally executives are impressed if you have done intensive research on the company and how your skills fill their needs.

9. Use Canadian employment agencies. Start contacting them in your home country before you leave to see what jobs are available and what qualifications are required before you relocate. Employment agencies do not charge you for finding you a job. Their fees are charged to the employer who hires you, so you as a qualified candidate are valuable to employment agencies. Employment agencies have their own data base of clients and they may have positions open that have not been advertised. Ask the employment agency to give you feedback on your resume, cover letter, soft skills and interview preparation.

10. Develop your soft job skills. Some important soft skills include proper grooming. Consider getting a haircut or hairstyle for the interview. Do not wear jeans. Do not show any tattoos or body piercing. Consider that an interview may not be the best time to make a statement on your appearance. Do not use slang. Don't be on time, **be early**. Leave a positive impression even though you may feel that the interview did not go well -- always thank the interviewer for their time. If most of your time has been invested in your education, it's now time to shift your thinking from student to employee. Make sure that you look like an employee rather than a student. Dress above the position that you are applying. Make the interviewer feel comfortable and make some eye contact. Personal grooming essentials include having no body odor and avoiding excessive use of perfume or cologne.

11. Multi-national work experience. Multi-national companies transfer employees all over the world and therefore any experience with them can serve as international experience.

12. Seek out immigrant-friendly employers. Go over the list of companies that are recognized for their employment of new Canadians. There is a whole section in this book on firms that have been recognized for their contribution in helping new immigrants. Introduce yourself to these companies and what you have to offer them. A good starting place would be the web site: http://www.canadastop100.com/diversity

13. Interview preparation. The North American job interview is built on a process on being asked a question and formulating an answer based on examples from past experience. Develop questions that you would be asked in an interview and review your answers. You don't have to memorize the answers but be prepared for potential questions and show that you've given it some thought. The following questions might be typical in a North American interview: What are your strengths and weaknesses? Some cultures may find that it is boastful to talk about personal achievements. However, the North American interview will require you to talk about your accomplishments and comment on how they were done. If your culture focuses on team performance, that's a valuable asset, so comment on how your performance made the team more successful. Weaknesses should be minimal and be addressed through training, etc. Some interviews involve situational questions where the interviewer gives you a question such as, "You are in a situation where you disagree with your superior on a course of action. How do you try to convince your boss that you have a better idea?" Some of the elements that you might consider in the answer are: an explanation of the results and how you got to them, a statistical analysis of your solution, is the company better off from a cost and efficiency viewpoint, focus on the facts and solution and not the personalities, show how your superior would gain with your solution. Sometime during the interview you will be asked if you have any questions. You should have at least one question on the company or position based on your research of the company and position.. When you leave your previous job leave on a positive note and do not leave anything behind that would give you a negative reference or negative interview question in a future job hunt. Do not forget to send a thank-you note for the interview opportunity. Do not ask about salary in the first interview. Learn from the interview process. It would be extremely rare for a candidate to get a job offer after only one interview for one job. Know more about the company in which you are seeking the position than the interviewer who is asking the questions. Do a lot of research.

14. Be Positive. Some people have said the search for a job is more exhausting than the full-time job itself. Be prepared to be rejected at times. That is just part of the process. Remember that Statistics Canada predicts that by the year 2011, new Canadians are expected to account for the entire net labour force growth. A lot can be read into facial and body expression. Pain or sadness on your face will show in the interview. A closed body position indicates a lack of confidence or a very private and shy individual. Everyone is a bit nervous at an interview and you should realize that the person conducting the interview may be inexperienced also and wants to feel at ease. A seasoned interviewer will feel energized if they interview a candidate who is relaxed, personable and informative and provides some key attributes to help the company. Even if you do not get the job look upon an interview as an opportunity to market your skills. Learn from the interview and prepare for the next one with lessons learned. The fact that you got an interview indicates that you were in the small number of candidates considered for the job.

15. Prepare in advance. Contact professional schools to get all of the information necessary before you leave your host country including qualifications, preparation for testing, testing, budget, time required, etc. You need to have complete information before committing yourself and your family.

16. Relocation. Mobility is important. Become informed about areas in Canada where you skills are required and there is a job for you. Canada is a big country and its opportunities are not the same across the country with some provinces experiencing higher growth rates and stronger employment possibilities than other provinces. In an article in the Globe and mail of Thursday, September 4th entitled "Immigrants bypassing Toronto to follow money West, study finds" the article highlights the opportunities available in other parts of Canada. The article pointed out that immigrants earn more money in Calgary, Regina and Saskatoon than they do in Toronto. The factors may be related to economic growth rates and supply and demand. The article goes on to say that immigrants often settle where family members live, but are also drawn by economic opportunities. The oil and natural gas booms in Alberta and Saskatchewan have led to huge labour demands and a rise in wages as business owners struggle to fill jobs. Smaller Canadian cities have less competition for higher paying-paying jobs and this goes for places like Calgary, Edmonton, Regina and Saskatchewan as it does for Charlottetown, Halifax and Moncton. The immigrant needs to learn about all of Canada and the job opportunities available across the country and not just in the major cities. A basic of employability is to go where the jobs are located and the competition is lowest. Form relationships with employment agencies and employers in communities where there are jobs in your field and you will have a much quicker path to success. If you visit Canada also visit smaller cities to the East and West.

17. Network with others. Network in your home country and in Canada within your skill, trade and profession, university clubs, your religious, social, cultural and political affiliations. Political associations are important in that like- minded people politically can help their fellow members in their hunt for jobs. Many jobs in Canada are obtained through personal contact before they are posted on job sites. If you are fortunate enough to have one networking associate who becomes a mentor to you then consider yourself to be very lucky. Many people have traveled the same path as you and they would like to help people in similar circumstances. Remember that if you are the only one that knows that you are looking for a job then it will be more difficult to find one. Also take advantage of professional networking sites to open up opportunities. You do not have to stop your job search while you wait for a response from an employer. You could miss out on an opportunity if you do not remain active. Utilize a web-site such as www.loonlounge.com where you can network with other immigrants in your country's community in Canada. You can also find out job opportunities. Remember that networking never stops. It will open doors for you through your whole career and use the networking opportunities to reciprocate and help some-one else along the way. If we all help each other and even make one person's path easier the whole country will gain.

18. Upgrading your skills by taking night school programs. Many people, both immigrant and Canadian-born have improved their job prospects by further training and education. There are courses in everything from language training which would be particularly helpful if you wanted to qualify for some of the bilingual jobs in Canada in government or customer service. These jobs are more plentiful, because of the qualifications, and have a smaller competitive candidate base and higher compensation. Other courses of benefit are computer courses, accounting, presentation and writing skills

19. Flexibility. If you are in a position where you do not have job prospects when you arrive in Canada then be prepared to take any job, even if it is not in your chosen field. There may not be openings in your chosen occupation so you may have to be prepared take a job where you can improve your language and communication skills in order to support yourself and your family. Consider these jobs not to be long term and not permanent. They are merely stepping stones that can lead you to your ultimate objective of employment in your area of experience. You are also not obliged to stay in one province in Canada when you arrive. You are allowed to move around the country to find employment but be aware that you need to inform Citizenship and Immigration Canada of an address change if you are to receive additional documents. Be flexible in your job search. Jobs may be scarce in your particular field of expertise in the area that you have chosen to live. Jobs are more numerous in areas of administration and customer service in which you might have specific skills and a much greater opportunity to find employment. The old adage that it is easier to find work when you are employed rather than unemployed may be particularly valuable.

20. Future outlook. Canada needs you. There are substantial opportunities in Canada but there may not be openings in your area of expertise in the area you have chosen to live. Canadian society is getting older with the aging of the 'baby boomers' (post Second World War babies). More people are approaching retirement age. Canada has a lot to offer. It's a rich country in natural resources including energy, food, water, and raw materials. It is a democratic country with a high standard of living and a universal health care system, a Charter of Rights and Freedoms and employment laws and protection of employees' safety. Today, Canada is even more of a land of opportunity than it was decades ago, as long as you're flexible. It can be an ideal place for you to build a solid future for you and your family.

Perhaps the most important item to remember is that once you get a job your education, experience and training never end. You should be constantly upgrading your skills through-out your life in order to retain your job, elevate your position and compensation, make yourself valuable to you employer in good times and bad and increase your future opportunities in Canada and the global economy. Some of the methods of improving your future prospects are:
 • go to courses at night to improve your English (French) language ability in speaking and writing- or language skills related to your area of expertise
 • computer skills such as Word, Excel, Access, or software related to your area of expertise whether it be accounting, business, or engineering can be taken at night
 • general business courses through night school
 • get a professional designation such as CGA, PMAC or a business degree
 • affiliations that improve your networking, social and speaking skills whether they be religious, political, or charitable
 • in the ever changing world economy you should be aware that companies come and go and jobs come and go and you need to protect yourself and your family You have started the journey with your first job. It is a journey along different paths of life experience and knowledge which never end.

Chapter Twelve
Getting Ready To Work In Canada
Important Documentation

Whatever your particular field of endeavor, there is a chance that are you already have what it takes to secure suitable employment in Canada. You have specialized skills, experience, and knowledge – valuable assets to offer Canadian employers. But in order to be successful in finding the job you want, you need to market those assets and match them to employers in need.

First and foremost, there are several key documents you need in order be adequately prepared for work in Canada. Your important documents include:
- A resume
- Cover letter
- Educational credentials, including any degrees, diplomas, certificates, or apprenticeship documentation translated into English by an organization such as WES
- Letters of recommendation from Professors, Deans, Lawyers, Doctors, Professionally certified people in your field of expertise, politicians, religious persons

Each component plays an important role. Begin gathering what you already have on hand including old resumes, certificates, and diplomas. Compile any letters of recommendation you happen to have from previous employers as they help verify your past performance and accomplishments.

Below are four government supported websites to help you find work in Canada:
www.directionscanada.gc.ca
www.workdestinations.org
www.hrsdc.gc.ca
www.theworkplace.ca

If you are coming to Canada as a business immigrant, you would be well advised to conduct your key research online, prior to your arrival. Doing so will enable you to locate key sources of financing, business opportunities, small business development, suppliers, potential customers, and more. The more preliminary work you do from your home country, the quicker and easier it will be to get established in Canada.

The following web sites can provide helpful information to business immigrants:

www.strategis.gc.ca

www.contractscanada.gc.ca

www.cic.gc.ca

Resume Writing Tips

Your resume is a crucial tool in eventually landing the job you want in Canada. I use the word 'eventually' because your resume, no matter how well prepared, will only advance you to the next step. In other words, your resume alone won't get you the job -- but it can place you in the running.

The primary task of your resume is to obtain an interview. That's it. Nobody gets hired without being interviewed at least once. But those who are granted interviews are commonly just a small fraction of the numbers of people who apply for a given position. Interviewees are selected in most cases based on the information presented in their resume and its relevancy and compatibility with the vacant position.

It's your resume that gets you the interview. But what draws attention to your resume, making it stand out amongst a stack of seemingly similar resumes from qualified applicants is the cover letter that accompanies it.

As important as it is, in preparing a job application, the cover letter is often overlooked entirely. But it's become an important job search tool. An effective cover letter gets noticed. It creates attention and interest and stands apart from the rest of the pack. It's the cover letter that literally draws prospective employers or agency representatives to your resume – giving you an inside chance at qualifying for an interview.

Since it's such an important self-marketing tool, I always encourage job applicants to send a cover letter with every resume they submit.

Writing an effective cover letter need not be difficult or elaborate. In fact, one of the keys is to keep your letter brief and to the point. Each position you apply for requires a customized cover letter. A generic letter will only get lost in the shuffle. In each case, your cover letter should aim at the specific job you're seeking and communicate the major reasons why you would be a solid choice for the position and an asset to the organization.

Now let's briefly review the major sections to include on your resume.

The Introduction segment should include your full name, complete mailing address, home telephone and cell phone numbers and an e-mail address. It's important to have an answering machine or voicemail activated to capture any messages left by prospective employers or hiring agencies. Check to verify the accuracy of all contact information.

Imagine that you are the person going through all the resumes collected for the position you seek. What is it about your resume that makes it jump out at the person scanning through dozens, or perhaps even hundreds of resumes from other candidates? Strive for a resume that sets you apart from the crowd. Fact is... you could be in direct competition with hundreds of other candidates. Everyone would like to be offered the job, but only one will get it. In order to make the first cut and be selected as an "A" list candidate, you need a resume that's a cut above the rest. You need something that communicates beyond the mere words contained on the page. A subtle difference may be all it takes as long as it makes you stand out from the competition.

Essentially, you only have about 10 to 20 seconds to make an impression on the person scanning the resumes. In that brief period of time, your fate is determined in relation to the available position. Either you pass the test screening, or you don't. Don't think for a second that any employer or agency will actually read every line of a resume to carefully consider each candidate. It simply doesn't happen that way. Judgments are made quickly and decisively, at least in the early stages as qualifying candidates are quickly whittled down to a much smaller and more manageable group.

Remember, the objective of the resume is to get an interview. But on average, only one interview is granted for approximately every 200 resumes received. Competition is a fact of life and that's why you need to take a proactive position in marketing yourself.

The best approach to take with your resume is to focus in on the needs of the employer, instead of your own needs. Yes, you need to find employment and this particular job could be ideal for you. But no employer hires anyone based on the needs of the prospective employee. Hiring decisions are made to suit the needs of the organization. So when you position yourself to serve a particular organization in a way that best meets its needs, you're communicating on the same level. When you do so, you're much more likely to capture the interest of those doing the hiring.

The Objective in Resumes

Another key element of the resume is the 'objective' section. In this segment, you have to be clear about your career direction. If you don't know where you are going, then how could you expect an employer to know and be willing to give you a shot at it?

Following are two sample Objectives directed towards the same job:

OBJECTIVE: "To obtain a sales position with an organization where I can maximize my skills, experience and education."

Clearly, this objective is focused on the needs of the candidate and not the employer. Your objective needs to be worded in an employer-centered way, rather than in a self-serving way. What are you going to do for this company or organization? How are you going to make them a better, more productive and profitable company, if you were to start working there tomorrow? When you begin to think from the employer's point of view, you're on the right track.

Below is an example of a much stronger objective:

OBJECTIVE: "To obtain a sales position in an organization that wants unparalleled sales growth by obtaining new accounts, surpassing sales targets and developing world class service."

This kind of objective draws employers to you. It says that you want to join a company with these objectives... that you want to be a part of their success... and that you have the talent to help make these things happen. See the difference? This second example offers an objective that merges with the direction of any growing organization.

The Summary in Resumes

Another key resume section is the summary. If you apply these ideas provided for the cover letter, objective, and summary -- you will make yourself stand out, rather than be buried with the masses.

The summary consists of several descriptive statements designed to direct attention to your qualifications and achievements and how they fit the needs of the company. A strong summary should also tie in with your stated objectives as indicated on both the resume and cover letter. Consistency is the key here.

Include your work experience as a designated professional and indicate your area of expertise. It's also a good idea to include some comment related to your personal skills such as leadership, teamwork, communication, or decision making. A brief description of outstanding achievements, references to awards, promotions, or performance can and should be included here.

Match the Ideal Candidate To You

Develop a list of all possible attributes the perfect candidate for this specific job would have to offer. Next, start a new list on a separate page. On this page, begin listing all of your abilities, interests, achievements, and talent related to the position you're vying for. Be completely truthful and honest here. But at the same time, don't shy away from highlighting your strongest skills and abilities.

Now look closely at the two lists. Highlight any skills, abilities or accomplishments that match what this company wants most. You may be surprised how your existing skills are compatible with the qualities sought by employers. Doing this exercise helps you recognize genuine marketable skills and abilities that you may have simply taken for granted.

Work Experience

In this section, list your work experience in sequence, beginning with your most recent employment. Include the name of each company, the timeframe of your employment, and a brief job description. Keep it brief and to the point. Your resume should not be a personal history lesson, but a one-page summary of your qualifications and attributes positioned in a way to answer the requirements of a specific position.

Round-out your resume by including a few significant details about your education and training. In the "Education" section, list the institution(s), years attended, and the diploma or degree attained. Here, the emphasis should be placed on the highest levels of academic achievement.

Under "training", indicate any computer, business, or industry-specific courses or specialized skills training you received. If you choose to include a section titled "Activities/ Interest" -- be brief. No company wants a lengthy list of your hobbies and interests, though they may want to know a little bit more about you on a personal level.

Most importantly, emphasize your teamwork skills and your well-rounded and multi-dimensional capabilities and you'll leave a positive impression.

References can be made in "Work Experience" section, or you can simply add a footnote suggesting that references are available on request. The reason for doing this is to keep your resume to one page, two pages maximum. Any resume over two pages won't get looked at and if you can boil down a top notch resume to one page you will make an impression on the reviewer. Just be sure you have your list of references and points of contact ready, for any employer or agency who requests it.

The following web site provides a lot of valuable information on resume creation and marketing yourself: www.rockportinstitute.com/resumes.html

Key Resume Points To Consider

Customize your cover letter and resume. Give it a unique look and feel that will set it apart from the kind of routine resumes employers see on a regular basis. A generic letter and resume is less effective than one that's custom-tailored to a specific job listing. Be sure to also describe your experience in terms of the job you're pursuing.

Customization shapes your resume to suit the position, making you a more compatible match. Sometimes the modifications made to a resume are subtle, yet the results can be profound.

Cover letters should be short, introductory messages that always fit easily onto a single page. Three to five paragraphs is all you need. Ideally your resume should be one page as well and never more than two pages.

Avoid including extensive details about your work experience. Resumes are always scanned quickly and too much detail will only cause yours to be passed by.

Use words and descriptions that convey a sense of creativity, completion, leadership, productivity and cost-reduction — all important traits sought by employers. Such words as created, completed, established, initiated, reduced, simplified, improved, and increased demonstrate these attributes through your past performance.

Proofread to correct any grammatical or spelling errors. It's always a good idea to have other people look at your resume to spot weaknesses and errors, or to offer constructive criticism or suggestions for improvement.

Content items that should never appear on your resume include:

1. The word "resume" in big bold letters across the top. Every employer and agency knows what a resume looks like. Labeling yours is a waste of space and gives the wrong impression about you.

2. Any information related to salary. Typically, the issue of salary is raised by the employer in the second interview, although it may be brought up earlier. The key point to remember is to always let the interviewer initiate the discussion on salary or wages paid.

3. Detailed information on former employers and references such as addresses, names of supervisors, associates, etc. Doing so only makes your resume twice as long and half as appealing, so anyone reviewing it might not even get to that section.

4. Reasons why you left previous jobs. If it's important, this question will be asked by the interviewer. Be prepared. You should have developed an excellent answer to this question. Be sure not to fault your former employer, superior or co-workers. There is no benefit in blaming others during a job interview.

5. Unexplained voids in your work history. Work experience should flow without blank spaces that cannot be easily explained. Most employers are looking for long-term solutions and stability in those they hire.

6. Changing fonts and styles through-out your resume in an effort to make you look different and creative. Let your accomplishments make you different and valuable and beware of too much creativity which might make you a quick trip to the wastebasket.

Personal Preparedness

For detailed information on this section the government has prepared an excellent web site and publication called: www.cic.gc.ca/english/resources/publications/guide/index.asp

There's also a PDF publication (Portable Document Format - a publication formatted for reading on any computer with the free Adobe Acrobat Reader) titled, A Newcomer's Introduction to Canada. This one shows all of the things that you need to do before leaving for Canada. The documents listed are all important, so be sure to check out these publications.

There are a number of essential documents you must have in your possession before arriving in Canada. These include:
  • A Canadian immigrant visa
  • An official document confirming permanent residence status for each family member arriving in Canada with you
  • If arriving as a temporary resident, you need a work permit PLUS a visa (if required) for each family member traveling with you
  • A valid passport for yourself and everyone with you
  • Two copies of a list of all the items you're bringing into Canada with you now PLUS two copies of a list of items due to arrive at a later date
  • Proof of finances ensuring that you and your family have the funds necessary to live in Canada for at least one year

Note: Do not pack these crucial immigration documents in a suitcase. Canadian customs and immigration officials will immediately request these upon your arrival. Keep all important documents with you at all times.

Other Important Documents

There are several additional documents you must bring with you as well, including:
- Birth certificates for all parties
- Marriage license or certificate
- Adoption, separation and/or divorce papers where applicable
- Educational records, diplomas or degrees

Note: due to the possibility of fraud, many companies and institutions may want original documentation mailed to them even though you have copies. I suggest setting up a file with an evaluation firm in Canada to handle this for you prior to your arrival in Canada.
- Trade and professional certificates (See note above as the same information applies)
- Letters of reference
- Resume
- Immunization and vaccination records
- Driver's license and international driver's license

Translation of Documents

Please make sure that all documents are translated into English (French, if you are settling in Quebec).

Any document you plan to submit to employers or educational institutions needs to be translated into English. Use only a certified translator to convert your documents into English. Be sure it's someone who holds the title of "Certified Translator" by the Association of Translators and Interpreters of Ontario (ATIO). To find a Certified Translator who can serve you, refer to the Yellow Pages, or contact the association directly at 1-800-234-5030.

Assessment and Accreditation

There are various resources available to help you get your education and qualifications assessed against Canadian equivalent standards. The following list by province will help you in this process. Any assessment you require should be completed long before your planned arrival in Canada, because it will definitely reduce the time it takes you to secure employment. Some federally funded agencies will do this work for free or a low cost. There are also many private companies operating in this field and all charge fees.

Humber Institute of Technology and Advanced Learning
Centre for Internationally trained Professionals
1620 Albion Road, 2nd Floor
Etobicoke, Ontario, M9V 4B4
416-745-0281

World Education Services-Canada
45 Charles Street East, suite 700
Toronto, On, M4Y 1S2
416-972-0070   www.wes.org/ca

World Education Services(WES) is a leading international credential evaluation service in Canada. Job Seekers, New Canadians and students come to WES for accurate credential assessment reports that they can give to Employers, Licensing Boards and Academic Institutions.

International Credential Assessment Service of Canada (ICAS)
Ontario AgriCentre
100 Stone West, Suite 303
Guelph, Ontario N1G 5L3
519-763-7282   www.icascanada.ca

International Qualifications Assessment Service (IQAS)
Alberta Advance Education
9th Floor, Sterling Place
9942-108 Street
Edmonton, Alberta T5K 2J5
789-427-2655   http://www.advanceeducation.gov.ab.ca/iqas/iqas.asp

International Credential Evaluation Service (ICES)
3700 Willington Avenue
Burnaby, British Columbia V5G 3H2
604-432-8800   www.bcit.ca/ices/

University of Toronto Comparative Education Service(CES)
315 Bloor Street West
Toronto, Ontario M5S 1A3
416-978-2190   ces.info@utoronto.ca

Academic Credentials Assessment Service-Manitoba (ACAS)
Manitoba Labour and Immigration
Settlement & Labour Market Services Branch
5th floor, 213 Notre Dame Avenue
Winnipeg, Manitoba R3B 1N3
204-945-0300   www.gov.mb.ca/labour/immigrate/work/recognition/acas.html

Centre d'expertise sur les formations acquises hors du Quebec (CEFAHQ)
Ministere de L'Immigrations et des Communautes Culturelles (MICC)
255, boulevard Cremazie Est, 8e etage
Montreal, Quebec H2M 1M2
514-864-9191   renseignements@micc.gouv.qc.ca   www.immigration-quebec.gouv.qc.ca

International Qualifications Assessment Service (IQAS) - Saskatchewan
The government of Saskatchewan provides this service through an interprovincial agreement with the Government of Alberta so please refer to the information for the province of Alberta.

Other helpful web sites related to assessment and accreditation include:
www.cicic.ca

On this site you will find the Canadian Information Centre for International Credentials.
www.cthrb.ca/Assessment

Here the Canadian Technology Human Resources Board has developed an online program where an individual can self assess their competencies versus Canadian standards.

It's important to develop a relationship with a recognized provider of pre-employment screening. A competent professional can help employers and universities verify your credentials and experience. If you establish a relationship before you leave your native land, it will be much easier and faster to get your qualifications and educational background assessed.

The government of Canada's new Foreign Credentials Referral Office (FCRO) helps internationally-trained individuals find the information and resources they need to have their credentials assessed and recognized. The Foreign Credentials Referral Office is a central source of authoritative information on requirements for working in Canada and labour market trends. It also assists people in the job search process.

If you want to work in a specific profession or skilled trade, the 'Working in Canada' tool connects you to the information you need and the path you must take to receive your license, do your job search, and begin working.

FCRO services are available at 320 Service Canada Centres
www.credentials.gc.ca   1-888-854-1805

Apprenticed Trades

An apprenticeship is a system of supervised training that leads to certification in a specific trade. Some apprenticed trades require a licence and others do not. At the following web-site you can learn more about apprenticed trades: http://workingincanada.gc.ca

If you want to work in a trade that is regulated and require a licence you must apply to the professional regulatory agency or apprenticeship authority in the province or territory that you will be settling in.

Job Interview Tips
Soft Skills For Job Interviews

A vital aspect of preparing for a job interview is personal grooming. Grooming fundamentals such as taking a shower, brushing your teeth, having clean hands and fingernails and combing your hair are important to making a positive first impression. If your interviewer smells you before you get into the office, either with body odor or excessive cologne or perfume, you've started off on the wrong foot, despite your qualifications for the job. Ensure that your hair is properly groomed and don't be afraid to get your hair done if it does not look neat.

As far as clothing is concerned, dress to the position that you eventually want to obtain at the company and not just the entry level position for which you are being interviewed. Dress for the desired role. Research has indicated that grooming and clothing do have an impact on being hired and on impressions left on the interviewer. If the person is untidy, overly non-traditional in clothing, language or style, are they a good fit for the corporate culture? Do you want to make that kind of statement about yourself at the interview? Think about the position you want to grow into with at the company and present yourself accordingly. An attempt to understand the corporate culture will pay dividends and is much more effective than making your own independent statement at the interview. It's also important to have a firm handshake when you introduce yourself to interviewer. The interviewer will expect something firm, not weak and not bone-breaking either, but a solid handshake that says you're confident about yourself. Items you should never wear to a job interview include:

- Jeans
- Hats, caps or toques
- Excessive jewelry or cosmetics

Wear a business suit, blazer and dress pants or conservative apparel. Show up early and prepared. If you are late, you've already lost the job. Clean and polish your shoes. You might be surprised to know how many people look at your hands, shoes, socks, and the pressing of your clothes. For men, the way your tie is knotted is a detail some people pay attention to, as is facial hair. For women, the depth of your neckline and your general appearance (hair, make-up, etc.) create first impressions – positive or negative. Don't give your interviewer anything to focus on that could deny you the job.

Be aware of body language you may be using such as having your arms crossed in front of your chest, or constantly touching or stroking your chin or face. Nervous habits won't help you.

Some individuals may be highly creative in their outlook on life and any recommendations are not meant to deter that positive aspect. However, your potential employer may not be looking for that attribute in your appearance at the interview and you may in fact be isolating yourself against other competitors for the job. Dress to fill the role. And remember, the interview is about moving forward and ultimately being presented with a job offer. If you choose, you can get more creative later.

Of course, the job interview apparel listed is for an office position. If you are being interviewed for a warehouse, assembly or manufacturing line position it would be advisable to follow many of the same guidelines except the clothing should be clean work wear. All companies require the wearing of steel toed workshoes or boots on the job so you should have a pair available to start work.

The Interview Process

If your resume and cover letter perform as intended, you'll be contacted for an interview. The interview is the next step in the hiring process and it's a crucial one. Your resume helped get your foot in the door. Now, it's up to you to show the interviewer(s) that you have what it takes and would be an asset to the employer.

The first step is preparation. That's a dominant theme throughout this book because it's something anyone can do at any time to improve their results. Being prepared for an interview is absolutely essential.

Familiarize yourself with the details you've included on your resume. In fact, it's a good idea to practice going through your resume from beginning to end. It's all factual information, but you probably don't think of yourself the same way your resume describes you. That's why you need to review the contents in detail and design a series of questions about you and your qualifications. Think of questions an interviewer is likely to ask and then practice the answers. Get a friend or business acquaintance to interview you and make a video recording of it. Today's technology makes this easy and inexpensive to do. Watch how you respond to the questions and then work on developing stronger answers and presenting them in a confident, capable manner.

You should have conducted the interview in practice many times before going to the actual interview. Rehearse your performance over and over again. Simulate the experience of the interview and when it's time for the real thing, you'll be calm and confident, while providing quality answers to all the interviewer's questions. It's just like you were studying for a final exam. You wouldn't arrive unprepared for an exam and you should never show up to an interview that way either.

Several web sites exist to help you. You can get numerous additional interview tips plus help in designing a series of questions for your area or expertise. Ultimately, you'll be better prepared for it in the interview process if you think through potential questions and develop strong responses in advance.

These free web sites that can help you prepare for an interview are:

www.Job-Interview.net

www.cvtips.com/job_interview.html

Should the interviewer ask if you had trouble finding the place, always respond by saying that you had no trouble whatsoever. The reason is that no one wants to hire a person who gets lost the first time trying to make his/her way to work.

Try not to be nervous in your interview. By preparing yourself well in advance and practicing your responses, you will reduce any nervousness. Act confident and self assured and you'll appear that way to others. Also, considering that many interviewers are inexperienced at the process themselves, they could be as uncomfortable as you are.

Consider the interview as an opportunity to market yourself and to make a positive impression and to advance you further towards a firm offer of employment. That's really what you can do in an interview. But you also want to assess the employment opportunity to make sure it's a good fit for you.

A good rule of thumb is to imagine that you are applying for a more prestigious position one that is higher on the pay scale that you are an applicant. Then, dress and act accordingly for that higher position. It communicates a degree of seriousness about your career and gives you an advantage over others who are simply looking for a job to pay the bills.

If you are being interviewed by a hiring agency, then treat that interview exactly as if you would treat an interview with the company. This is important. You've got to make a significant positive impact to have any chance at the job. Remember that you are always marketing yourself in every situation. Are you at your best?

Greet the interviewer with a firm handshake and address him/her by Mr., Mrs., or Ms

– followed by their last name. If they prefer to be called by their first name, they'll tell you so. Never assume this yourself. Be professional and business-like at all times. Do not sit down until you are offered a seat.

Avoid smoking and chewing gum. If you are a smoker, have your clothes dry-cleaned before the interview. Steer clear of foods like garlic and onion that can negatively impact your breath. And be sure to show up to your interview freshly-showered, well-groomed, and impeccably-dressed. That's the best way to make a great impression early on.

If you agree to a coffee, keep in mind the risk of spilling it on the interviewer's desk. That's not the kind of impression you want to make. It's better to respectfully decline at the time of the interview. When it's over, go enjoy a cup of coffee or tea. Take notes on your performance after the interview and strive to do better the next time.

Establish eye contact with the interviewer as this conveys sincerity. If you look away from the person asking the questions, they'll have a tendency to not trust you.

Stress your accomplishments, knowledge, and unique experience -- without making it sound boastful. You can accomplish this by sharing some actual results. Be upbeat and optimistic. Act with energy and enthusiasm. Show that you're interested in the company and the position.

Avoid simple 'yes or no' answers. Elaborate by sharing brief details or examples, while at the same time limiting your answers to a maximum of one minute each. You want to provide interesting, informative details, without boring the interviewer or losing any positive momentum you have already built up.

Conduct your own research on the company prior to your interview. The best-informed candidates make the most favourable impressions. With today's technology, information is readily available. All you have to do is make the effort to find it. Your research will benefit you if you are asked if you have any questions. Interviewers are impressed with candidates who have made a serious attempt at doing a lot of research on the company and including that information in some of their answers.

Job Hunting Tools

Many jobs in Canada are obtained through employment agencies which select a short list of candidates for employer interviews. You are first interviewed by the agency which reduces the number of candidates to a "best list" of three or five of the most qualified individuals. This list is then submitted to the employer.

Candidates can use such job board sites as Workopolis and Monster to apply to agencies. Agencies can also be found online, or through the Yellow Pages telephone directories.

Many government-sponsored agencies (not for profit) help candidates with their job searching skills and training and help them find job openings, but the actual placement is secured by the candidate or agency. Employment agencies do not charge candidates, they charge the employer if the candidate is hired.

Religion at Your Place of Work

The Canadian Charter of Rights and Freedoms protects the right to religion and religious expression. What this means is that every employer is obligated to accommodate such things as time away from work, as well as the scheduled date and time of meetings.

The employer is not obligated to provide accommodation to the point that it causes undue hardship to the organization however. Freedoms of belief, expression and religion are extended as long as they don't go beyond what's acceptable to the business. This could include financial hardship, disruption to the normal functioning of a company, or placing the health and safety of the workforce in jeopardy.

In the case of days off, all employees are entitled to paid time off equal to the number of Christian days recognized as statutory holidays in Canada. All provinces and territories in Canada have a number of statutory holidays each year, including New Year's Day, Good Friday, Canada Day, Labour Day and Christmas Day.

Victoria Day, Thanksgiving Day, Remembrance Day and Boxing Day are also recognized as holidays in a number of jurisdictions, not to mention special holidays which are specific to individual provinces and territories, such as Family Day in Alberta and Ontario, British Columbia Day, New Brunswick Day, Saskatchewan Day, St. Jean Baptiste Day (Quebec), Discovery Day (Yukon) and the 1st Monday of August (NWT, Nunavut). In total, Newfoundland and P.E.I. have 5 statutory holidays; New Brunswick and Nova Scotia, 6; Manitoba and Quebec, 8. All others, including Ontario and the three territories have 9 statutory holidays.

To be eligible for a paid vacation day, an employee must ordinarily meet certain requirements, such as working a minimum number of hours or days in a given period prior to the holiday.

If the individual wants time off with pay for a major cultural celebration then he/she should resolve the issue with the employer, well in advance. Most employers will allow workers time off in such cases, if the employee is using his/her own vacation time and provide the employer adequate notice. Just remember that it's always the responsibility off the employee to inform the employer of such a request. Never assume that these additional requests will result in paid time off.

Key Point Summary

- Crucial Canadian job-search documentation includes a resume, cover letter, educational credentials, and letters of recommendation
- Research your best opportunities online in advance (this applies to all types of immigrants)
- The role of your resume is to get you the interview
- The role of your cover letter is to direct the attention of a reviewer to your resume
- Create a resume that sets you apart from other candidates
- You only have a few seconds to make an impact
- Focus on the needs of the employer – be company-centered rather than self-centered
- Write you objective in a way that merges with the company's goals and direction
- Use the summary to concisely capture your best attributes
- Anticipate the qualities each company seeks and assess how you can best measure up

- Customize your cover letter and resume for each position or listing
- Keep your letter to a few short paragraphs on a single page
- Resumes can be one or two pages – but one page is better
- Avoid including unnecessary details
- Prepare, preview and rehearse for each interview
- Anticipate questions and develop excellent answers
- Dress above what you think the position entails
- Be well-groomed with clean clothes and show up with an upbeat attitude
- Act with professionalism and poise
- Be sure to have all vital documents with you when you arrive in Canada
- All foreign language documents need to be translated into English (or French)
- Seek official accreditation before submitting your supporting documents

Companies Recognized For Their Contributions in Helping New Immigrants

The face of Canada's workforce is indeed changing. And as Canada's domestic population ages and its workforce retires in larger numbers, employers are becoming increasingly dependent on new Canadians to fill vacant positions. Immigrants are an increasingly vital component to the economic growth of the nation and the standard of living Canadians enjoy.

Employers right across the board are going to have to pay attention to this issue because new Canadians are one of the few growing sources of qualified and skilled employees.

Leading edge organizations have not only recognized this developing trend, they've actually done something about it. These companies have acknowledged immigrant employees as valuable assets and have implemented programs to help new Canadians adjust to life in Canada. In essence, what these organizations have endeavored to do is simply pay more attention to the issues of today's immigrants and to offer means of assistance.

Essentially, it's a matter of creating an environment that's accommodating and supportive of immigrant employees. Recognition of work experience and educational qualifications from outside Canada and providing language training programs are two ways companies are making the adjustment to life and work in Canada a little easier for recent immigrants.

Some of the more visible immigrant-friendly employers include:

Institutions
  The Federal Government
  Provincial Governments
  Municipal (city) Governments
  Universities
  Colleges

Financial Services
  TD/ Canada Trust
  Manulife Financial
  Ernst & Young
  KPMG

Media/ Communications Companies
   CBC Television
   Bell Canada

Charitable Organizations
   Goodwill
   Salvation Army

Retailers
   Wal-Mart
   Safeway

The web site below lists 20 Canadian businesses from across the country. Each was cited for their immigrant-friendly programs such as recognizing foreign qualifications and education, having a coaching or mentoring program to help integrate new employees into the Canadian work environment, and offering management training on multiculturalism and inclusiveness.

Finalists were selected from over 200 submissions from across the country. Winners represented all key categories of employment. The Top 20 recognized companies include: Associated Engineering Group Ltd. of Edmonton, Enbridge, Inc., Business Development Bank of Canada, Ernst & Young LLP of Toronto, Keane Canada Inc. of Halifax and TD Bank Financial Group of Toronto.

A complete list is available at: www.canadastop100.com/immigrants

Another list to check out is the top 100 companies to work for in Canada. You can find this list here: www.canadastop100.com/national

Still another list to check is the 50 Best Employers to Work For listed in the Globe and Mail of Wednesday, January 14th 2009. Such companies as Protegra Inc. in Winnipeg, Miele Canada Limited in Vaughan and Gibraltar Solutions Inc. in Mississauga are listed.

But it's not only the larger national companies that are working to accommodate new Canadian workers. The Toronto Region Immigrant Employment Council recently announced the winners of its second annual Immigrant Success Awards. Those winning firms are as follows:
   Small Employer Award - Steam Whistle Brewing
   Honourable Mention - Microskills Development Centre
   Mid-size Employer Award - Xerox Research Centre of Canada
   Large Employer Award - Toronto and Region Conservation Authority
   Influence Award - George Brown College
   Honourable Mention - Career Bridge

Another organization that is friendly to immigrants is the CBC (Canadian Broadcasting Corporation) which has a specific interest in representing all cultures of Canada and the growing number of new immigrants to this country. One of the most recognizable individuals is Ian Hanomansing, a Trinidadian immigrant of Indian descent, who is a news anchor for the CBC.

Wal-Mart leads the way among retailers in employing new Canadians. Another firm that has been in the forefront of hiring a diversified workforce is Safeway, a large food and drug retailer mostly in Western Canada.

In the October 2007 issue, Profit Magazine identified the following Canadian companies as having excellent growth potential: Equitrans Global Logistics, Advatum Services Inc., and Auctionwire Inc. were listed among those positioned to experience a high rate of growth over the coming years. For a complete list, please refer to the October issue of the magazine.

The Toronto Daily Star of April 3rd, 2008 announced the winners for the 2008 awards for Canada's Best Diversity Employers. Firms listed in this survey include:

Air Canada (Montreal-based national airline)
Boeing Canada Technology Ltd (Winnipeg aerospace component manufacturer)
Catholic Children's Aid Society of Toronto (Toronto social services for children)
Ernst & Young LLP (Toronto-based accounting firm)
Hewlett-Packard Canada Co. (Mississauga computer products and services)
HSBC Bank Canada (Vancouver-based banking and financial services)
IBM Canada Ltd (Markham computing products and services)
KPMG LLP (Toronto financial services)
Proctor and Gamble (Toronto manufacturer and marketer of consumer products)
Enbridge Inc. (Calgary natural gas distribution and services)

All of the companies from across Canada are listed on the following web site:
www.canadastop100.com/diversity

The Toronto Star of Saturday, October 18th, 2008 announced its Top 75 Employers for 2009 in the GTA. Companies included many of the companies listed above along with some others including:

AMEC Canada Inc
Bank of Montreal BMO
Barclay's Global Investors Canada Ltd.
Capital One Services Inc
AGFA Healthcare Information Inc
BD Canada Inc
Bayer Inc
BBM Canada
CH2M Hill Canada Ltd
The Compass Group Canada
Gay Lea Foods Co-Operative Limited

The National Post (March 1st, 2008) published an article on Canada's 50 Best Managed Companies. Companies mentioned included engineering firm, ADI Group of Fredericton, New Brunswick and Losani Homes Ltd. of Stoney Creek, Ontario. For the complete listing of "Canada's 50 Best Managed" companies, visit: www.canadas50Best.com

The TRIEC (Toronto Region Immigrant Employment Council) 3rd Annual Immigrant Success Award Winners announce in January of 2009 were:
- RBC Best Immigrant Employer Award to Nytric Limited located in Mississauga,On
- RBC Best Immigrant Employer Award to CH2M Hill Canada Limited located in Toronto with offices across Canada
- TD Financial Group has proven to be an immigrant-friendly organization and have a multitude of programs in place that support diversity in the community.

The TD Bank Financial Group is one of Canada's top corporate donors. In 2006, they provided over $33 million to more than 1,600 charities and not-for-profit groups. On top of their financial contributions, TD has implemented programs and policies to provide diversity in corporate leadership, encourage diversity in the workplace, and improve service to diverse customer groups. TD Financial Group's proactive approach leads the way in today's multicultural Canada.

Specific programs and policies employed include a Diversity Leadership Council. The purpose of the council is to spearhead diversity initiatives internally, while encouraging businesses to include diversity in their business plans. Another initiative is a mentoring program that matches new Canadians with professionals who share the same occupation or skills. This sets up a "career bridge" to help place and acclimatize new Canadians to the Canadian work environment. TD also supports the African-Canadian community by promoting black history.

Additionally, the TD Bank Financial Group has taken a leading sponsorship role with *CareerEdge* -- Canada's Internship Organization that helps new immigrants gain valuable Canadian experience. Other notable organizations recognized by *CareerEdge* include: Bell Canada, Accenture, and TakingItGlobal.

Chapter Thirteen
Business Section
Investing in Canada

Canada ranks high as a country to invest and do business, when compared to the other leading nations of the world. Canada is the best country among the G7 Group to invest and conduct business as rated by the Economist's Intelligence Unit which is a world leader in global business intelligence. It's an assessment that spans the years from 2005 to 2009.

The key factors contributing to Canada's leading-edge position include:
• A capable, intelligent and skilled workforce (As a portion of GDP, Canada spends more dollars on education than any other country in the world)
• Canada has and continues to develop its pool of sophisticated knowledge workers
• Canada is a leading world economy and is considered more technologically advanced than Japan, Germany, United Kingdom, and France
• Canada's technology industries have been growing much faster than traditional industries
• Canada is a quality place to live and holds a premier position in relation to the other G7 countries

Canada ranks first in providing equal opportunity. We are one of the world's most multicultural and multilingual societies. Canadians enjoy an overall quality of life that is second to none, with one of the lowest costs of living of any developing nation. Canada is one of the safest places in the world to live and offers the optimum in terms of human development.

The World Trade Magazine ranked Canada in the top 3 nations for Investment and Trade opportunities. Canada guarantees investors the overall lowest tax rate among developed countries and the most preferable R & D (Research and Development) tax credit program among all G7 countries.

In an article published by the Toronto Daily Star March 28th 2008, titled "Canada Low-Cost Business Spot" the firm KPMG ranked Canada as the second best country behind Mexico.

The survey noted that while Canada had lost the previous cost advantage to the United States due to our rising currency valuation, we had gained ground on European countries. If you're an investor or entrepreneur, you should check to make sure you have all of the requirements of operating a business in Canada.

Canada has also introduced numerous incentives to ensure that new businesses will be successful here. To be eligible for most of these incentives, you have to establish a company in Canada.

Canada has a NAFTA (North American Free Trade Agreement) advantage in that Canada is America's largest trading partner. This means that any company located in Canada has access to more than 425 million consumers and a combined GDP of more than 11.4 trillion dollars.

As revealed in a Globe and Mail article (October 31, 2007) Canada's Minister of Finance, Jim Flaherty, is attempting to make Canada the most competitive corporate tax system of all the Group of Seven countries. To do so, the finance minister has set what he believes is an attainable target. He intends to lower the federal corporate tax rate to 15 per cent by 2012.

Immigrant Investor Program

The Immigrant Investor Program is a program sponsored by both the government of Canada and the government of Quebec to help in the process of immigration to Canada for business investors. The guidelines are listed in the Investor Class section of the Avenues of Admission chapter of the book. Immigrant investors receive permanent resident visas leading to Canadian citizenship. Many of the banks, including HSBC, have programs that make investment more accessible for immigrants to Canada.

Business Investors Information - Federal and Provincial

The Ministry of Small Business and Entrepreneurship operates Small Business Enterprise Centres in communities across all provinces. New entrepreneurs will find a variety of services and resources to enhance their business development. At each office the services offered include:

A. consultant services
B. publications
C. seminars

The prime web-site is:
www.canadabusiness.ca

Each province has programs for the small and medium sized business investor including foreign investment by New Canadians.

Listed below are the various programs in effect in the Province of Ontario. For any other Province look up the web-site for the Ministry of Economic Development and Trade.

Enterprise Toronto. It is one of 55 small Business Enterprise Centres throughout Ontario who provide a myriad of information and advise small business entrepreneurs. The link is: http://www.ontariocanada.com/ontcan/search/search/search.do?name=offices&arg2=Toronto

The next link provides information for immigrants about starting a business in Ontario:
http://www.2ontario.com/bi/bi_startingabusiness.asp   (place underscore in space)

Another link to services to help immigrants who want to start a business in Ontario:
http://www.2ontario.com/bi/bi_services.asp

This link provides lots of information about immigrants investing in a business:
http://www.2ontario.combi/bi/_businessimmigration.asp

This link provides all sorts of ways to start a small business, with info on financing, taxes, business registration:
http://www.sbe.gov.on.ca/ontcan/sbe/en/start_en.jsp

This info will help grow the business once it is underway:
http://www.sbe.gov.on.ca/ontcan/sbe/en/grow_en.jsp

Newcomers can also access skills training programs offered by Employment Ontario. The Apprenticeship Training Tax Credit (ATTC) encourages Ontario businesses to hire apprentices by providing up to $15,000 towards eligible apprentices' salaries and wages for the first 36 months of training by private sector employers.

Rueben Moitra

Rueben Moitra is a consultant with HiTech Research Consultants in Toronto(Ph:416-524-4874). HiTech Research Consultants is a firm which specializes in SR&ED refund claim (scientific research and experimental development, government programs). They offer consulting and full preparation of your R&D claim. Essentially, they will try to capture all of the time a business would have spent on new product development, new process development along with improved products and processes. Rueben has an education and background in business and accounting and has helped over 100 Canadian companies receive Research and Development refunds from the government.

Rueben has some advice for immigrants starting up a business in Canada:

A. in order to make your business, just a "little busy", you may have to make many tracks to get your business engine running, try doing cold calls, warm calls, referrals, demo days, trades shows and the like. You may have to make 50 calls to get 1 new client, but don't be afraid to work!

B. develop a relationship with an accountant who can provide you all of the information necessary to start a business in Canada- use references to locate an accountant who is experienced in handling the affairs of small and medium sized businesses in Canada

C. ensure that you have all of the information regarding Federal and Provincial taxes, GST, PST and a business licence along with application for such items as a liquor licence if that is part of a food and beverage establishment

D. know your numbers-market, sales figures, profit margins, sales and profit forecasts, number of employees-prepare a business plan even if you are providing your own financing because it will be a roadmap for your business and a measurement device for the future

E. if you do not have any numbers or need help in their development there are various people that can help you such as- your accountant, consultants like HiTech or various marketing consultants, government agencies and web sites

F. take small steps rather than moving in large commitments that might take you into a vulnerable business position

G. if you are looking for financing from a banker of investment firm you should figure out all of the questions in advance and provide detailed answers to them. This action indicates that you have the business acumen to run a profitable company

H. if you are creating a new product a firm such as HiTech can assist you in applying for government grants or refunds on the research work that you are doing along with advising you on the correct documentation and records required to apply and maximize the amount of your refund

Small Business Start-up in Canada

Two important web-sites in providing information on small business start –up in Canada are:
www.sbinfocanada.about.com
www.canadaone.com/tools/startingabusiness

One of the first and most important steps in Canadian small business start-up is developing a business plan and its necessary components.

1) The Main Elements of a Business Plan are:

The Executive Summary which is actually a summary of all of the listed elements and is placed at the front of the business plan to give an overview before the details are reviewed in detail.

The Industry

A Market Analysis

Competitive Analysis

Marketing Plan

Management Plan

Operating Plan

Financial Plan

It would not hurt your business plan to have a section on Customer Service in the Marketing Plan and read up on customer service practices.

The quality and accuracy of your business plan will directly impact your firm's success and your ability to get financing from any number of institutions.

Along the way it is important to get proper business advice from a professional accountant and business lawyer.

2) Choose a form of business

Your form of business determines the legal structure of the business and you must get the proper advice and documents drawn up by a business lawyer. If you decide to incorporate your business you should look at the advantages and disadvantages of incorporating provincially or federally.

3) Choose a name for your business and register your business in a province/territory along with linking to the Provincial Sales tax information for that province/territory.

4) Find small business financing either determining if you as an owner can do it or you need help from others including financial institutions.

Financing for Canadian Small Business Start-ups
Three important web-sites for finding information on small business financing are:
www.canadabusiness.ca
www.ic.gc.ca/epic/site/csbfp-pfpec.nsf/en/Home
www.sbinfocanada.about.com/od/finanacing/a/financinghub.htm

The Canada Business Service Centre

The Canada Business Service Centre offers an interactive on-line business planner available on this web site: www.cbsc.org
 The interactive online business planner assists entrepreneurs in preparing a three year business plan for their new or existing business.
 The business development Bank of Canada also offers a business plan guide at:
www.hdc.ca/en/business_tools/business_plan/

Opportunities for Canadian Business and Educational Institutions At Home and Abroad

 Canadians must now look at the world as a global opportunity to expand their business and expertise into far reaching markets and invite business investment into this country. There are businessmen around the world who are looking for Canadian expertise in their countries which effectively creates more jobs in Canada. The world is at our fingertips and we no longer have to travel around the world when most business will be conducted from our virtual homes and offices through the internet and communication systems. Opportunities exist for these types of business both in Canada and with Canadian expertise abroad:
- education- opening branches of Canadian colleges and universities abroad
- the marketing of Canadian educational institutions abroad
- business interests in the field of healthcare pharmaceuticals, geology, mining and oil exploration in which Canada excels
- tourism and tourist attractions
- telecommunication and transportation
- civil engineering

Employment and Labour Law in Canada

Laura Williams

Laura Williams is a partner at Crawford Chondon and Partners LLP, which is a law firm specializing in providing advice and representation to employers in the area of labour and employment law. Laura is also a principal and shareholder of The Employers' Choice Inc., a human resources consulting firm.

In her practice, Laura provides strategic advice and representation to employers on a full range of labour and employment law matters and human resources issues. Laura's clients range from small owner-operator enterprises to large multi-national corporations.

Laura speaks frequently at employment law seminars and conferences, and regularly conducts workshops and training for employers, supervisors and human resource professionals.

An Overview of Employment and Labour Law in Canada
Laura K. Williams, Crawford Chondon & Partners LLP[1]

There is probably no other area of law in Canada that undergoes such a rapid evolution as employment and labour law. The legislatures, courts and various administrative tribunals all have roles to play in the regulation of the employment relationship, as they develop and modify laws and practices to strike the appropriate balance. This presents a challenge for employers, who must keep abreast of changes in employment laws to ensure compliance with workplace requirements and to avoid being exposed to additional risk in the event of a breakdown of the employment relationship. As a result, the law can often seem intimidating to employers operating in Canada, and particularly to foreign businesses unfamiliar with the political structure of government in Canada. In addition, new employers in Canada can be confused by the many legal forums through which employees are able to seek remedies, depending on the nature of the employment or labour issue raised.

The purpose of this article is to provide a general roadmap for employers unfamiliar with the Canadian labour and employment legal landscape, to help businesses navigate their way through the complex maze of laws governing the employment relationship. Provided below is an overview of the most salient features of this ever-evolving area of the law.

Division of Powers in Canada

Canada is a parliamentary democracy, where power is divided between the federal and provincial governments. The division of powers between the federal and provincial governments is set out under the *Constitution Act, 1867* (the "*Constitution*"). For the purposes of labour and

---

1 By Laura K. Williams, Partner, Crawford Chondon & Partners LLP This overview has been drafted as a general guide to provide general information to prospective employers who are considering doing business in Canada. It is intended to be summary in nature and not intended to set out a complete analysis of the law, a legal opinion or advice from Laura Williams or any member of Crawford Chondon & Partners LLP.

employment law, the determination of whether an employer is subject to federal or provincial legislation is dependent on the nature of the business activity in which it is engaged. Section 91 of the *Constitution* empowers the federal government to pass legislation applicable to those businesses engaged in inter-provincial activities such as communications, broadcasting, banking and transportation, including inter-provincial trucking, railways and airlines. The provincial government has the authority, pursuant to Section 92 of the *Constitution,* to legislate in areas of business activity that do not fall within the federal domain, including almost all of the manufacturing and service industries, as well as issues related to health and education.

Legal Landscape

Employment relationships in Canada are governed by both legislation and the common law which arises out of the decisions made by the courts and various administrative tribunals. Claims of wrongful dismissal and certain breaches of occupational health and safety legislation are most frequently dealt with by the courts. In the context of a wrongful dismissal claim, certain terms and conditions of employment between an employee and his/her employer are also informed by the common law. The most fundamental obligation imposed upon employers by the common law is to extend beyond statutory minimums the obligation to provide employees with reasonable notice of termination of employment, or pay in lieu of reasonable notice, in the absence of just cause for dismissal. Since just cause for dismissal is extremely difficult to prove in the employment context, employers generally opt to terminate employment by means of providing employees with reasonable notice or pay in lieu of notice.

The legal landscape in Quebec, which is Canada's second largest province, is unique and distinct from the rest of Canada because it has protected its constitutional right to regulate business operating in that province in its own way. Unlike the rest of Canada, Quebec operates under a civil law regime and as a result of its history and largely French-speaking population, Quebec is also distinct as businesses must recognize French as the official language of the province and must be capable of conducting business in French. The *Charter of the French Language* also imposes other French language requirements on businesses operating in Quebec, including the requirement to have a French version of the company name, French language advertising and product labeling, and business forms, (including employment applications).

While many of Quebec's labour and employment laws are similar to those in other Canadian provinces, a business planning to operate in Quebec should seek specific advice on the legal requirements that apply to the employment context within that province.

The balance of this article will apply to general labour and employment law conditions that exist in Canada's common law jurisdictions, excluding Quebec.

The Courts - Wrongful Dismissal

Where an employer decides to end the employment relationship however fails to provide an employee with reasonable notice or pay in lieu of notice to allow the employee to obtain other employment, it is open to the employee to sue the employer for wrongful dismissal. In considering the amount of notice an employee is entitled to receive, the courts will generally consider the age of the employee; the employee's length of service; the position held by the employee and the employee's level of compensation.

In instances where the employer is found to have engaged in any aggravating or "bad faith" behaviour, in dismissing the employee, a court may extend the reasonable notice period as a method of increasing the damage award.

It is also important to note that individuals who choose to pursue this route run the risk of incurring cost consequences if they do not consider a reasonable offer to settle, or if they lose their case. Generally, Canadian courts penalize the losing party by awarding costs against them; however costs awards rarely result in 100% recovery for the successful party.

Occupational Health and Safety Prosecutions

Every Canadian jurisdiction has enacted legislation that aims to provide employees with a safe working environment to minimize the risk of workplace accidents. While the standards may vary from province to province, the common thread in all of the legislation is the duty imposed on employers to take all reasonable precautions to protect the health and safety of their employees.

In addition to the duties outlined in the various legislations, there are very detailed regulations that accompany most occupational health and safety statues. These regulations tend to impose specific responsibilities on employers in certain industries to ensure the safety of their respective workers. Other regulatory responsibilities often found in the regulations relate to the usage and handling of toxic substances and hazardous materials.

Occupational health and safety legislation also provides employees with the right to be informed by their employer about hazards in the workplace and the right to refuse to work if employees reasonably believe that it poses a danger to them. Employers are not able to discipline or otherwise commit a reprisal against an employee who exercises his or her right to refuse work that is believed to be dangerous.

Employees also have the right to participate in workplace health and safety committees to assist in dealing with health and safety issues in the workplace. In Ontario, for example, employers who employ more than 20 employees are required to create a Joint Health and Safety Committee.

Health and safety inspectors are generally empowered to enforce occupational health and safety legislation. These inspectors have a broad range of powers at their disposal to investigate potential violations of the legislation. Where an inspector finds that an employer has failed to comply with the legislation, he or she can typically order that the violations be remedied within a certain time frame, may issue work stoppage orders and/or sometimes lay charges under the specific legislative provisions.

The potential liability for an employer who fails to comply with occupational health and safety legislation can be staggering. A failure to comply can result in quasi-criminal prosecution of both individuals and corporations, often leading to fines for anyone convicted, whether they are an individual or a corporation. In addition to fines, Canada's *Criminal Code* was recently amended to expand corporate liability for serious breaches of health and safety violations and workplace accidents. Senior managers, officers and directors of corporations now face the prospect of criminal sanctions for a failure to ensure the health and safety of their workplaces. Accordingly, it is of the utmost importance for employers to be duly diligent to prevent the occurrence of accidents or injuries in the workplace.

Employment Tribunals

With the exception of wrongful dismissal claims, and certain breaches of the occupational health and safety legislation referenced above, the trend in Canada has been to devolve more responsibility on specialist tribunals, created by legislation for the enforcement of employment-related issues. While judicial review of tribunal decisions is still available to litigants, the courts tend to be deferential to those tribunals that have focused purposes and demonstrated expertise in their respective subject areas. The following is a brief overview of the various tribunals that adjudicate employment-related issues.

Employment Standards Tribunals

Employment standards legislation in both the provincial and federal branches of government is aimed at establishing minimum standards for all employees, unless they are specifically exempted from the legislation. Employers are not able to contract out of these minimum standards unless they provide rights that are superior to those contained under the legislation. This is called the "greater right or benefit" analysis.

Employment Standards legislation addresses such issues as:
- minimum wages;
- hours of work;
- vacations and holidays;
- pregnancy and parental leave;
- emergency leave; and
- termination of employment.

In the event that a provision of employment standards legislation is breached, an employee can complain to the employment standards tribunal in his or her jurisdiction and employment standards adjudicators have a broad range of remedies available to them, which include but are not limited to:
- reinstatement of the employee to employment;
- compensation for lost wages and other financial compensation; and
- damages for emotional pain and suffering.

Human Rights Tribunals

Each Canadian province, as well as the federal government, has established comprehensive legislation that provides for a system of investigation and resolution of issues related to discrimination in the workplace. The status of human rights legislation is treated as "quasi-constitutional", meaning that decisions rendered under the human rights regime are usually given more weight in the event that there is a conflict between a human rights decision and that of another tribunal. This results from the broad consensus in Canadian society that all individuals should be treated with respect and dignity.

Generally, human rights legislation in the employment context provides for an individual's right to equal treatment in the workplace, and prohibits discrimination in employment based on certain prohibited grounds, which vary slightly from province to province. The most common grounds include:

- place of origin
- place of residence
- creed
- sexual orientation
- family status
- political beliefs
- ancestry
- disability
- marital status
- pregnancy
- sex
- age
- race

In addition to the obligation placed on employers not to discriminate or permit harassment in the workplace, human rights legislation has recently been infused with the notion that an employer is under a duty to accommodate employees to the point of undue hardship, particularly on the grounds of disability, religion and family status.

The enforcement of human rights legislation is largely complaint-driven. Most provinces have established a human rights commission that provides assistance and investigates the complaints of individuals who believe they have been discriminated against. These commissions often perform a "gate-keeper" function, in that they will only refer a complaint to the adjudicating human rights tribunal if that complaint is found to have merit and is not made in bad faith. Recently, legislative reform of the *Human Rights Code* in Ontario has resulted in the elimination of the investigative and screening role of the Commission. Complainants who allege an employer's breach of the Ontario *Human Rights Code* are now able to file their complaint directly to the Tribunal.

Human rights tribunals have a broad range of remedies at their disposal, including the power to award reinstatement of a terminated employee, award damages for loss of income, or damages related to the loss of enjoyment or hurt feelings and the ability to require employers to institute anti-discrimination policies or other initiatives to encourage compliance with human rights objectives.

Labour Relations Tribunals

In all Canadian jurisdictions, legislation exists that regulates trade union organization and collective bargaining activity. The most fundamental principle that is entrenched in all Canadian labour legislation is the right of employees to organize and to be represented by a bargaining agent, without employer interference, through a certification process. Following certification, the parties must bargain in good faith in an attempt to reach a collective agreement. During the life of a collective agreement, strikes and lockouts are not permitted. While various provincial labour law statutes differ in significant respects, they have several characteristics in common, which include the following:[insert bullet points here]

- While an employer has the right to communicate with employees during an organizing drive, such communication is constrained to ensure that the employer does not unduly influence employees;

• Many protections exist in labour legislation for preserving union bargaining rights and the collective agreement in the event of a sale of a business;

• When certified, the union is recognized as the sole representative that represents employees in the relationship with their employer. The employer is then prohibited from dealing on an individual basis with employees to establish terms and conditions of employment;

• Bargaining rights are obtained by unions through a process of employees joining together for membership in the union. The union will then proceed to make an application for certification as the exclusive bargaining agent by applying to either the provincial or Federal Labour Relations Board. Membership evidence then dictates whether the Board certifies the union as the bargaining agent, dismisses the application, or calls for a vote of all eligible employees to determine their wishes;

• Following a successful certification application, the union becomes the exclusive bargaining agent for employees in its bargaining unit, and the employer has an obligation to bargain in good faith with the union to achieve a collective agreement; and

• As referenced above, strikes or lockouts are prohibited during the life of the collective agreement.

The vast majority of collective agreements in Canada are negotiated without the parties resorting to strikes or lockouts. However, where strikes and lockouts do occur, employees are able to picket the employer's premises to communicate their positions to individuals entering and exiting the employer's premises. Secondary picketing, which involves picketing third parties dealing with the employer, is also permitted in certain circumstances. Employers may be able to obtain injunctions from the courts to limit picketing activity where the strikers violate the standards of conduct established by the courts and legislation.

Picketing is regulated by the criminal law and the law of torts in addition to labour relations legislation. Picketers are only able to communicate information and are prohibited from engaging in forms of intimidation, including verbal threats, physical assaults or blocking access or egress to and from the employer's premises.

Workers' Compensation Boards and Tribunals

All Canadian provinces provide comprehensive no-fault insurance schemes which compensate, or provide income replacement to, employees who have injuries or illnesses that result from or arise during the course of employment. Participation in the plan is compulsory for employers engaged in an industry or activity covered by the insurance plan, as determined by the specific statute.

In exchange for relieving employers of tort liability to the employee as a result of workplace accidents, employers are required to contribute to the insurance plan in accordance with a rate schedule that corresponds to the type of industry or business activity in which they are engaged. Generally, the greater the degree of risk of accident in the workplace or business activity, the higher the premium that employer will be required to pay. In some provinces, workers' compensation legislation provides for a system of experience rating which may mean that an employer's claim history may impact the premium rate it pays if it is found that the employer has a poor claim history. Conversely, an employer with a good claim history may receive a rebate.

Under most workers' compensation schemes, a certain percentage of the injured worker's salary is paid subject to maximum entitlements established under the legislation. The legislation also usually provides for temporary benefits for recovering employees and permanent benefits for employees who are found to have a permanent impairment of their earning capacity as a result of the workplace accident. Workers' compensation boards are also responsible for providing rehabilitation services through their own operations and/or other facilities that provide rehabilitation services. In most cases, an employee is limited to the compensation and other benefits provided under the plan. The employee is statute-barred from proceeding with a civil action for damages in the courts.

Workers' compensation legislation also imposes additional obligations upon employers. In most cases, employers are required to report any accidents that occur in the workplace within a specific period of time. Employers are also required to work with employees to prevent injuries and to assist in returning them to work.

Employers covered by the applicable workers' compensation plan must also register with the workers' compensation board in their jurisdiction and make the necessary payments under the legislation. If not done voluntarily, the process is usually triggered when an employee sustains an injury resulting from a workplace accident, makes a claim for benefits, which is then reviewed by the workers' compensation board. In situations where the employer raises issues in writing about the employee's entitlement, the agency may investigate the claim in further detail and then make a determination regarding whether the employee is entitled to benefit coverage or not. Employees who are denied benefit coverage are generally entitled to appeal the decision through the specific workers' compensation appeal process. Employers also have rights of appeal where they disagree with how a claim has been adjudicated.

Federal and Provincial Privacy Legislation
Privacy legislation and regulation in Canada has been a relatively recent phenomenon. To date, only the federal government, British Columbia, Alberta and Quebec have specifically legislated in this area. The federal legislation, *Personal Information Protection and Electronic Documents Act (PIPEDA)*, applies to commercial activities of federally regulated companies in any province that has not enacted its own companion legislation.

The central goal of *PIPEDA* is to govern the handling of personal information of individuals by organizations in the course of commercial activities, and *PIPEDA* specifically applies to how federally-regulated employers handle the personal information of their employees. However, the scope of the federal legislation does not extend to personal information relating to employees of provincially-regulated employers who operate in provincial jurisdictions that have not enacted their own privacy legislation; in such cases *PIPEDA* only applies to the collection, use and disclosure of personal information in the course of commercial activities. As referenced above, only Alberta, Quebec and British Columbia have enacted privacy legislation that specifically regulates how employers handle the personal information of their employees. Currently, in provinces without privacy legislation, the use of employee personal information by private sector employers is unregulated. However, the principles set out in *PIPEDA* and other provincially-enacted privacy statues are increasingly being viewed as desirable best practices, and that it would not be surprising to see other provinces enact similar legislation in the future.

Franchising

J. Perry Maisonneuve

Much of the information in this chapter was provided by franchise consultant, J. Perry Maisonneuve. Perry is the Founder and Principal of Northern Lights Franchise Consultants Corporation. For more than fifteen years, Northern Lights has served franchise owners in all key areas of business ownership including planning, finance, franchise sales, marketing and operational support .

Perry has also developed kits specifically to help the entrepreneurial immigrant choose a franchise that best matches his or hers skills and aptitudes. This approach dramatically improves the franchisee's rate of success.

Although we rely on Perry's expertise to advise new immigrants in the area of franchising, he is also an expert in all areas of business management and development. Perry provides advice and guidance in all areas of owner-managed business and the experience gained by franchisees can be valuable to any business owner.

You can contact Perry Maisonneuve directly through the following methods:
P: 905-812-1219   E: jpmaisonneuve@franchiseservices.ca   W: www.franchiseservices.ca

Franchising has proven to be an effective and practical approach to business ownership. It works so well in most instances that franchising has become a widely-accepted global business strategy with over 17,000 franchise systems around the world, supporting over 1.2 million franchisees, and more than 12.5 million employees. Clearly a significant number of people all over the world and right across Canada are involved in some capacity with a franchised business.

While franchising has traditionally dominated the food service and retail sectors, the franchise system has now been applied to such diverse industries as: business services, health care, education, information technology, and customized manufacturing and assembly facilities.

Companies that offer franchises have already blazed a trail. They've established what works and what doesn't and have created a duplicable system that can be repeated over and over again, in numerous geographic locations.

Should you decide to pursue franchising, it's important to find an opportunity that suits you well. Finding the business that's right for you can make all the difference. Not all business opportunities or available franchises are created equal, so it's essential that you investigate thoroughly before investing any money.

Finding a good fit between the business and franchisee is also of vital importance to the franchisor. Any organization driven to succeed is looking for a person with specific skills and attributes – someone who is quite capable of representing the brand and making their individual operation a successful one.

Essentially, there are three methods to starting a business of your own:

1. You could start your own business from scratch. This is definitely the cheapest way to get started operating a business of your own. Unfortunately, it's also the method that puts you at the greatest risk financially. Without any direct guidance, 80 to 90% of these businesses fail within the first 24 months.

2. You could buy an existing business. This may or may not work well, depending on the specifics of the business and the cost of acquisition.

3. You could invest in a franchise. A franchised business provides the valuable elements of business ownership, with a lot less risk. Investing in a franchise represents a compromise between the two options above.

What are the key advantages of franchising?

• Franchising provides the franchisee with a well-established model to follow and a systemized approach to all aspects related to the operation of the business.

• Greater funding capacities. A solid franchise is much easier to finance. Banks provide greater access to capital for established franchised businesses versus non-franchised enterprises.

• Faster expansion into new markets. A recognized franchise makes breaking into new markets easier due to brand awareness and built-in customer loyalty.

• An advertising fund pool that all franchisees contribute to and benefit from. With franchising, the advertising aspect of operating your business has already been created and tested.

• A motivated business owner. You're no longer on your own. You have procedures to follow, targets to meet and a considerable investment to recoup and turn into an ongoing profit.

• A commitment to achieving success. Access to a proven system and brand recognition comes with obligations. Your contractual arrangement as well as your personal investment into the business forces you to remain committed to long-term growth and success.

It should be understood that a franchise is not the right choice for everyone. Owning a franchise can pay off in a big way. But it involves a substantial investment, tremendous dedication, and hard work for many years. That's why you must ensure that the franchise is a proper fit for you, before taking the plunge.

No serious franchisor will automatically accept an applicant. Before granting you a franchise, the corporate office will need to be satisfied that you will make it a success. Even though your capital investment can be substantial, that's only one qualifier. You'll have to also meet the organization criteria.

Utilizing the services of someone like Perry can be a big help because he matches the attributes of the potential franchisee with whatever franchises are available at the time. This is the reason why various franchises are not recommended by name. The selection process is individual in nature and is based on a whole group of factors provided by prospective investors. Just because a particular brand is successful doesn't mean it's the right franchise for you. The business that's a good fit for one individual may not necessarily be a good fit for the next. Making the right decision from the start is critical.

Franchises are particularly valuable to new business immigrants because they provide immigrants with an entry point into Canadian business culture. Follow the formula as outlined in the operations manual and your chances of success are much better than if you were to start any other type of business in your new country.

Banks are also more accommodating to the immigrant business investor when they are provided with complete business plans involving location, revenues and projections, training manuals, brand recognition, and professional marketing and advertising programs.

That's where franchised businesses have a huge advantage. It's not just estimated projections you present, but the actual figures based on the performance of other franchises within the chain. But when you start a business from the ground floor, your numbers are merely estimates because there's no track record to base those estimates on.

Success stories of franchising in the Toronto area include "Popeye's", a chicken restaurant chain, which has over 35 locations in the city. The original franchise holders in Toronto were Muslim and they were given permission by the corporate office to sell Halal chicken at their Popeye's locations. "Halal" most frequently refers to food that is permissible according to Islamic Law. Consequently, the franchise holders have gained a large following within the Muslim community, which has helped their business to continue to develop.

Another success story involves a couple of Canadian immigrants of professional backgrounds who ventured into the education franchise, Oxford Learning Centres. Today, their partnership includes 8 Oxford Learning Centre locations. This example clearly demonstrates the importance of finding a business that is the right fit.

Franchising is an ever-changing industry that adapts to the general economy as we move from primarily a product-based economy to a service economy. These economic winds of change have lead to the rapid development of service-oriented franchises in areas of business, health care, and education.

Language skills start to become more important as the franchise holder has to be able to communicate and market his service on a one-to-one basis. The older, more established food service franchises do not require the same high language skills that service skills demand. On the other hand, service-based franchises do not require the expensive equipment or facilities that food and retail businesses need, so start-up costs are lower and margins higher.

Some immigrants prefer to bring their whole family with them and involve them in a food business where they usually bring experience from home. Most business immigrants have developed a nest egg to invest in a restaurant business in Canada and have all kinds of expertise, making it a good fit for them.

General Information on Franchises

Recent statistics indicate that 56% of today's franchises are in the food business, 20% in the service sector, while retailers account for the remaining 24%. Franchises could be classified on three different levels:

1. Emerging Business – This is one which is less than 5 years old, with less than 20 franchise holders in total. There is room to grow but you need to consider whether they will be a growing concern, or are they just based on a founder's name.

2. Mezzanine Level – This franchisor has more than 5 years experience, with 20 to 60 franchise units, a solid track record with notable experience and effective business practices in place.

3. High Level Franchisor – 60+ franchise units with mature experience and an international presence. These are the most established franchisors. But there may not be too many opportunities at this level because of the lack of available prime locations, as well as the waiting list for any new openings that may arise.

There are also two types of equity that are important in selecting a franchise:

Consumer Brand Equity - This type of equity involves the recognition of the brand by the consumer. Does the franchise have a strong brand presence with its customers that the business has built up over the years? Are there line-ups at the counter for the franchise's products? These are two strong indicators of solid brand recognition in the marketplace.

Investor Brand Equity - Is there a waiting list for a franchise? Does it have a recognizable and popular brand name and unique products? Does the franchise have a proven business record that offers a low risk opportunity to new franchisees? As a potential franchise owner, these are important points to consider before moving ahead.

The process of selecting a franchise should begin with a broad overview. Start by taking a look at a large number of franchises and begin to narrow down your list to a small group, based on the various parameters of greatest importance to you.

Legal Rights of Franchisees

The Ontario government passed a "Franchise Act" in 2000 which has three key principles:

1. A duty of fair dealing
2. An obligation of full disclosure targeted at franchisors
3. The unrestricted right of franchisees to associate and organize

Each franchisee is expected to practice due diligence in their dealings with a franchisor and it is recommended that every potential franchisee get professional advice early in the selection process. This is very important. Do your research before investing. That's the best way to produce satisfactory results.

Specifically, the legislation states that:

• The franchisee is not to sign any agreement or pay the franchise fee for 14 days from the date that they are given the disclosure documents. This is essentially a cooling off period, one that allows investors to be sure before moving forward with what is usually an investment of considerable size.

• Each franchisee is to receive full disclosure of documents including all material facts, copies of agreements to be signed, financial statements, a listing of the officers and directors of the franchisor, etc.

• Each franchisee is to receive a list of all franchisees in the province and may contact any franchisee they like, provided they follow a protocol that does not interfere with the franchisee's business.

• Franchisees are free to join as groups or bodies and form associations with any other franchise owner or organization.

Franchising represents an unmatched opportunity for today's business immigrant. Although the costs are considerable, you're getting a proven system that's essentially a turnkey operation, easier access to funding, and a step-by-step plan that increases your odds of success.

It's a safer, tried and true approach to business. You'll get customers almost automatically – without spending huge amounts of capital to do it. But that doesn't mean owning a franchise is easy. It takes a lot of work to make your business a success. You are guided every step of the way, but you still need to put in the effort to make it work.

A franchise gives you everything you need in business. It's not just a mapped out business plan. Instead you have the plan, plus real world numbers to plug into it. Every piece of the puzzle fits because it's all been figured out for you in advance. Any business owner who follows the formula they're given stands a good chance of succeeding.

Above all else, due diligence is vital. Conduct as much research as you can. Seek professional help as it's required. And use your own good judgment. That's the best approach to making sound decisions and establishing your own profitable franchise business.

CAMSC

Canadian Aboriginal and Minority Supplier Council(CAMSC) is an organization that aims to encourage the economic development of minority-owned businesses in Canada by developing relationships with large and medium sized Canadian businesses. It operates as a private sector, non profit organization. As such, CAMSC is governed by a board of directors consisting of executives from major multinational corporations in Canada.

The objectives of CAMSC are to...

1. Provide and continually strengthen an information network, linking major corporations and institutions with visible minority and Canadian Aboriginal-owned businesses.

2. Encourage the visible minority and Aboriginal businesses to use this network to promote their goods and services and help market their products.

You can become a certified CAMSC supplier if you meet the requirements. One of the major requirements is that you are a minority-owned business and the owner of the company is a member of a visible minority or is Aboriginal.

CAMSC is also affiliated with the National Minority Supplier Development Council (NMSDC) in the United States. CAMSC offers a variety of programs and services to its corporate members and certified Aboriginal and visible minority businesses.

Below is a listing of some of the core services: For Aboriginal and visible minority business enterprises to become certified suppliers the following qualifications are required after the initial screening, interviews and site visits. The applicant must...[insert bullet points here]

• be a 'for-profit' enterprise
• operate in Canada
• be able to operate as a supplier of products or services to other businesses
• be owned by a minority or aboriginal (meaning that the business is at least 51% owned by such individuals.)

The Advanced Management Education Program is a customized executive education program with intensive training and technical assistance for CEO's of Aboriginal and visible minority-owned firms interested in accelerated growth. This training is offered in collaboration with the NMSDC at the Kellogg School of Business.

Another available tool for minority businesses is the Business Information Centre. This Centre is a resource for dissemination of vital statistics and information pertinent to the changing picture of corporations, industries, and Aboriginal and minority-owned businesses. CAMSC also presents various procurement fairs, conferences and seminars where minority and Aboriginal businesses are encouraged to interconnect with large and medium-sized Canadian businesses in order to promote their products and services. CAMSC also holds an annual awards dinner where Aboriginal and minority owned businesses are honoured along with major companies who sponsor diversity in their workplace and practices.

Chambers of Commerce and Business Organizations in GTA

Organizations in the Toronto area that can help the immigrant businessperson develop contacts and promote his/her business within their own cultural group:

Indo-Canada Chamber of Commerce
45 Sheppard Ave. E., Suite 900
Toronto, Ontario M2N 5W9
416-224-0090

Goan Overseas Association of Toronto
PO Box 5667 Station "A"
Toronto, Ontario M5W 1N8

Kannada Sangha Toronto,
PO Box 23545 Dexter PO
Leslie St. Willowdale, Ontario M2H 3R9

Telugu Cultural Association of Greater Toronto
 bose_vemuri@rogers.com

The Vedanta Society of Toronto
120 Emmitt Ave.,
Toronto, Ontario M6M 2E6
society@vedantatoronto.ca

Centre for Spanish Speaking Peoples
2141 Jane St. 2nd Floor,
Toronto, Ontario M3M 1A2
416-533-8545   info@spanishservices.org

Markham African Carribean Association
1661 Denison Street #76532
Markham, Ontario
905-294-5033   www.markhamafrican.com

The Jamaican-Canadian Association
995 Arrow Road
North York, Ontario
416-746-5772

Black Business and Professional Association
416-504-4097   http://www.bbpa.org

Carribean Association of Peel
440-B Britannia Rd. East,
Mississauga, Ontario L42 1X9
905-890-2676   http://www.caribpeel.org

Mississauga Chinese Business Association (MCBA)
1550 South Gateway Road, Unit 213
Mississauga, Ontario, L4W 5G6
905-625-6222   mcba@mcba-canada.com

Toronto Chinese Business Association
1220 Ellesmere Road, Suite 13
Toronto, Ontario M1P 2X5
416-595-0313

Vietnamese Association of Toronto (VAT)
1364 Dundas St. W.,
Toronto, Ontario M6J 1Y2
416-536-3611

Mississauga Board of Trade (MBOT)
701-77 City Centre Drive
Mississauga, Ontario L5B 1M5
905-273-6151   info@mbot.com

Toronto Board of Trade
Downtown Centre, 1 First Canadian Place
PO Box 60,
Toronto, Ontario
416-366-6811 (also locations in Scarborough, North York and Etobicoke)

Philippine Chamber of Commerce of Toronto (PCCT)
Cora dela Cruz, President
21 Canadian Road, Unit 4
Scarborough, Ontario M1R 5G2
416-925-0013   info@pcct.ca

Canada China Business Council - Toronto Office
Suite 407-100 Adelaide Street West
Toronto, Ontario M5H 1S3
416-954-3806   ccbc@ccbc.com

For other Chambers of Commerce across Canada please refer to the following web-sites:

The Canadian Chamber of Commerce- www.chamber.ca

Newfoundland and Labrador- www.ic.gc.ca

Nova Scotia- www.nschamber.ca

PEI- www.southshorechamber.pe.ca

New Brunswick- www.frederictonchamber.ca

Ontario- www.ontario.org

Manitoba- www.securegwn.com

Saskatchewan- www.saskchamber.com

Alberta- www.abchamber.ca

British Columbia- www.bcchamber.org

TRIEC

Kevin McLellan is currently manager hireimmigrants.ca at the Toronto Region Immigrant Employment Council (TRIEC). He joined TRIEC in 2005 after launching an award winning labour market initiative in Durham Region in collaboration with educators, employers and NGOs. He spent fifteen years in the advertising industry working with clients such as General Motors and the Canadian Tourism Commission.

He has a B.A. from the University of Windsor, a certificate in Business Administration from Seneca College and is a provincially licensed ESL instructor. His community work has included serving as a Board Director for the Durham Region Unemployed Help Centre.

He is currently serving as a member of the National Steering Committee for the Information and Communication Technology Council's project Building an IT Framework for Internationally Educated Professionals.

In the 2007 TRIEC Annual review the goals of the organization are highlighted." The Toronto Region Immigrant Employment Council is working to remove the barriers immigrants face when entering the labour market, while at the same time helping organizations benefit from the talents and skills immigrants bring with them to Canada.

Since 2003, TRIEC has facilitated collaboration among a diverse group of stakeholders including employers, post-secondary institutions, employment service providers, regulatory bodies and all three levels of government."

The goal is to assemble these key players to find and implement local, practical solutions that lead to meaningful employment for skilled immigrants. By bringing together government representatives through TRIEC's Intergovernmental Relations Committee, engaging employers through The Mentoring Partnership and hireimmigrants.ca, and working with organizations in the community, TRIEC is finding solutions, ensuring actions, and connecting partners in new and unique ways. You can find out more by visiting: www.triec.ca.

At the heart of what TRIEC is trying to do is to make business more accommodating to the skilled immigrant and inform business on the competitive advantage that firms have in hiring skilled immigrants. TRIEC provides awareness in the business community on the value that skilled immigrants provide to companies and the Canadian economy.

Part of TRIEC's mission is to break down the barriers that inhibit immigrants from finding rewarding employment and careers in Canada. The three major barriers that immigrants have with Canadian companies when they are trying to find employment are:

1. Language
2. Lack of Canadian experience
3. Employers inability to evaluate foreign education and credentials

TRIEC has done research on what businesses have to do to hire and retain skilled immigrants. The research indicates that there needs to be a shift in attitude and practice in order for business to capitalize on the skilled immigrant talent pool. TRIEC has developed case studies of practices that companies can utilize to attract skilled immigrants and integrate them most effectively into their workforce. These practices include:

- ways to access the skilled immigrant talent pool-either through an agency or an internship program
- help from an HR expert
- HR workshops
- credential assessment services
- language training
- bridging and mentoring programs
- government and other programs which may help

TRIEC's main focus is on the employer because they do not want to duplicate the efforts performed on behalf of the immigrant by the social agencies and placement agencies. TRIEC does believe though that the immigrant can address some of the barriers directly on their own and meet the employers together to knock them down. Some companies have incorporated language training into their overall training programs, however, any English language training and communications skills upgrading taken by the immigrant in his home county or on his/her arrival will serve them well in their job search and integration into Canadian corporate and social culture. Some of the methods that TRIEC is using to educate and inform business about skilled immigrants are included in their 2007 annual review are:

hireimmigrants.ca
The hireimmigratns.ca program provides employers with the tools and resources to accelerate the integration of skilled immigrants into their organizations. In 2007 the focus was placed on reaching small and medium-sized enterprises (SME's)

How-to Workshops for HR Professionals
In 2007 hirimmigrants.ca partnered with the G. Raymond Chang School of Continuing

Education at Ryerson University to develop a series of how to workshops for SME's.

Mentoring Partnership

The Mentoring Partnership (TMP) is a collaboration of community organizations and corporate partners that brings together skilled immigrants and established professionals in occupation-specific mentoring relationships. The Mentoring Partnership includes a large number of Canadian companies in all areas of expertise.

In 2007 TMP completed over 1150 matches. This brings the total number to more than 2,600. Nearly 80 per cent of the individuals in the mentoring partnership are now employed and 85 per cent of those are employed I those working are in their field of choice.

TRIEC brings the company mentors to the table and forms a database of mentees and mentors who can be matched together. The various government agencies help the skilled immigrant candidate or mentee to acquire the skills so that they will be effective for the company taking them on in the mentorship program.

The Mentoring Partnership has been so successful that the model is being implemented in the Waterloo, and considered in Ottawa and Niagara regions.

Immigrant Success

The Immigrant Success (IS) Awards are given to employers in the Toronto region with a proven track record of achievement in recruiting, retaining and promoting skilled immigrants in the workplace. Individual awards are also presented to an HR professional and individual champion who has gone above and beyond to assist skilled immigrants in the workforce.

IS Awards

The IS Awards have two objectives: to recognize and celebrate employer and individuals that demonstrate excellence, and to build employer awareness of the issues and the solutions in which they can participate. TRIEC is trying to make the business case to hire new immigrants and how to do it by having business talk to business and set role models.

Best Employers for New Canadians

Launched in 2007, the Best Employers for new Canadians competition is a new national award presented by Medicorp Canada, editors of Canada's Top 100 Employers, in partnership with TRIEC. This special designation recognizes employers with the best initiatives and programs to assist recent immigrants in making the transition to a new workplace-a new life in Canada. The names of the award winners for 2008 are listed at the following web-site: www.canadastop100.com/immigrants.

TRIEC has also partnered with WES (World Education Services) in helping skilled immigrants get their education and credentials recognized in a way that makes it easier for Canadian employers to appreciate their skills.

Since small and medium sized companies are a major factor in employment TRIEC has focused on assisting them in identifying skilled immigrants as a major workforce contributor. These companies do not have the large HR departments that multinational organizations have but they will be a major generator of jobs in the Canadian economy.

It is through this solution based action approach that TRIEC aims to help employers increase their capacity to attract and retain skilled immigrants and make them the valuable human resource that Canadian business needs to grow and be competitive in the world economy.

Diversity: Good for Business

There is a strong and ever-growing case for diversity in business. This book has discussed Canada's aging population, declining birth rate, and the global competition for talent over the coming decades.

Replenishment and net growth of human resources in the Canadian workplace can only be accomplished through immigration. Immigration is crucial to Canada's ability to sustain its standard of living and continue to grow economically.

Diversity in the workplace provides Canadian organizations with many advantages, including the following

• Diversity provides a large, global pool of capable and qualified talent. (A greater number of candidates from which to choose typically results in better selection of employees)

• Diversity helps resolve the problem of internal staff shortage more easily than searching within the domestic market alone

• Diversity presents a business with a broader, more up-to-date corporate image by having people of diverse backgrounds on staff.

• Diversity adds to any organization's creativity and communication resources, allowing it to gain opportunities in marketing to diverse groups, both domestically and internationally.

The borders of the world have been eliminated by technology and the internet. Today's communications systems means a global market for even the smallest of businesses is easily within reach. Smart companies are now marketing to diverse market niches, both inside Canada and around the world. When you have people who represent various cultures and backgrounds working in your organization, you gain by the unique perspective and intelligence these folks bring to the table.

Your people are representative of your organization and your products. A diverse representation conveys an image to others that is more welcoming on a global scale. When viewed in this positive light by more groups of consumers, sales naturally increase. You effectively open doors

Some employers have been reluctant to hire new Canadians because many of them speak with an accent, although to most, their English communication is acceptable. But aware employers remember that many immigrants over the years had accents from the British Isles, Europe, etc. and they made out just fine. Most were able to fit in well and made exceptional contributions in Canada.

With a significant shortage in skilled personnel looming, companies may want to develop internal language and communications training. This would serve to satisfy their staffing needs and allow for the hiring of particularly skilled people who might otherwise be overlooked because of their language abilities.

Canadian companies which are leading the point on diversity have begun to place new Canadians in higher positions of management. This makes diversity not just an HR function, but a focus and direction for all staff development.

The European Business Test Panel (EBTP) survey found that 83% of 495 companies are convinced that diversity initiatives have a positive effect on their business. Though actual statistics are not available at the time of writing, my experiences and contacts suggest that Canadian results would mimic those results of the European business Test Panel. Yet the Conference Board of Canada says that 42% of companies surveyed have no strategic plan for diversity and 50 per cent have no diversity training for employees. Research conducted by the Maytree foundation has shown that only 1 to 2 percent of corporate Canada is made up of visible minorities. If visible minorities around the world believe that Canada does not provide them with the growth and opportunity that they desire they may decide to stay in their won country, or look elsewhere.

One company which embraces diversity is Microsoft. Microsoft has established a number of initiatives to promote and integrate diversity into the entire fabric of their organization and at every level. Microsoft has also started programs which demonstrate their commitment on a local, national and global level. Their "Diversity Education Program" gives employees the tools to appreciate the diverse makeup of their organization and maximize those differences in order to compete effectively in the marketplace.

Organizations will not be able to optimize the impact of diversity unless education programs are put in place because the process will be slow to progress without educational programs. "Microsoft Outreach" also helps with student scholarships in the computer sciences to help students who are underrepresented in those scientific fields.

Another perspective on diversity in the workplace was covered in a National Post article titled, "Invited into the Inner Circle" which discusses people of diversified cultures in positions of management in companies. Catalyst and the Diversity Institute surveyed 17,000 managers, professionals and executives in 43 of the largest firms in Canada. Major findings as a result of this research included:

1. Visible minorities were less satisfied with their careers than their Caucasian counterpart. The visible minorities felt that they were not part of the networking community which is fundamental to advancement.

2. Some men and women in visible minorities felt that they could not become part of the company hierarchy over time.

3. The cultural soft skills brought from their home country are not recognized in Canada.

4. The visible minorities question whether they will be allowed to move up the corporate ladder or remain at a middle management level.

5. The experience in the workplace has shown that more and more women are participating in the business world, but they are not yet present in large numbers at the higher level positions in corporations. Progress has been slow and visible minorities feel that their situation will be similar.

An article on the web-site www.hireimmigrants.ca, which offers advice to business on the best ways to implement diversity programs, titled Resource Room- Success Stories on Mount Sinai Hospital in Toronto. The article states that in 2007 Mount Sinai took on a workforce survey to measure whether the diversity efforts of the organization were successful. The old saying of what gets measured, gets done is particularly applicable to diversity initiatives. It is not a program that can run on its own initiative but needs leadership, inspiration, measurement, policies and training and education to optimize its goals. In summary the article goes on to say,

"Diversity has long been an integral principle and driving force at MSH. In 2000, a diversity and human rights office was established with a mandate to create organizational change by:

- addressing harassment and discrimination complaints
- providing training on human rights and related issues
- developing policies to ensure equity it the workplace"

The hireimmigrants.ca article goes on to say," Once the office was established the office focused on ensuring that fair opportunities in employment existed for all members of the community and all hospital employees. It appeared that while the MSH workforce is diverse, that diversity was not moving all the way up the ranks."

The Mount Sinai experience is very illustrative of how a diversity program should work and that it is a never ending quest for inclusiveness.

Another area of extreme importance is the staffing requirements of small and medium-sized companies. Every business needs human talent and these small to mid-size companies will be major drivers of the Canadian economy over the next couple of decades. That is, if they can find the talent to sustain their growth.

Smaller firms don't have large human Resources departments to strategize the new demands for global talent. Instead, many rely on government to help meet their needs. That's reason enough for governments to listen more closely to the pressing need of the small business community.

In an article in Macleans magazine October 13th, 2008 titled " Diversity or Death" it was stated that Canadian business "depends on hiring immigrants. Currently, one-fifth of Canada's workers are immigrants, and by 2011, it's estimated that New Canadians will account for all net labour-force growth." In the article, Joerg Dietz, an international business professor at the Richard Ivey School of Business says," If you don't start working on diversity management today, you might not be around tomorrow.

Welcoming Immigrants into your Workforce

"Do we stand in their way and create barriers to immigrants trying to enter our companies or do we embrace them and use their ideas and contributions and propel Canada to a leadership role in the global economy? Make every wall that is a barrier an opportunity to change into an open door." Terry Sawh

In an article published by hireimmigratns.ca, a TRIEC program, entitled " Promising Practices and Tips for Integrating Skilled Immigrants Into the Workplace" they highlight certain areas where companies can improve their ability to integrate immigrants into Canadian companies.

Some of the ideas include:
- choosing a diversity champion in a company who is a high level executive who will promote diversity at the same level as profit, safety, etc with specific goals and measurement
- create awareness and education in the company about why diversity and immigrants are so important so to the company's future- such issues as a larger labour pool to obtain the best talent with the ageing of the Canadian workforce, and the possibility of obtaining new

domestic and international markets.

• use internship and mentoring programs such as CareerBridge and AISEC to provide entry into the Canadian business culture. Provide in-house mentors to help integrate immigrants.

• providing accommodation to different religions who worship during the day at work

• providing in-house English or French language training customized to your business and communication systems

• provide diversity training for every-one at the company just as you would for any human resource program

• follow the lead of such companies as TD Financial Group who have a diversity leadership council, surveys and measures performance, has mentoring programs, has quiet rooms for worship and has diversity training for every-one.

In a workshop presented by hireimmigrants.ca the presentation revolves around creating metrics that analyzed the value that skilled immigrants bring to the Canadian workforce.

The objective of the workshop is to assign numerical values that develop an understanding how and where skilled immigrants contribute within our companies and track the progress of the results. The end goal is to provide hard numbers on why companies should employ skilled immigrants.

The topic is important to HR, executive and marketing individuals because it defines skilled immigrants into a range of identifiers and then relates these identifiers to a company's specific enviroment and criteria. The enviroment and criteria could relate to these objectives of the company:

• a business driven by innovation and a search for global talent

• a business wanting to expand globally or penetrate some domestic ethnic markets

In a Public Policy Forum from 2004 on "Bringing Employers into the Immigration Debate: Survey and Roundtable" 2091 companies were asked questions on the hiring of immigrants. The study was performed by Sandra Lopes, research Associate and Yves Poisson, Director of Special Projects.

In the section "Benefits of Hiring Immigrants" and the perceived impact on organizations of employing immigrants the following items were viewed as positives:

Skills in language-63 per cent- the ability to speak different languages is actually looked upon as a positive because the company can deal with its customers in more global languages and penetrate new markets

Capacity to generate new ideas-69 per cent- the addition of immigrant talent will help the company look through the eyes of the world and come up with global ideas for its products and services.

The organization's reputation- 64 per cent- the organization is looked upon as a global company that recognizes international talent and is planning to grow its business in the future.

Development of products and services for multicultural markets- 63 per cent- in some of Canada's major cities the New Canadian percentage of the population is reaching 50 per cent – there is an opportunity for companies to tap into these new domestic markets and use their immigrant base to export their business around the world

The Public Policy Forum goes on to say that the major challenges that Canadian companies have regarding immigrants are:
- HR Departments are overlooking immigrants in their company strategy
- Processes have to be changed in the hiring of immigrants to accommodate the difference between immigrants and Canadian born hires

Another firm that has been doing and excellent job of providing advice and leadership on integrating immigrants and other non-traditional talent into the workforce is Graybridge Malkam. They have a series of newsletters under their web-site: www.graybridgemalkin.com

The newsletter contains such information as:
- sourcing non-traditional talent by emphasizing job competencies rather than past experience
- hi-lighting the organization's commitment to diversity in their corporate policies and training
- advertising in non-traditional talent pools that attract diverse candidates
- be inclusive in your search and avoid ruling out part of the talent pool
- people from different countries develop their resumes differently so your selection people should be aware of the differences and use them as a positive rather than a negative
- look at international experience as a long term value to your organization and search it out
- start conducting interviews with candidates that knocks down the barriers related to language, accent, appearances affected by race or religion and focus on the qualifications and contribution to the company's global position

According to the CareerBuilder.com web-site various programs are being used to promote diversity in the workplace. These programs include:
- Diversity training for employees
- Surveys and focus groups to see how diversity is regarded with-in the workplace
- Mentoring groups for diverse members
- A diversity council to provide the promotion of diversity
- A special day to mark diversity

Small Business and Immigration

In an effort to provide information to the government on how to better respond to Canada's skills and labour shortage, a report titled "Immigration and Small Business" was developed by the Canadian Federation of Independent business (CFIB).

A major contributor to economic growth in Canada will be the jobs generated by small and medium sized businesses. Yet, according to the report most owners of small and medium-sized businesses have serious concerns about the shortage of qualified labour.

Current labour shortages are just the beginning. It's a problem that's expected to get much worse. These smaller enterprises see the problem as one that will seriously hamper their ability to grow and stimulate the economy. They feel that immigration must provide the solution to their increasing shortages of talent simply due to Canada's declining birth rate and retiring workforce.

The study succinctly summarizes the needs of businesses by stating that "the permanent immigration system does not come close to matching the needs of Canada's small and medium-sized businesses, particularly for trade and entry level jobs."

In our research, we've seen some of the problems with the current immigration process. For example, the points system seems to aim at the cream of the educated and highly-skilled crop, even though these individuals may have difficulty finding jobs in their chosen field and location.

The report also points out that "overall, about half of the shortages are in occupations that do not require formal education beyond secondary school." It's important to recognize that a great many of these occupations are not "unskilled" positions, but may require on-the-job training gained informally, rather than through traditional education channels.

One indicator of a strong economy is how workers can move from unskilled or semi-skilled to the ranks of skilled workers. Canada needs young tradespeople who will learn and apply their trades here. Entry-level clerical people, service staff, along with general labour and light industrial workers are also required to help grow our economy. The Ontario Chamber of Commerce has predicted a shortage of 100,000 skilled labour positions in the province of Ontario alone in the next 15 years alone.

Immigration processing, with its common delays, presents a problem to small firms who need people to address labour shortages now. Labour market opinions are required for many permanent and temporary positions which introduce lag time into an already sluggish system, while businesses continue to suffer from the very shortages that inhibit economic growth.

The essence of the study is contained in this statement, *"Professional and managerial occupations account for only 8% of the labour shortage reported by small and medium businesses. In contrast, 74% of economic immigrants and 34% of foreign workers are in these skill categories."*

Are we bringing the right talent and the right volumes of immigrants into Canada to efficiently and effectively grow our economy? Or is it time that we as Canadians made major revisions to immigration policy and procedures?

A research poll conducted by Nik Nanos on policy options cited the main reasons why Canadians feel that immigration is important. The reasons in order of priority were: economic necessity, family compassion, and being a refugee.

The feeling is that the system will accept candidates who will provide the skills necessary to assist the Canadian economy in its development and growth over time. Many refugees can make valuable contributions in the major economic areas of retail, service, semi-skilled trades and construction. Canada was built on the skills and labour of many immigrants from Europe after the Second World War. Many of these people had some skills, but limited language ability. Many of today's refugees could help the Canadian economy and make a direct contribution. What Canada requires is someone who will work hard and meet the needs of the economy in whatever job role they're qualified to fulfill.

Chapter Fourteen

"When I arrived in Canada I was totally alone and had no relatives or friends or social agencies to help me out in my new country. It is different now for the New Canadian who in many cases has family and friends to greet him/her on their arrival in Canada and there is a network of social agencies providing assistance to the new immigrant. Remember my advice about visiting Canada first so that you get an idea of the country, its customs and people. Also remember that with each day things will get better for you and your family because it takes some time to get used to all of the dynamics of your new country."

- Terry Sawh

Settling In and Adjusting To Life In Canada -
Now That You Have Arrived
Arrival in Canada
The Day Of Your Arrival

By this point, you've submitted all the required forms, supporting documentation, and fees. At the same time, you've done your homework and have researched the job market and started marketing your own skills and expertise to employers in Canada. Perhaps you have a job offer, or interviews arranged in advance. And you've officially been granted legal immigrant status in Canada. Congratulations and welcome!

Be sure to follow the exact guidelines specified by Citizenship and Immigration Canada in your entry kit. This includes having all the required documents in your possession, as well as any secondary documents as support. If you have your passport and all the essential documents, you will find it much easier to enter Canada.

Upon your arrival in your new country, you will be interviewed by a Canada Customs officer. It is part of the process every new immigrant goes through. It would probably be beneficial if you practiced a mock interview with someone in your home country already familiar with traveling abroad, or more specifically, to Canada.

It's the duty of the Canada customs officer to question you. It's standard operating procedure, something that everyone simply has to endure. One concern of the officer is what you are planning to bring into the country with you, so you'll be required to provide a list that includes every item.

The officer is also interested in determining your personal status and will therefore want to see your passport, work permit, visa, etc. Passports and/or visas will also be requested of everyone who's traveling with you too. You'll also be asked questions similar to those on the immigration application form. They may also ask to see proof that you have the required funds as outlined earlier. Once the officer is satisfied with your documentation and the information you provided, he or she will sign your Record of Landing or Confirmation of Permanent Resident Status.

If your arrival is via one of the major Canadian airports, you will be handed a booklet "Welcome To Canada - What You Should Know". This booklet is also available on the sites below, so you really should review it prior to coming to Canada. There are also immigrant reception services right at the airport. These people can help provide you with any additional information you may need.

The booklet is available at:
www.cic.gc.ca/resources/publications/guide/index.asp

Reference: Citizenship and Immigration Canada
www.gc.ca/english/newcomer
www.directioncanada.gc.ca

Arrival in Canada: Your First Week
Your First Week In Canada:
Important Action Steps You Should Take

There are several things you need to do when you first arrive in Canada, in order to prepare you and your family for the months and years ahead. Take the time necessary during your first week in Canada to accomplish the following important tasks:

1. Apply for a Social Insurance Number 1-800-622-6232 www.servicecanada.gc.ca. You must have a Social Insurance Number to work anywhere in Canada. Every employer is legally bound to request and record the SIN number of everyone they hire.

2. Apply for your Health Card. You'll need this card whenever you require medical or hospital services of any kind. If there is a waiting period, as there is in some provinces, you should have arranged private health insurance in advance. You need to immediately seek full medical coverage for you and your family, until your provincial health coverage kicks in.

3. Open a Canadian bank account at any local branch. I heartily recommend the TD Bank, HSBC or Scotiabank as immigrant-friendly financial institutions that offer a full range of banking services and options to suit your individual needs.

4. Locate the Settlement Agency closest to your chosen location. (Please see the resource section for a full list of options)

5. Investigate to discover the Health Care Centre, Medical Clinic, and Hospital nearest your new residence. Get to know where you should go before any medical treatment is required.

6. Locate the closest Employment Resource Centre. Make use of the resources available to you for finding work in your chosen area.

7. Find out where the nearest Public Library is located. Libraries offer a wealth of resources including computers with high-speed Internet access. You can also conduct valuable research to help you land a job.

8. Identify where the closest schools are that your children will be attending. Bring their immunization records with you when you visit to register.

9. Get local street maps and public transit schedules. Familiarize yourself with your new neighbourhood and community. Get to know where various products and services are available and how to get there.

10. If you're not already fluent in English, check out any English language schools that may be in your area and obtain a copy of class schedules.

Health Care

Canada has one of the finest health care insurance services in the world. It is known federally as Medicare, however, on a provincial basis it may be identified by a name such as OHIP (Ontario Health Insurance Plan). Under Medicare you do not have to pay directly for most health care services. They are paid through your taxes. If you are new to Canada and looking for a doctor it may be difficult to find a family doctor as soon as you arrive. Many Canadians take advantage of clinics where you do not need an appointment to see a doctor but you may have to wait for the doctor to have an available time slot. You need to present your health card or private health insurance identification anywhere you seek medical services – including walk-in clinics.

Your health, as well as the health of loved ones settling in Canada with you, is of primary importance. Universal health care is something Canadians hold near and dear to their hearts. It gives everyone fair access to a wide array of medical services, including emergency treatment. You should apply for a health card for yourself and every family member, as soon as you arrive in Canada.

Everyone in Canada with permanent residency, including newborn babies, is covered by Canada's universal health care program. But foreign students and temporary workers need to arrange private health care for themselves. In the case of temporary workers, private health care may be arranged by an employer.

Applications are available to anyone through each region's provincial health office. You can also pick up the required application form at any family doctor's office.

Be aware that in the provinces of Ontario, New Brunswick and Quebec, there is a three-month waiting period before anyone qualifies for universal health care. So if you're settling in any one of these provinces, you will have to obtain private health insurance coverage for your first three months here. You won't qualify for standard coverage until you've been in Ontario, New Brunswick, or Quebec for 90 days.

In order to get health insurance when you are visiting Canada or if you are a student or on a temporary work permit or are immigrating to the Province of Ontario, New Brunswick or Quebec for the first ninety days, consider one of the Canadian firms listed below. The following organizations can provide health coverage for you:
- Blue Cross Visitors to Canada Travel Insurance
- RBC Travel Insurance
- Your travel agent

Bear in mind the conditions of any firm that you get medical insurance from as these do vary. Some get you to pay upfront for medical services and then reimburse you later, while others cover your medical costs directly.

I strongly recommend that you obtain private health insurance for provinces that have a waiting period. This also applies to temporary workers and students as well. You will find that life will be more comfortable and secure with such coverage in place.

It is advisable that you visit the Citizenship and Immigration web site to update yourself on information on Canadian health care.
www.cic.gc.ca/english/newcomers/fact_health.asp

Provincial medical plans do not cover prescription drugs. Some provinces offer subsidies to people on low incomes and who have high drug costs and some provinces offer a prescription drug plan for seniors.

Obtaining a family physician in Canada may be challenging so many immigrants first use the resources of day walk-in clinics. Some of the best ways of finding a family physician is through family and friends and asking around at local pharmacies.

Health and Safety in the Workplace

The following highlights of the Occupational Health and Safety Act apply to every worker in Ontario and Alberta. Similar acts are in place in Canada's other jurisdictions. All workers have the right to:

1. Participate and be part of the process of identifying and resolving workplace health and safety concerns...
2. Know about potential hazards in the workplace and implement the Workplace Hazardous Materials Information System (WHMIS)...
3) Refuse work if they think that the workplace is dangerous to themselves or others.

A Joint Health and Safety Committee becomes part of any organization that regularly employs 20 or more workers. The committee itself acts as an advisory group and typically consists of both worker and management representatives.

This workplace partnership of management and staff is there to improve the health and safety for everyone working within the organization and its facilities.

Each committee meets regularly to discuss health and safety concerns and review the progress made on any earlier recommendations. Any member of a company's Joint Health and Safety Committee who is 'certified', has the right to stop any work process that may be dangerous to any worker.

Social Insurance Number(SIN)

Obtaining a Social Insurance Number and card should be a priority for every new immigrant to Canada. You need to have been assigned an official Social Insurance Number (one that is yours alone) in order to work at any job, anywhere in Canada.

This number identifies you for work in Canada and tracks you for Income Taxes, Unemployment Insurance, and Canada Pension. Once a number has been designated, it's yours for life. There is never any need for another number. Even if you lost your card and needed a replacement, it would still carry the same number.

Social Insurance Number applications are available through the Human Resources Development Canada Centre near you. Any regional office can be easily located in the blue Federal Government pages of the phone book or online.

Employment Insurance

When you begin working in Canada, a percentage of your income will go to the government for various benefits. One of those benefits is called Employment Insurance, or EI. If you are laid off from your job, you might be eligible for EI benefits. This fund is set up to help you (and any laid-off worker in Canada) for a short period of time, while you search for other employment.

Your employer should give you an itemized stub with your paycheque showing you the quantities deducted for taxes, pensions and benefits such as Employment Insurance. You are not allowed to be paid in cash to avoid these taxes and benefits.

Employment Standards Act

Each province has a law that sets minimum standards for workplaces. We will highlight some of the important sections of the Ontario Act which is available to you at the web site: www.labour.gov.on.ca

Who is protected by the Employment Standards Act? (ESA)

If you work in Ontario you are most likely covered by the ESA. There are exceptions and special rules for some workers such as federal workers who are exempt from the Act.

Hours of work

Generally, employees cannot be required or permitted to work more than the hours listed below:
- 8 hours a day - or the number of hours in a company's established work day
- 48 hours per week

An employee can agree in writing to work longer than these hours listed but the employee must receive an information sheet outlining the hours from the act and sign off that they received that information.

Minimum Wage
Minimum wage is the lowest hourly rate an employer can pay an employee and these numbers are outlined on the web site.

Payday
Employees must be paid on a regular and consistent payday and given a statement showing their wages and deductions.

Vacation Time and Pay
Most employees earn at least 2 weeks of vacation time after every 12 months of employment. In lieu of vacation time employees are entitled to be paid 4% of their total wages earned.

Public Holidays
A public holiday is a day off work with pay. Ontario has nine public holidays each calendar year and most employees are allowed to take public holidays off regardless of how long they have worked for the company.

Pregnancy Leave and Parental Leave
Eligible employees are entitled to take 17 weeks of pregnancy leave and 35 weeks of parental leave (if they have taken pregnancy leave). All other eligible parents can take up to 37 weeks of unpaid parental leave.

Personal Emergency Leave
If an employer regularly employs at least 50 people, its workers are allowed to take up to 10 days a year of unpaid, job protected emergency leave.

Family Medical Leave
Employees can take up to 8 weeks of unpaid leave to care for an ill family member.

Termination Notice and Pay
Employees must be given advance written notice, or termination pay instead of notice, or a combination of both, if the employee has been working continuously for the company for 3 months and their job was terminated. Severance packages for long term employees should be reviewed by an employment lawyer to ensure that the package is fair and equitable under Canadian law and employment practice.

Not All Employees Qualify For All ESA Rights
Not all employees qualify for all ESA rights. An example would be temporary workers hired by an employment agency.

Employment agencies have a practice called elect to work which is used for temporary workers. There is no guarantee of full-time work for the employee, but the employee can leave the job at any time and the employer can release the employee from work at any time and with little or no notice. The employee is still protected by the Health and Safety Act and Human Rights Code. The temporary employee has deductions taken off for Income Taxes, Canada Pension and Employment Insurance along with receiving vacation pay, but would not receive any of the benefits normally given to a full-time employee such as paid statutory holidays, health benefits and paid time off.

Workers Compensation

All Canadian provinces provide comprehensive no-fault insurance which compensate or provide income replacement to employees who have injuries or illnesses that come from or arise during their course of employment. Participation in the plan is compulsory for the employer who is in an industry or activity covered by the plan. Employees do not pay for the plan, employers do. It's designed to help workers financially who are temporarily off the job due to work-related injury or illness.

Workers' Action Centre

Deena Ladd emigrated from the UK in 1987. She has a Social Work Degree from Ryerson University. From the early 90's onward Deena has worked for various organizations helping newcomers, immigrants, women, workers of colour and people in low wage occupations that had experienced difficult working conditions. Deena now works for the Workers' Action Centre located in Toronto.

The Workers' Action Centre was created due to the large increase in precarious types of employment and worsening conditions for workers in jobs where low wages and employment standard violations were high. Precarious work includes temporary work, temporary agency work, contract, independent contract work and part-time work. The Centre found that for many workers in precarious jobs there were health and safety hazards for the worker, no access to health benefits, violations of rights, discrimination, etc. Workers did not have anywhere to go with their problems or complaints and could not get the proper information related to legislation such as the Occupational Health and Safety Act, Workers' Safety and Insurance Board, Ontario Human Rights Code and Employment Standards. The Workers' Action Centre is a non-profit organization which is funded by mainly private foundations and some government funding. The Workers' Action Centre evolved from a research project in 1999 which researched and interviewed over 200 workers in precarious jobs.

What the Workers Action Centre Does

The Centre operates a phone line in six languages where people can phone in with their problems and get advice. The Centre provides information sessions and clinics every week and every other week in Scarborough. They go out into the community and provide educational workshops. They train front line workers in immigrant serving organizations on employment standards and other issues facing workers. The Centre also works with employers directly to solve complaints. The centre does research and policy submissions to the government on various employment issues. One of these submissions was the Submission to the Ministry of Labour Consultation on Work through Temporary Help Agencies submitted on June 6, 2008. The Centre partners with legal clinics to help in any complaints requiring legal interpretation and follow-up. The Centre uses the skills of various professionals including lawyers, law students, social workers, Human Rights and Employment standards specialists and educators. Many workers, especially newcomers are not familiar with the process of filing complaints at various government departments or getting assistance with workplace problems. The Centre helps workers figure out which strategy to address their workplace problem would be best.

Issues that the Workers' Action Centre are involved in WAC is a membership based organization. The major issues that the Workers' Action Centre is involved in are:

Unpaid Wages

Access to Statutory Benefits such as holiday pay and vacation pay

Employment standards

Addressing the rise in precarious work through Employment agencies and contract work

Human Rights Code

The Minimum Wage

Wages and the minimum wage

The minimum wage was frozen at $6.85 an hour for eight years from 1995 to 2003 which caused many people to fall behind and fall deeper into poverty. The impact of such a low minimum wage has put workers and their families under enormous pressures. Many low wage workers are forced to take two and three jobs just to feed their families. With a hold put on minimum wages for such a long time a period of catch up would have to take place eventually. The current government plan is to raise the minimum wage over time to $10.25 an hour by 2010. However, organizations such as WAC are still fighting for an increase to be introduced earlier and would like to ensure that the minimum wage is linked to the poverty line and indexed to inflation.

Employment Standards

The Workers' Action Centre feels that all employees whether they be part-time, temporary or permanent should be entitled to the same standards of employment.

Employment Agencies

The Workers' Action Centre feels that some companies are using temporary agencies to avoid their responsibilities in hiring workers directly. Some agencies are registering employees as independent contractors with the employee not having any access to Employment Insurance, Canada Pension Plan, paid overtime and holiday pay. The use of employment agencies also brings up issues such as liability for wages and employment standards. WAC believes the client company and the agency should be held jointly liable for all working conditions and wages.

Statutory Holiday Pay

Currently many employers or agencies are avoiding their obligations to pay public holiday pay to temporary agency workers under an "elect to work" option in the Employment Standards Act. The Workers' Acton Centre wants all workers to have this statutory benefit regardless of employment status.

Employment Fees

Some firms acting as employers are asking for a fee from the immigrant workers for training which, in effect, is a hiring fee. Immigrants should not be paying a fee to either an employment agency or any employer asking for a training fee.

Canadian Justice System

Canada is a free and democratic society. This means that everyone has the same fundamental freedoms including freedom of opinion, religion, and association. Everyone with Permanent Resident Status is free to locate in any part of the country they choose.

Every citizen of Canada has the right to vote in elections. They can also enter, remain in, or leave Canada at any time.

Everyone here has the right to life and liberty and is expected to behave in accordance with the fundamental laws of our justice system.

Like most Canadians, it's unlikely that you will be involved in any crime. If you want more information on the Canadian court system, it is available online at sites such as www.Wikipedia.org.

Police-Dealing with them

Police departments across the country have Newcomer Outreach programs or communication programs with the public. As an example the Toronto Police Service Newcomer Outreach Program in intended to provide new immigrants with information on police services in Toronto. This information includes how to access those services and some of your rights and responsibilities under Canadian law.

On this website you will find lots of information about police services that you can download or order free of charge. Some of the topics covered in the information are listed below:

• Contacting the police
• Use of 911 emergency phone number
• What do I do when the police come to your home
• What if someone doesn't understand or speak English
• Do you have to answer the officer's questions or identify yourself?
• What are my rights if arrested?
• What should I do if an officer approaches me on the street?
• What should I do when an officer stops me while I am driving?

The various languages the booklet is translated into are:
Chinese
English
Farsi
French
Italian
Korean

Portuguese
Punjabi
Russian
Spanish
Tamil
Vietnamese

The web site for information on the Toronto Police Services is located at: www.torontopolice.on.ca/publicinformation

You might meet a police officer at a spot check or in public. Throughout the year, police setup roadside inspection units called 'spot checks' in order to look for impaired drivers. These spot checks are located in many different areas including highway entrances. Please remember to never drink and drive. If you are stopped by the police, politeness and respect are good words to live by.

Play by the rules and cooperate with the police, whenever or wherever the situation arises. He or she is only enforcing the laws as they are required to do. You always have the right to challenge any charge in court. It is forbidden to offer the police any type of compensation in settlement of a problem or charge. Do not even think about attempting to negotiate with a policeman because the police will charge you. If you want any further information on police forces across Canada refer to Wikipedia, Law.

Canadian Charter of Rights

The Canadian Charter of Rights and Freedoms is a bill of rights entrenched in the Constitution of Canada. The Charter guarantees certain political and civil rights to people in Canada from the policies and actions of all levels of government. Under the Charter, persons physically present in Canada have numerous civil and political rights. This means that all persons who are in the country are entitled to a list of political and civil rights. These people do not have to be citizens of the country to gain these rights. Only in the sections 3) and 6) is it required to be a citizen of Canada. The rights in those sections include the right to vote, hold political office and the right to enter and leave Canada and move to any part of Canada. The primary rights and freedoms enshrined in the Charter include these sections:
  • Section 2 contains the fundamental freedoms of religion, expression, freedom of the press and freedom of peaceful assembly and association
  • Section 3 contains the right to vote for citizens and right to hold political office
  • Section 6 contains the right to enter and leave Canada and move to any province
  • Section 7 is the right to life, liberty and security of person
  • Section 8 is the right from unreasonable search and seizure
  • Section 9 is the freedom from arbitrary detainment or imprisonment
  • Section 10 is the right to legal counsel
  • Section 11 is the right to be presumed innocent until proven guilty
  • Section 12 is the right not to be subject to cruel and unusual punishment
  • Section 13 is the right against self-incrimination

• Section 14 is the right to an interpreter in a court proceeding

Canadian Elections - Federal and Provincial Politics

Canada has elections at the municipal (local town or city), provincial and Federal level. You may vote in the provincial and federal elections if you are a Canadian citizen. Immigrants who take out Canadian Citizenship are encouraged to participate in the election process and many immigrants have gone on to become elected to government at the provincial and federal levels.

The list below represents a brief sampling of visible minorities who have gone on to be elected federally and provincially. Visible minorities are encouraged to participate in the democratic process of elections and there are opportunities to be elected at the municipal (towns and cities), provincial and federal level in all of the political parties.

Immigrants have been making significant strides in the political spectrum of Canada. The list clearly shows an increasing number of ethnic MPs and MPPs. This trend will continue in the same pattern and in my opinion, it is a practical reality of the changing demographics in Canada.

Federal Members of Parliament across Canada
Omar Alghabra, Liberal, Mississauga-Erindale, Ontario
Navdeep Singh Bains, Liberal, Mississauga-Brampton South, Ont
Vivian Barbot, Bloc Quebecois, Papineau, Quebec
Olivia Chow, NDP, Trinity Spadina, Ontario
Ujjal Dosanjh, Liberal, Vancouver South, BC
Sukh Dhaliwal, Liberal, Newton-North Delta, BC
Ruby Dhalia, Liberal, Brampton-Springdale, Ontario
Nina Grewal, Conservative, Fleetwood-Port Kells, BC
Rahim Jaffer, Conservative, Edmonton-Strathcona, Alberta
Wajid Khan, Conservative, Mississauga-Streetsville, Ontario
Gurbax Malhi, Liberal, Brampton-Gore-Malton, Ontario
Kotto Maka,Bloc Quebecois, Saint-Lambert, Quebec
Maria Mourani, Bloc Quebecois, Ahuntsic, Quebec
Deepak Obhrai, Conservative, Calgary East, Alberta
Yasmin Ratansi, Liberal, Don Valley East Ontario
Pablo Rodriguez, Liberal, Honore-Mercier, Quebec
Eve-Mary Thi Lac, Bloc Quebecois, St.-Hyacinthe-Bagot, Quebec

Hon. Gurbax Singh Malhi, Privy Council, MP – Bramalea – Gore – Malton(elected member of Federal Parliament)

Interviewer: Kaisree Takechandra – Friday, July 4, 2008.

Takechandra: Hon. Malhi, please tell me where you were born.
Malhi: I was born in Punjab, India, in a small village named Chuga Kalan, in the district of Ferozpur.

Takechandra: Did you obtain your education in India?
Malhi: In 1972 I graduated from the University of Punjab with BA in English, Political Science

and History. I then studied 2 years at the Agra University Law School, India. I did not complete the law degree.

Takechandra: What led you into politics?

Malhi: I was raised in a single parent home. My mother inspired me. She was always actively involved in community activities and assisting people, especially the poor and underprivileged and I would go with her. I would also accompany her to meet with government representatives on issues affecting the village. We did not get to meet the politicians. They were always unavailable. These experiences inspired me to get involved in politics – it was in my blood. In college, I was involved in the Students Association.

At national elections I would go and assist candidates that I supported, in their campaign. Becoming a politician became my dream. I believe that politicians must listen to the people and meet with them. I have set aside every Friday for meeting with the public. I also meet with people who are not in my ridings. I gave out my home and cell numbers so that people can contact me. I made a commitment that once elected to political office, I would be accessible, approachable and accountable to the people who elect me.

Takechandra: When did you migrate to Canada?

Malhi: I got married in 1975 and migrated at the end of April, 1975.

Takechandra: What was the push/pull factor (s) that caused you to migrate to Canada?

Malhi: My wife sponsored me.

Takechandra: What expectations you had about coming to Canada?

Malhi: Better opportunities.

Takechandra: Did you have prior knowledge of job opportunities & living conditions coming to Canada?

Malhi: I had the opportunity to visit Canada before migrating. My wife was living here since 1972. I was not surprised when I migrated. I worked in a factory as a general labourer, I drove taxi and did delivery jobs. In 1985 I obtained my Real Estate License and worked with Homelife Realty. I became one of the top sales people and remained in real estate until 1993. I was also involved in various community activities, including the temple, volunteering my service as required.

In 1990, I was elected President of the ridings – Bramalea – Gore – Malton and was re-elected in 1991. In 1992, I was nominated candidate for the Liberal Party and in 1993, was elected the official candidate for the Liberal Party and won the seat. I was re-elected in 1997, 2000, 2004 and 2006. I am the first turbaned Sikh to be elected to the Canadian House of Commons.

Takechandra: Would you say that your initial work in real estate and community services would have created the opportunity for exposure to your present constituency and laid the foundation for your political career in Canada?

Malhi: Yes

Takechandra: What will be your recommendations to an immigrant who would like to enter the Canadian Political Process/

Malhi: He/she needs to work in the communities, doing volunteer work etc. He/She must know the policies and procedures of the party that he/she supports and must be honest and hard working. He/she must be willing to meet with people and provide feedback.

Takechandra: Could an immigrant enter the Canadian political process before being a citizen?

Malhi: If one is not a citizen, he or she cannot run for public office in Canada. However, he/she could become a member of any political party of his/her choosing, in Canada.

Takechandra: Our experience interviewing immigrants tells us that most of them coming to Canada did not have prior knowledge of what to expect. For example, they did not know of the difficulties obtaining a job in their profession and that they would have to upgrade their qualifications to Canadian standard etc. Given your experience, what would be your recommendation to immigrants coming to Canada?

Malhi: It would be better to visit Canada for 2-3 months to understand the requirements and demands. I understand the difficulty in obtaining a visitor's visa but an opportunity to visit before migrating would be good. Secondly, visit the Canada website and write the Consular requesting information about the skills that are required and available opportunities regarding your profession. Thirdly, try to obtain as much prior information as possible, including understanding the language and vocabulary used in Canada.

I have been advocating for the government to have a website advising prospective immigrants that even if they have qualifications they would not get a job in their profession right away. As Parliamentary Secretary to the Minister of Labour, I had called on the Associations to have a meeting to determine the issue of recognizing the credentials of foreign trained professionals. Before they come to Canada they should know if they are going to get a job, if not what they should do. I also suggested to the Canadian government that systems can be put in place where the required exams etc. could be done in the home country prior to migrating and on arrival in Canada, the immigrant would go through an internship/training, with payment from the government.

Takechandra: Are you satisfied that you have achieved your expectations in Canada?

Malhi: I am satisfied.

Takechandra: Thank you Hon Malhi for taking time off from your busy schedule to accommodate this interview.

Provincial Members of Parliament for Ontario

Bas Balkissoon, Liberal, Scarborough-Rouge River
Michael Chan, Liberal, Markham, Unionville
Vic Dhillon, Liberal, Brampton West
Kuldip Kular, Liberal, Bramalea-Gore-Malton
Yasir Naqvi, Liberal, Ottawa Centre

Shafiq Qaadri, Liberal, Etobicoke North,
Harinder Takhar, Liberal, Mississauga-Erindale

Human Rights Code
Each province in Canada has legislation regarding human rights. The following outline is about the Ontario Human Rights Commission. The Ontario Human Rights Commission was created in 1961 to promote and protect the rights of everyone in Ontario, under the Ontario Human rights Code. The Code says that you have the right to be free from discrimination and harassment at your workplace, accommodation, goods services and facilities and in vocational associations or trade unions.

Discrimination means unfair treatment because of your ancestry, ethnic origin, colour, race, religion, sex, disability, age religion, or sexual orientation. If you feel that you have been discriminated against you can call the Ontario Human rights Commission to get more information or file a complaint.

The Human Rights Amendment act 2006 took effect June 30, 2008. The new law creates the human rights Legal Support Centre to provide legal support. The Human Rights Legal Support Centre will offer independent human rights related legal and support services to individuals ranging from advice and support to legal representation.

In Canadian corporate culture some companies have moved very quickly to an enviroment that advocates and educates their employees on human rights while other companies may not have moved as quickly and may need some time to fully integrate human rights into all levels of company life. It is in the same vein that some companies have adopted diversity into their culture while others haven't, although diversity is not a legislated position in Canadian companies.

Drivers License
Owning Your First Vehicle
Driver's licenses in Canada are issued by each individual province. In Ontario, all drivers must carry a valid driver's license at all times. It's a simple, plastic identification card that includes a photograph of the licensee.

Ontario has a graduated Licensing System (GLS) in place. It's a two-step process that takes a minimum of 20 months to complete. A period of up to 5 years is allowed as a maximum, for new licensees to meet the official requirements.

You must be at least 16 years of age and pass both a vision test and knowledge test that's based on the handbook the Ontario government publishes. No one is permitted to drive a vehicle unless you pass these tests first. After passing the test, each new driver receives a Level One (Class G1 or M1 for motorcycle) license. This license has strict restrictions on when, how and where you can drive.

A G2 License can be obtained after 12 months as a G1 licensee. The G2 has fewer restrictions. To qualify for a full license, drivers must pass two road tests monitored by Ministry of Transport officials.

The graduated system was introduced several years ago to provide more real driving experience for new drivers and reduce the number of younger driver injuries and deaths on our roads.

Canada has a reciprocal licence agreement with the following countries: Austria, Belgium, France, Great Britain, Germany, Japan, Korea and Switzerland. If you are a licensed driver with two or more years of driving experience from one of the above jurisdictions you may get full class licence privileges without taking a knowledge or road test. However you must pass a vision test and show acceptable proof of your previous licence status and driving experience.

If you have less than two years of driving experience, you may get credit for your experience for graduated licensing and be issued a Class G2 or M2 licence. Once you have a total of two years of driving experience, you may take the G2 road test to earn full driving privileges.

Requirements for jurisdictions that do not have reciprocal agreements with Canada are different. This means you must do the following:

• Declare your driving experience on the driver's licence application form
• Present a valid foreign driver's licence translated into English or French
• Pass a vision test and a written knowledge test on Ontario's traffic rules
• Provide adequate proof of foreign driving experience. Applicants who fulfill these requirements will qualify for a G1 license. Information on requirements and licence restrictions are available at the following web site: www.drivetest.ca

If you are looking for a driver's licence in any of the other provinces information can be obtained on the following web site: www.cnadaonline.about.com/od/driverslicence

International Driver's Permits are issued by automobile associations in your home country and are available to tourists to Canada only. They are authorized by a UN treaty among nations of the world, for the purpose of allowing motorists to drive vehicles in international traffic without further tests or applications. It's proof that the holder possesses a valid driver's licence issued by a competent authority in their home country of residence. International Driver's Permits are not valid for immigrants seeking temporary or permanent residency in Canada.

It is advisable -- if learning to drive in Canada as an adult or a teenager -- that you attend a driver education program. The type of program will give you good instruction on the rules of the road and will help you get lower insurance rates, while learning how to drive defensively and safely.

Driver Training Schools
Two of the major driver training schools in Canada are the CAA and Young Drivers.

CAA (Canadian Automobile Association)
1-800-268-3750 General Information and Membership
Greater Toronto Area 416-221-4300

Driver Training
5859 Yonge St., Suite 105

Toronto, On M2M 3V6
416-223-8870   driver@caasco.ca

Young Drivers of Canada

Go to the web site for Young Drivers of Canada -- http://www.yd.com/ -- and enter your postal code and city and the menu will direct you to the nearest location.

There are many good private driving schools in Canada and we recommend that you get references and search out the best ones in your area. Also talk to you insurance company and get their recommendation and what type of discount they will give you for the course. Many of the high schools also provide driver training for teenagers.

Owning Your First Vehicle

A car is an expensive luxury. With a vehicle of your own, your costs are continuous. Even if you were in a position to pay cash for vehicle, there are numerous additional costs involved in the operation and ownership of it. And those added costs never go away.

Some of the things that you need to consider in owning your first vehicle are the cost and maintenance of that vehicle versus your budget for transportation, housing, food, clothing, etc. When you factor in all the associated costs tied to having a car (maintenance, parking, gas, and insurance) you may want to take public transit for a period of time at first. That way you can see if you are generating the kind of money required to own a car. This could easily reach $300 to $500 a month -- even more. The cost of a litre of gas has just recently increased from $1.00 a litre (or $4.00 a gallon) up to approximately $1.25 per litre ($5.00 a gallon). These costs have been reduced at the time of writing this book due to world economic crisis and are now around 80 cents a litre.

Depending on your budget, you may prefer to take public transit for a period of time to see if you are generating the kind of money required to own a car. If not, the decision is easy: stick with public transit. But if you can afford a car, it does provide an added degree of freedom. By trying public transit and then reassessing your individual situation later, your decision will be based on real data and your capability to manage the added expense of a car. With this approach, you won't go into the hole, only to discover later that perhaps purchasing a vehicle was not a prudent choice for you.

Getting a car is a big step that shouldn't be taken lightly. Once the decision has made to get a car, investigate all of your options. Choices are numerous. Do you get a new or used car? Do you buy or lease?

Resources like Consumer Reports can point you towards vehicles with low maintenance and solid performance records. Do your own research. Check out numerous brands and models. Uncover other people's experience with each model, than narrow your choices down to a car that is the best fit for you, your family and your budget.

Every vehicle has an assigned registration number (through the Ministry of Transport) which must be renewed every year for a fee on the owner's birthday. Insurance is mandatory if you wish to drive in Ontario and the other provinces. Insurance coverage typically includes:

- **Liability Insurance** - Protection when someone else is injured or killed or their property damaged.
- **Accident Insurance** - Benefits to you or your estate if you are injured or killed in a car accident.

• **Collision Insurance** -- Coverage for damages caused to your own vehicle and coverage for fire, theft, or vandalism.

It is my recommendation that you use a recognized automotive dealer of one of the major brands to buy even a used car. These dealerships are supported by their brand and you have recourse in the case of any disagreement by going to the corporate head office. The major brands also have a reputation to uphold on their new and used cars and they have their maintenance and warranty commitments should be strong.

Also, you should always be provided with the repair and accident record on the car that you are purchasing. There is an association between price and quality and some people buy a very low priced car and end up paying enormous maintenance and repair costs. Buy a car that has a good service repair record and this information is available at a public library through a magazine called "Consumer Reports."

Driving Rules

Drinking and driving on any road in Canada is strictly forbidden. Severe penalties are imposed on those found guilty of this type of offense and the roads are regularly monitored for anyone suspected of driving under the influence of alcohol. The maximum permissible blood-alcohol level is .08 ml of alcohol per 100 ml of blood.

Better to be on the cautious side and have a designated driver who is not drinking at all. The police set up roadblock 'spot checks' to catch impaired drivers. Some of these spot checks are set up on highway ramps others on main arteries. But rather than avoid these police checks, simply avoid drinking whenever you plan to drive.

Seatbelts are mandatory and fines are given to anyone caught in a vehicle not wearing one. The law also requires that baby seats be properly installed and safely secured.

Drivers are encouraged not to speed. Police may allow speeds of up to 10 kilometres over the limit, but go beyond that and you could be handed a ticket. Often this results in a court date, where a conviction could cost you a substantial sum of money and more.

Drivers convicted of certain offences (including but not limited to driving under the influence) have "demerit points" recorded on their driving records. These points stay on your driving record for two years from the date of the offense. Collect enough points and you could lose your driver's license.

New laws have been introduced in Canada to deter people from racing on the roads because there have been many deaths caused by this practice.

It's vitally important that you obey the rules of the road. This means to always signal for lane changes, avoid tailgating and zigzagging between lanes, and stop at all stop signs and red lights. If you are a considerate, safe, and defensive driver, chances are you'll be fine on Canada's roads and highways. Also remember when an emergency vehicle such as ambulance, police or fire truck have their sirens running you are expected to get out of their way and pull over to the right hand curb and stop. You are also expected to give emergency vehicles the right of way even if you have green traffic light and they have a red light.

The following web site will assist you in obtaining your Driver's License in Ontario: www.mto.gov.on.ca.

Public Transit in Canada

Although it is difficult to cover all of the public transit services in every location in Canada we will focus on the major cities and describe the various services available to the users in the urban centres.

Toronto

The city of Toronto offers a public transit service which includes a subway, bus and streetcar system run by the Toronto Transit Corporation.

One way fares are $2.75 per adult and $1.85 per student with a valid student card. Routes are available on the following web-site and fares can be obtained at a lower rate if buying in volume or on a monthly pass basis. Routes are with-in the limits of the boundaries of the City of Toronto. You must obtain a transfer pass after you have paid the fare if you wish to transfer to a different mode of transport or travel on a different route or zone. A GTA weekly pass is available which provides transportation services within the total Greater Toronto Area (GTA) including Mississauga, Brampton and York.

Determining your route if you were to travel from outside Toronto into the Greater Toronto Area can be more complicated and will usually require some information gathering on your part. You are best to get information from people who travel the route and try it yourself a few times before your first day of work or an appointment. The web site for the Toronto Transit Commission is: www.toronto.ca/ttc/index/htm

This web site shows maps of the various routes for subways, buses and streetcars throughout the entire city. Mississauga Transit for service in Mississauga and Brampton has a web site for information on routes and fares located here: www.mississauga.ca/portal/residents/publictransit

Weekend services for all forms of transit may have different schedules than during the work week so those times should be checked separately. Various special services are available for people with disabilities so theses services should be looked into if you are disabled.

GO Transit is a commuter train and bus service operated by the government of Ontario. The service provides bus service to main commuter connections to the east, west, north and south of Toronto and then train service into the city where the individual can connect with the city services. Parking is provided at the main train stations although the lots tend to fill very early in the morning. A typical rate for the train one-way Oakville to Toronto would be $5.85. The web site for all GO Train and GO bus routes and fares is: www.gotransit.com

The city of Toronto has a huge road system servicing it which includes multiple highways and a toll highway called the 407 which bypasses the city to the north. There are free parking lots for car pooling in the outer GTA and special car pooling lanes are starting to be introduced on the highway system. Car congestion is heavy during rush hour and the car can quickly become an inefficient method of getting to and from work. Parking is also extremely expensive in the city.

Montreal

Montreal is serviced by buses, subway and a paratransit for persons with disabilities. One-way fares are $2.00. The main web sites for routes and fares are:

www.ville.montreal.qc.ca/portal

www.stm.info

Edmonton

Edmonton is serviced by bus and a rail system (LRT). One-way fares are $2.50. Information on schedules, maps and fares are on the following web site:

www.edmonton.ca/portal/server.pt?space

Calgary

Calgary is serviced by bus and a rail system (CTrain line).One-way fares are $2.50 Information on fares, schedules and maps is available on the following web site:

www.calgarytransit.com/html/about_ct.html

Vancouver

Vancouver has a bus service along with a system for downtown called the Sky Train and also water connections called Sea Bus. One-way fares are $2.50.

Information on fares, schedules and maps is available on the following web site:

www.city.vancouver.bc.ca/residents.htm

Key Point Review

- Preparation gives you an advantage
- Know what to expect upon your arrival in Canada and have all documentation with you
- Anticipate the types of questions you may be asked by customs officials so you can handle them easily and smoothly and pass through customs in as little time as possible
- Use your first week in Canada to: obtain a Social Insurance Number, apply for your Health Card, open a Canadian bank account, and to familiarize yourself with essential and helpful services in your neighbourhood
- Universal health care covers necessary medical services and care, but in some provinces, you have to wait 3 months in order to qualify
- Health and safety in the workplace is a fundamental right of every worker and should be an important concern of everyone
- You must have a Social Insurance Number in order to work in Canada
- Driver's licenses in Canada are issued by the provinces after applicants pass both a written and practical driving test
- Owning a car in Canada can be an expensive luxury with many additional and unavoidable costs
- Vehicle and liability insurance is mandatory in Canada
- Setting up a bank account in Canada is easy and it serves multiple purposes
- Credit cards can be easy to obtain, but prudent financial management is crucial too so proceed with care
- Housing costs can be higher than expected in densely-populated areas

• Everyone earning income in Canada is obligated to pay taxes and file an income tax return each year
• Depending on your chosen province, you will have anywhere from 5-9 statutory vacation days each calendar year

Sports and Recreation in Canada

Below is listed a varied selection of sports and recreational activities available in Canada at various times throughout the year:

Summer
Boating, Canoeing, Kayaking
Swimming
Hiking
Camping
Fishing
All water sports
Golf
Cricket
Soccer (youth participated soccer is one of the fastest growing sports in Canada)
American football
Baseball

Winter
Skating
Skiing (Downhill and Cross-Country)
Snowboarding
Snowmobiling
Sledding or toboggan
Hockey
Ice Fishing
Basketball

Fall
Hunting
Hiking

Professional Sports Available for Watching
Hockey
Basketball
Baseball
Soccer
Indoor Lacrosse
Cricket at a community or club level
Car racing
Golf
Canadian (American style) football
English Rugby at a community or club level

Soccer in Canada

Soccer is one of the many popular recreational sports in Canada and for the past two decades soccer has overtaken ice hockey as the sport with the most registered players in the country.

One of the reasons why soccer has become more popular in recent years is because of its low infrastructure cost and low participant cost. In addition, soccer offers all of the benefits of fitness, skill, team play, and a relatively low number of injuries, compared to some other sports like hockey or football.

In 2005 there were 841,000 registered soccer players in Canada. That's a huge number of Canadians playing the game. Soccer is played by boys and girls, teenagers, and men and women in organized leagues of various skill levels. The most senior levels involve play at the professional level and compete in FIFA tournaments, although Canada is a relatively inexperienced newcomer, as far as world soccer competition is concerned.

Cricket in Canada

Cricket has a long history in Canada, where records exist of cricket being played by the Royal Navy and the British Army. Participants stayed relatively low until the last two decades when immigrants from former British colonies brought more interest and participation in the game.

In the last decade the number of participants has steadily increased and now there is cricket participation in every province. The web site listed below will give you an idea of the Canadian Cricket structure and the affiliated Provincial Organizations. www.canadacricket.com

The inflow of immigrants from countries where soccer and cricket are extremely popular sports has created a demand for more and more facilities in Canada. All levels of government have become involved in developing and financing facilities for these two sports.

There are also plans to make cricket a sanctioned school sport in York region (just outside of Toronto). The Royal Bank of Canada is sponsoring a program to introduce cricket to elementary schools. The sport of cricket does require additional facility funding and also a coaching and training structure to prepare players for international competition. There is also a problem with corporate sponsorship and media support, both of which are required to significantly grow the game in Canada.

Many supporters of cricket believe that it will undergo the same growth and popularity as soccer did over the last 30 years in Canada starting with participation at younger ages and moving on to the professional levels bringing along fan and financial support over the years. Cricket has also designed a new game format which reduces playing time to three hours to encourage fan interest. The growth of immigration from cricket-loving countries such as India, Pakistan, Sri Lanka and Jamaica ensures a growing interest in the sport of cricket in Canada.

Cricket and soccer in Canada have been gaining tremendous momentum, which reflects the pattern of immigration to Canada. Many municipal authorities are supporting these new sports by creating bigger and better facilities and increasing visibility. The current attention paid to the Indian Premier League has generated a major international buzz and captured the attention and interest of Canada's many cricket fans.

Shopping in Canada

Listed below is a very short list of major food, home furnishing, automotive, and clothing chains in Canada. This list is compact and does not represent the smaller chains that exist in each province in these categories.

There are national grocery chains that retail across Canada and if you want groceries that are particular to your own ethnic group the names and locations are available in ethnic newspapers.

Canadian Tire - Automotive, Home appliances, Sporting Goods

The Brick - Home furnishings

Wal-Mart - General Merchandise and some Food

Leon's - Home furnishings

Home Depot – Do-it-yourself home renovation, appliances, tools, lumber

Sears - Home Furnishing, Clothing

Staples - Office Supplies

The Bay - Clothing, fashion, home furnishing

Shoppers Drug Mart - Drugs, Cosmetics

Zellers - Clothing, toys, household supplies, and general merchandise

We recommend these names because they are known to offer good value and have very good policies on customer care and service. These stores also have a national presence. Since Canada is one of the most diverse countries in the world there are a number of retail stores which cater to various ethnic tastes.

Chapter Fifteen
Your Personal Finances in Canada
Banking

It is advisable that you establish relationships with people such as your bank manager, professional accountant, financial advisor -- as well as a lawyer. Locate these experts through friends, family and references. Ask questions and review performances and the reputations of these professionals within your own inner circle of acquaintances. These advisors will help you pay the proper amount of tax on your income and also educate you on accounting methods to reduce your taxes paid.

It's important for all new immigrants to establishment a relationship with a bank in Canada as soon as possible. This is important because A) It gives your place of employment a bank account in which to directly deposit your cheques... B) It gives you an account to manage your money and pay your bills... and C) It helps you to establish a track record in Canada.

Costs for accounts can vary among the banks in Canada, so you should shop around to determine the best value for you.

HSBC

I recognize that one of the problems facing new immigrants is the ability to secure a financial institution to take care of their banking needs. HSBC has special provisions for new immigrants and provides a unique list of services to fulfill their needs. During my review of banking services, I discovered HSBC's Passport Account – a bank account that thoughtfully addresses the needs of new immigrants.

One of the easiest ways for a new immigrant to start banking in Canada is with an HSBC Passport Account. In order to qualify, you must have arrived in Canada within the last 2 years and have a minimum deposit of $100.00 in Canadian currency. Additionally, you will have to show proof of either landed immigrant or foreign worker status. What you get from an HSBC Passport account are the following benefits:

• Unlimited monthly banking transactions, with no monthly fee for 6 months

- An HSBC Bank Card for all your shopping needs
- Access to the largest surcharge-free ATM (Automatic Teller Machine) networks in Canada through HSBC Bank Canada
- 24 hour access to your account with Personal Internet Banking
- Telephone Banking, where you can simply pick up any phone and enjoy a complete range of banking services
- A one time discount of $10 on a Safety Deposit Box
- Discounted international money wire transfers
- Discounts and offers from other merchants

You can sign up for the following extra services, each with additional benefits for Passport account customers:
- High Rate Savings Accounts, with in-branch and online access and no monthly fee
- Transaction fees are waived for Passport account customers for the first year
- Direct Savings Account with online-only access offering a high interest rate with easy access 24 hours a day and no minimum balance or monthly fees are required
- One year redeemable GIC plus a bonus ½% on the posted rate for amounts of $3500 or greater and it's redeemable after 90 days

You can also access a range of borrowing solutions to help you reach your goals, big or small. With a Passport account, your credit approval is based on your income and wealth in Canada.

A personal line of credit lets you have additional money to use however and whenever you want. HSBC MasterCard is widely accepted around the world and offers convenient access to cash.

To open a Passport account before coming to Canada, please contact the International Banking Center (IBC) at the following:
1-888-280-4722 (North America Toll Free)
1-604-419-4169 (International / Call Charges may apply)
hsbcinternational@hsbc.ca

The IBC operates between 6 a.m. to 5 p.m. Pacific Standard Time (PST). After working hours, please leave a message and contact number where the IBC can reach you.
Account features are subject to change. For the most current information on any of our services please refer to our web site: www.hsbc.ca

A chequing account is good for most cash-management functions, but it's not the best place to keep your savings because the interest provided by banks is low. You'll always get better interest rates on a savings account. If you eventually get to the position of savings into a Registered Retirement Account, the bank can offer you options along with various investment consultants outside the bank.

You need to assess your costs and measure these against expected returns, but the money is tax-free as long as you stay under your entitled limit and you don't withdraw any of this money. If you're planning for the long-term and saving for your retirement years, this is generally a solid path to take.

You will be issued slips which are in turn submitted with your income tax return, giving you a deduction for Retirement Savings Plans. The banks will also offer you your own credit card, which is best-used sparingly, until you are in a good financial position to pay off the balance each and every month. This is important because carry-over balances usually have exorbitant interest rates (over 20 per cent in some cases) attached to them.

Canada has had some experience with identity theft just as have many countries around the world. The technology of credit cards is starting to reach the point of having a chip imbedded in the card so identity theft becomes much more difficult.

For the time being there are methods that you can use to minimize the possibility of identity theft. One method is to have an online account for your pay deposits and then transfer the money once a month to your chequing account. Be sure to get a monthly printout of all your transactions and keep this for your records. What this does is separate your pay balance from your monthly bill payments, giving you strict control on the movement of the funds in your account.

Credit in Canada- Establishing Credit
Credit History in Canada

In North America and in most of the developed countries there is a heavy emphasis on consumer credit. For most new immigrants, obtaining credit has been a challenge. We have interviewed TransUnion's Canadian President, Ken Porter, in order to provide comments and recommendations for New Canadians and immigrants coming to this country.

TransUnion has credit data files on over 24 million Canadians and has 175 associates in offices across Canada. TransUnion receives information from credit grantors such as banks, lending institutions and credit card companies and maintains active files on individuals' credit histories. To access this information, institutions must have a permissible purpose, such as a credit related inquiry (whether an application for a credit card, a loan or mortgage). This process is part of the consumer protection program that is in place for the release of credit information. In addition, privacy legislation in Canada generally requires consent for the collection, use and disclosure of personal information.

Every Canadian is entitled to view his/her credit file (consumer disclosure). TransUnion provides several methods whereby consumers can view their own credit history. TransUnion's offices have a consumer relations centre where individuals can request a copy of their consumer disclosure, in person, when they provide appropriate identification. Individuals can also access their credit report via the mail with proper identification. TransUnion also has a telephone system with an integrated identification tool to access one's credit history. The goal of this program at TransUnion is to help and educate individuals on the value and importance of their credit standing. In addition, TransUnion works with several organizations that provide TransUnion's information to consumers online.

Credit Scores - 5 steps to a higher credit score

1. Be punctual- pay all of your bills on time. Late payments and collections have the greatest negative effect on your credit score. As long as you make the minimum payment on time you have the potential to maintain good credit, however, there is a problem with carrying

over large credit card balances because eventually you might not be able to pay them.

2. Check your credit report regularly and take the necessary steps to remove inaccuracies-it is in your best interest to monitor your credit report and ensure that it is accurate and that there isn't any-one else using your credit cards which will have a direct impact on your ability to get credit and loans

3. Monitor your debt- keep your balance below 35% of your available credit. If you have a credit limit of $1,000 then you should keep your balance below $350 and this will also give you an idea of how much you should pay above the minimum balance if you don't pay off the whole balance

4. Use time to establish a good credit rating- it takes time to establish a good credit history-you may also want to keep the oldest account on your credit profile open which will add history to your credit profile

5. Avoid excessive inquiries to potential creditors as they are sometimes indicative of opening a large number of accounts to cover debt that you cannot repay.

Credit Rating - Why is a Good Credit Rating Important to you?
- Healthy credit is a foundation for everyone who wants to get a financial footing
- You need to validate the information appearing in your credit report in order to ensure that there isn't any fraudulent activity occurring or that an error is not present in the report
- Good credit history can help you obtain loans and mortgages and it is to your advantage to have the same information as the financial institution when you go in to negotiate a loan or mortgage because a good credit rating can translate into a more favourable rate
- Companies provide an online service for a modest fee in order to help you keep on top of your credit information and monitor changes to your information. TransUnion works with several organizations to bring this monitoring service to consumers. You should monitor your credit as you would your health. You would not think of having your investments unattended for years on end.
- ª Credit is individualistic, so a married couple may have two separate credit reports
- If you have co-signed on behalf of a friend or relative you need to be aware of their payment behaviour because their history will affect your credit rating

What if a New Canadian wants to have a credit card but has not been able to find employment and has been told that employment is a condition of granting a credit card
- there are a few methods which might help the New Canadian obtain credit- pre-paid cards are available to individuals who are not currently employed- these cards require a deposit but they allow the individual to show that regular payments are being made to "top up" the balance available and may assist the individual to acquire credit once a positive pattern is established- ensure that you are punctual with your deposits
- find a relative or sponsor in Canada who will co-sign for you on the credit obligation

but ensure that you follow prudent credit management and are punctual because you are affecting two credit ratings
- every New Canadian comes with cash or a bank draft of money to help in their settlement-negotiate the deposit of this money in a bank if they help you obtain a low limit credit card
- some banks are global in nature and you may be able to have sponsor in your home country who has an account with the same bank co-sign for credit approval in Canada

Life Insurance

Life insurance is very important to protect you and your dependents, particularly in the developing years of family life. Although Canada has a social health care system it does not cover the cost of life insurance, disability insurance, dental, or drug costs. Talk to your financial advisor about your own personal insurance and your ability to cover your family's debts if something happened to you. Some employers offer these services but you have to take care of them yourself if you are self-employed. It is also important to protect your assets from fire and theft even if you are living in an apartment.

Pensions and Pension Savings Plans

As soon as you begin to work in Canada there are deductions from your paycheque for Canada Pension Plan benefits. This benefit means that each employed individual has a CPP account set up for them to pay them a pension when or if they stop working at 65 years of age based on their years of work and total contributions. The Canada Pension is paid on a reduced basis between the ages of 60 to 65. You could collect this pension if you were not employed and earning income under the age of 65.

The Canada Pension is meant to replace about 20% of your average income. There are income supplements to the Canada Pension which can be applied for after the age of 65. It is obvious that individuals need to supplement their Canada Pension Plan with additional investment plans such as Retired Savings Plans (RSP) because the Canada Pension Plan will not support individuals or families on its own. The following is a description of the types of plans available. Any-one over the age of 65 is entitled to receive Old Age Security benefits which are based on the length of time that the individual has resided in Canada with a minimum residence requirement of 10 years..

Retirement Savings Plan (RSP)

Retirement Savings Plans are investment accounts that are designed primarily for saving toward your retirement years. Although a new immigrant or recent arrival might not think of retirement as a priority, they should look at these options fairly early in their employment years because of the large number of options available from these plans. Some of the benefits of the plans are:

1. An RSP will supplement your retirement income and your CPP and allow you to maintain a similar lifestyle to the one that your have been accustomed to.
2. Contributions to an RSP are tax deductible so that you reduce your taxable income and

many times you earn an income tax refund with an RSP. The government will tell you what your RSP limit is each year once your income tax has been filed.

3. Money that stays in an RSP account and grows is not taxed until it is withdrawn which is normally later in life when your taxable income is lower. This would be called tax deferred investment income because your RSP is placed in growth funds, stocks, bonds, etc. which increase in value within your account over time. Your bank or investment dealer can advise you on the best method for you and the type of risk that you want to take with your money. Please remember that these RSP's are part of the overall investment community so that the potential for a high return provides for a higher risk and you could lose some portion of your investment if you apply too much risk. The lower the risk on such things as bonds and government investment certificates provide for predictably lower returns but also more confidence in not losing portions of your principal investment. In 2008 and 2009 the recent economic downturn has dramatically affected the value of stocks, mutual funds, etc. which form a large component of RSP's. Many people have lost substantial portions of their RSP's because they were trying to get a reasonable rate of return. In reaction to this uncertain enviroment investment consultants and banks have started to offer RSP plans which have a guaranteed return on your RSP investment although it may be very low but it may appeal to some people who are concerned after losing part of their retirement savings.

There are mutual funds which provide a blend of investment vehicles that provide a good return and low risk over time. These investments are meant to be kept for longer periods of time. But these funds can be withdrawn, although you will pay taxes on the withdrawal and have to report any withdrawal on your tax return.

Your investment dealer could also place various charges against a withdrawal so this information should be obtained beforehand. RSP's are also an important vehicle if you find that you are laid off or without work for an extended period of time. The RSP is meant to be used for retirement but if you lose your job your income is low or non-existent so your tax rate will also be low and the RSP will be taxed at the lower rate. Some people making under $35,000 a year, for example, may not find that RSP's are a priority at this point in their lives when they could pay down their debts or get insurance. You should always get sound advice from your financial advisor first.

4. Your employer has your interest in mind and will offer you different types of Pension Plans that are part of their employment package:

TD Canada Trust has an excellent web site with information on RSP's and other investment vehicles. That site can be found here: **www.tdcanadatrust.com/rsp/introrsp.jsp**

Defined Contribution Plan

This plan provides an individual account for each participant. In many cases the company matches or puts in a percentage against each employee's contribution. The contributions by the employee are tax deductible. The accounts are investments and rated by the degree of risk desired by the participant for the degree of return. They do not guarantee a monthly amount such as the CPP.

RSP-other uses

RSP's can be used to purchase your first house. This is a one time use of an RSP and can be used by a husband and wife for up to $20,000 per RSP. Information on this option can be obtained from your investment dealer who holds your RSP.

An RSP could also be used by you for educational purposes if you need re-training to find work. Ask you financial advisor for information on the use of RSP for your own personal educational upgrading.

It is highly recommended that every individual in Canada prepare for their retirement years with some kind of savings and investment plan of their own. Without your own savings, you may only have less than a thousand dollars a month to live on. That won't support much of a lifestyle during your golden years, so it's best to begin preparing on your own as early as possible in your working life.

Registered Education Savings Plan (RESP)

The Registered Education Savings Plan (RESP) is a plan which helps provide for your child's education. The plan is an investment account established with your child as a beneficiary and when the money is withdrawn when the child is at a post secondary school it is taxed against the income of the child which is normally much lower. More details are available at this web site: www.tdcandatrust.com/resp/edu_planning.jsp

Real Estate in Canada

Harvey S. Margel

Harvey S. Margel, BA, LLB is a Barrister, Solicitor, and Notary Public practicing real estate law in the north end of Toronto. Harvey's advice to the Canadian newcomer is from the beginning to find employment and provide a stable future income. Most newcomers start as renters until they build up a steady and predictable income and form a down payment for a house. In the book we have stressed the need for preparation and research and real estate is no different. Harvey advises that you research the area that you want to live in. Visit houses for sale in the area and get prices, condition of other street residences, traffic, location to schools, shopping and location of religious institutions. Learn about the real estate in the area. A real estate agent is compensated when the transaction occurs so their best interests may not be your best interests. You need to make your own decisions regarding the purchase and selection of a home based on a buyer beware attitude. Any legal advice regarding the offer to purchase or sale will be provided by a lawyer, not the real estate agent. The lawyer will not give you business advice, this advice should be provided by your own experience and possibly a financial planner. It is not up to the lawyer or the real estate agent to provide for advice on the financing of the house. You have to do that on your own by negotiating directly with a financial institution or a mortgage broker.

Canadians, in general, feel that the purchase of a house is a valuable and important acquisition in their lives. The sale of a principal residence in Canada is tax free, however,

Canada does not provide for any mortgage interest tax deduction such as some other countries do. The tax free status of a principal residence is a valuable tool in building a retirement fund for many Canadians.

The real estate lawyer's principal duty in a real estate transaction is to ensure that the individual involved gets exactly what they are paying for according to the terms and conditions of the offer to purchase or sale contract. The title to the house is properly searched and the house is legally clean and free of any liens and obligations. The average cost of a lawyer for a real estate transition is $450 dollars plus expenses. Some lawyers charge less and others charge a lot more. You should be able to get a quote on a lawyer's services and typical expenses by asking at the first dialogue. When you consider that the average house price in Canada is in the $300,000 range an expenditure of under $1000 is not expensive and well worth the cost.

Remember to get advice also from a financial planner when deciding to buy a house because he/she will have guidelines on how much of your income you should be spending on a house. They can also show you a monthly house cost including mortgage, taxes, utilities and maintenance as a portion of your income.

Harvey S. Margel is willing to provide a free 1/2 hour of real estate consultation to any New Canadian at his office in Toronto. Harvey is located at 2365 Finch Avenue West, Suite 202 (Finch and Weston Road) , Toronto, On M9M 2W8. Phone 416-745-9933. Email: harveymargel@rogers.com

Renting an Apartment - Owning a House In Canada

In paying rent, what you can expect to pay will vary with each Canadian city. Rates are predominantly affected by supply and demand. In major cities like Toronto or Vancouver, you can expect the monthly rent for a two-bedroom apartment to range anywhere from $1200 to $2500. The actual figure often depends on how close you want to be to the business centre of the city, or to major transit arteries.

According to the National Post ("The Mortgage Trap" - September 27th,2007) average house prices in the major centers are as follows: Vancouver $589,916; Calgary $459,889; Toronto $411,224; Montreal $226,453. House prices in the Province of Quebec are lower than the rest of Canada, but bear in mind that you must speak and write in the French language in Quebec and your children will be educated in French.

A real estate agent is not usually the best person to give you advice on buying a house. The best person to give you this advice is your financial advisor who can determine if you can afford the principal, interest, taxes, utilities, and maintenance that come with home ownership. You also want to buy your property at the right time of the market cycle due to price fluctuations. Real estate in Canada is generally a solid investment. But if you buy at the wrong time, you could end up losing money on the deal.

It should be understood that in Canada there is no mortgage interest tax deduction available. But when you sell your principal residence, there is no capital gains tax on the sale. Based on the above prices, a mortgage payment on an "average" house could run over $2,000 a month. Additionally, there are other expenses related to your home including property taxes, utilities, telephone, and other services.

Many Canadians cannot afford these payments in their younger years and tend to postpone the purchase of a house until they are in solid financial shape and have solid long term work experience and also have built up the required down payment..

The following web site has good information regarding renting in Ontario: www.settlement.org/site/HO/rentng

If you are in need of subsidized housing until you get financially established, the following services may be able to help you.
- Non-profit housing owned by a group such as a church
- Co-op housing managed by the owners of units and a board of directors
- Public housing owned by the province - but waiting list for homes are long and it could take you several years to acquire a suitable place
- Rent supplements which are managed by the province

One of the better web sites for getting information on Canadian vacancy rates and home costs is the Canadian Mortgage and Housing web site.

If you are settling in the GTA (Greater Toronto Area) you can contact the Toronto Community Housing Corporation and request assistance in finding accommodation. Their web-site is: www.torontohousing.ca

It is highly suggested that any-one renting an apartment or owning a home obtain property insurance on the contents and liability for an apartment and insurance on your house, contents and liability if you own a home. A fire or theft can cause you considerable personal pain and in some cases have a lifelong negative effect on you.

Income Taxes

Once you are assigned a Social Insurance Number, it becomes the principle tracking tool for the deduction of Federal and Provincial Income Taxes, Employment Insurance and Canada Pension Plan contributions from your gross income.

Every working Canadian contributes a percentage of their income accordingly. Contributions are a major source of government revenues, which are then used to build and support Canada's infrastructure and social programs, among other things.

With each paycheque you receive, your employer automatically deducts the above taxes and contributions. Around February of each year, all employees in Canada receive a T-4 slip, which lists your exact income for the previous year and the taxes and contributions deducted. Separate slips are issued for Retirement Savings Plans deductions which could be handled by an investment agency, or yourself.

You are required to file an income tax document every year even if you do not owe the government any money. If you do owe the government money they will charge you interest on your outstanding taxes. You also need to file an income tax return if you are claiming any refund from the government.

There are firms that will prepare your income tax return for you. Such a firm is H & R Block. H & R Block is a "general purpose" type of income tax preparation service.

If your taxes are more complicated with investments and tax reduction programs, you could use a tax accountant. Your accountant would be advising you over time the best ways to minimize your tax payments.

There are different types of software for filing Canadian taxes but they would require some basic understanding of the tax system for you to fill them out and they do not give you advice along the way.

With any other investments (including interest earned from bank accounts) you will receive separate documentation once a year for income tax purposes. Once a year, every individual who has worked and earned income in Canada must file an income tax return. It is against the law not to pay income tax on income earned. This means that all income must be reported.

Standard tax forms are automatically mailed out by the federal government if you have filed a tax return in the previous year. But they can also be picked up at any Canada Post outlet across the country. Once completed, returns can be sent to the Canada Revenue Agency by mail, or submitted electronically.

Income tax checklist for immigrants to Canada:

1. If your current (non-Canadian) home is rented out for a brief period after your immigration to Canada, you may be required to pay withholding tax by the country you are leaving on any continuing rental payments. You should investigate whether you can pay tax on a net income basis.

2. If your current (non-Canadian) home is sold, taxes may be required in the foreign jurisdiction.

3. Consider the use of a non-resident trust where investment income is significant.

4. If the former country's tax rate is more favourable, try to ensure that you receive all remuneration prior to assuming Canadian residency (employment bonuses).

5. An Individual who is continuing to receive foreign employment income, may be subject to Canadian withholding tax requirements.
6. Consider obtaining provincial medical insurance as it may be more comprehensive than what is offered by the foreign country.

7. Consider selling stocks that are currently in a loss position to avoid possible deeming provisions by Canada which may result in Canadian capital gains.

8. Consider obtaining an exemption from participation in the Canada Pension Plan, if you are covered by the U.S. Social Security Agreement or any similar agreement.

9. Continued participation in foreign pension plans may reduce the ability to use Canadian tax-deferred savings plans, such as registered retirement savings plans (RRSP's).
10. Since moving expenses are not deductible for moves into and out of Canada, consider having

your employer reimburse you for your moving expenses. If the expenses being reimbursed are reasonable in the circumstances, these payments would not be taxable.

As a Canadian resident, you are required to pay tax on your worldwide income, so consider carefully the date you are choosing for Canadian residency. Tax implications in this regard are complex and can be managed with proper tax planning, therefore, any individual planning a move to Canada should seek the advice of a tax professional.

The government has a web-site for new immigrants to Canada that concerns Income Tax. The information provided relates to the first tax year that the immigrant is a new immigrant in Canada. It gives the new resident information on their tax obligations, forms and filing dates. Please refer to the following web-site for more information:

www.cra-arc.gc/tax/nonresidents/individuals/newcomer-e.html

As a Canadian resident, you are required to pay tax on your worldwide income, so consider carefully the date you are choosing for Canadian residency.

Tax implications in this regard are complex and can be managed with proper tax planning, therefore, any individual planning a move to Canada should seek the advice of a tax professional. The government has a web-site for new immigrants to Canada that concerns Income Tax. The information provided relates to the first tax year that the immigrant is a new immigrant in Canada. It gives the new resident information on their tax obligations, forms and filing dates. Please refer to the following web-site for more information:

www.cra-arc.gc/tax/nonresidents/individuals/newcomer-e.html

Child Tax Benefit

The Canada Child Tax benefit (CCTB) is a tax free monthly payment made to eligible families to help them with the cost of raising children under the age of 18.

The conditions required to get CCTB are:
- you must live with the child
- the child must be under the age 18
- you must be primarily responsible for the child
- you must be a resident of Canada and you or your spouse must be a Canadian citizen, a permanent resident, a protected person or a temporary resident living in Canada for the past 18 months

More info is available at the web site: www.cra-arc.gc.ca/benefits/cctb

Wills

It is probably a good idea to have a will drawn up by a lawyer for you and your spouse so that all of your family matters and assets are organized. The experience also acts as the source of information for the family assets and wishes and provides for management of your affairs if you are incapable of handling them.

Chapter Sixteen

Valuable resources Section websites, agencies and magazines

The following web site should be among your first stops online when considering coming to Canada. It's one of the best and most comprehensive resources for prospective immigrants to Canada. You will find it here: http://cic.gc.ca/

It's an official government web site operated by Citizenship and Immigration Canada. What this site lacks in personality, it more than makes up for in information. Dig in and you'll find a tremendous amount of detail on the process and all of the requirements for of immigrating to Canada.

You'll find authentic information on such topics as: Visiting Canada, Working Temporarily in Canada, Studying in Canada, The Refugee System, About Immigration, Living in Canada, and gaining Canadian Citizenship.

The web site supplies the necessary information for you to visit, live, and work in Canada. The information you'll find there is specific and government related. This resource also provides you with a list of agencies that can help you with various challenges that could come up. For example, YMCA's and YWCA's in every community have links to social agencies that help immigrants and this is part of their mandate. Ask about getting your education and qualifications assessed for free, or at a very reasonable cost.

You can get an application for Canadian citizenship from a Canadian Immigration Citizenship call centre or download it directly from: http://www.cic.gc.ca

Provincial Nomination

All provinces in Canada have a process whereby they have a more direct impact on attracting immigrants to supply worker shortages. Immigrants arrive in Canada with the goal of employment and perhaps permanent citizenship down the road. Simply apply directly to the province of your choice

Anyone applying via this program has the skills, education, and work experience to make an immediate contribution to the provincial economy. The criteria for provincial nomination are determined by the individual provinces and not the federal government, so they can change without notice. Therefore, it's important to monitor the web site regularly to note any changes. You'll find it here: www.cic.gc.gc/english/immigrate/provincila/index.asp

Canadian Citizenship

You can apply for Canadian Citizenship if you are: eighteen years of age, have been a permanent resident for three out of the previous four years, can communicate in English or French, and have basic knowledge of Canada -- including the rights and responsibilities of citizenship.

If you meet these requirements for Canadian citizenship, then you can get an application form from the call centre or download one here: http://www.cic.gc.ca

Home countries where visas are required

Immigrants from some countries and territories from around the world also need a visa in order to gain entry to Canada. The list of countries is too long to record here but is available on the web site: http://www.cic.gc.ca/english/visit/visas.asp

Immigrants need to understand that the government of Canada wants to maintain some control over people crossing the border and choosing to reside in this country. That's why additional documentation is required in some cases.

If you're applying to Canada as a Skilled Worker, you'll find the required application forms here: http://www.cic.gc.ca/englishinformation/applications/index.asp

Before hiring an immigration consultant or lawyer, take the time to seriously review the two web sites below to gain a better understanding of immigrating to Canada.
www.cic.gc.ca/english
www.canadavisa.com

These two web sites are loaded with all the relevant information, guides, forms, and questions and answers. If the immigrant can master this information from the government web site, they could certainly fill out their own forms and save money in the process.

Trades

To learn about internationally-trained trades people, visit:
www.edu.gov.on.ca/eng/training/foreign.html

For information about apprenticeships and a list of all the trades in Ontario, visit:
www.apprenticesearch.com and click on the "About Trades" link.

If you are interested in pursuing a career in one of the trades, contact the Ministry of Training, Colleges and Universities for Ontario. The ministry's Workplace Support Services office manages apprenticeship training and regulations.

Workplace Support Services Office
Toronto District Office
625 Church Street, 1st Floor, Toronto
416-326-5800

A full list of jobs under pressure in Alberta and British Columbia is at the following site:
www.paceimmigration.com/canadian /jobs_in_demand.php

Major City Services across Canada
For an inventory of Programs and Services offered by individual cities in Canada, visit:
www.ipds.iwin.ca

Language Training in English
Language Instruction for Newcomers to Canada (LINC) Program
Community Development Council Durham
134 Commercial Avenue
Ajax, Ontario L1S 2H5
905-686-2001 www.durhamLINC.ca

Assessment Centre
Centre for Language Training
263 Queen Street, Unit 14,
Brampton, Ontario, L6W 4K6
905-595-0722 x4101 www.tcet.com/clba

English Learning Centre
150 Central Park Drive, Suite #304
Brampton,On
905-790-1910

English Learning Centre
3075 Ridgeway Drive, Unit 5
Mississauga
905-828-2001

YMCA- Rexdale Youth Resource Centre
1530 Albion Road, Suite 83
Etobicoke, Ontario M9V 1B4
416-741-8714 www.ymcatoronto.org

Language Instruction for Newcomers to Canada (LINC)
West End of Toronto 416-397-6194
Central Toronto 416-397-6194
Scarborough 416-397-6046
North York 416-397-6591

Halton Assessment Centre
(Burlington, Oakville, Milton and Georgetown)
100 Elm Drive West
Mississauga, Ontario L5B 1L9
905-875-3851, x227

Assessment Centre
(Mississauga)
2 Robert Speck Parkway Suite 800
Mississauga, Ontario L4Z 1H8
905-279-0024 x1369   www.tcet.com/ciba

Catholic Crosscultural Services
LINC English Program
1200 Markham Road
2425 Eglinton Avenue
416-289-6766

Enhanced Language Training for Employment
500 Cummer Ave
540 Jones Ave
2267 Islington Ave
Toronto, On
416-395-3669

Enhanced Language training for Immigrant Women
2267 Islington Ave.
Etobicoke, On
416-396-4435
3660 Midland Ave, Suite 103
Scarborough, On
416-396-4434

YMCA
4580 Dufferin Street, 2nd Floor
North York, Ontario M3H 5Y2
416-635-9622   www.ymcatoronto.org

ILVARC
910-7th Avenue South West
Room 1401
Calgary, Alberta T2P 3N8
403-262-2656   www.calgaryimmigrantaid.ca

LARCC- Language Assessment Referral and Counselling Centre
10709-105th Street
Edmonton, Alberta TT5H 2X3
780-424-3545

Western ESL Services
208- 2525 Commercial Drive
Vancouver, BC V5N 4C1
604-876-5756

IELTS Testing Moncton
FutureInn
40 Lady Ada Blvd
Moncton, NB, E1C 8P2
506-852-9600

IELTS Administrator
8888 University Drive
Burnaby, B.C.
Vancouver, BC
V5A 1S6
604-291-5930

IELTS Kitchener
Conestoga College
299 Doon Valley Drive,
Kitchener, On

IELTS-Toronto
Humber College
205 Humber College Boulevard
Etobicoke, On

IELTS-Toronto
Centennial College
755 Morningside Avenue
Toronto, On

IELTS-Ottawa
Algonquin College
1385 Woodroffe Avenue,
Nepean, On

IELTS-London
Fanshawe College
1460 Oxford St. E.
London, On

IELTS Test Centre Halifax
English Canada World Organization
7071 Bayers Road
Halifax, Nova Scotia
B3L 2C2

Web sites:
www.conestogac.on.ca/ielts/testlocations.jsp
www.ielts.ca
www.csic-scci.ca
www.vec.ca/english

CIIP-An Agency in Your Home Country Helping You Immigrate To Canada and Find Work (Canadian Immigration Integration Project)

CIIP is a project funded by the Government of Canada and managed by the Association of Canadian Community Colleges. The project is designed to help immigrants under the federal Skilled Worker Program prepare for integration to the Canadian labour market while they are still in their country of origin completing final immigration requirements.

CIIP Locations
Services are offered free of charge in the following locations:
- Guangzhou, China
- New Delhi, India
- Manila, the Philippines

What Does CIIP Offer?
- Information on the Canadian labour market occupations, and the steps required for integration
- advice and guidance to assist in planning successful entry to the Canadian labour market
- practical assistance in identifying and contacting Canadian organizations for further assistance

Eligible applicants are informed about CIIP and provided with a registration form by Citizenship and Immigration Canada (CIC) during the final stages of the immigration process for the federal Skilled Worker Program.

Although I feel that Canada has a long way to go in its efforts to attract and integrate immigrants into Canadian business and life, it is admirable that an organization such as CIIP exists. Throughout this book I've talked about the need for advance preparation and the amount of work that can be done prior to the immigrant coming to Canada. We have seen that such preparation makes the transition much smoother for he immigrant and his or her family. It also makes the initial years, when many of the problems and difficulties occur, more successful. I hope to see such programs expanded to other regions and countries because they are proactive in nature and address many of the difficulties that immigrants encounter when they arrive in Canada.

Through planning, preparation, and education, we could easily have more immigrants who are happy and productive from their first day in Canada. In the end, everyone benefits. We help the immigrant and in reality we help Canada become a stronger competitor in the global economy. The CIIP Project Head Office is located at the following address:

Association of Canadian Community Colleges
200-1223 Michael St. N.
Ottawa, Ontario
Canada, K1J 7T2
1-613-746-7506   ciip@accc.ca

Information and Technology Training
New Program preparing internationally educated professionals for Canada's Information and Technology Sector (ICT). A new program announced December 1, 2008 which was initiated by the Information and Communications Technology Council (ICTC) aims to improve the integration of internationally educated professionals (IEPs) into the Canadian Information and Technology workforce. Tools such as ICTC's on-line workshops will help internationally trained professionals integrate more easily into the Canadian workplace. The workshops will teach essential knowledge about working in Canada and include the process of coming to this country along with ICT employers need and resources available to improve competencies in this important business segment. For more information go to this web-site: www.icti-ctic.ca

Advice from the Experts
Erica Martin - Team Leader
Employment Settlement Specialists, Vaughan Welcome Centre
Erica Martin leads a team of Employment Settlement Specialists, working for Job Skills, at the Vaughan Welcome Centre for Immigrant Services. This Welcome Centre, funded by both the federal and provincial governments, is a collaboration of 5 agencies – COSTI, Catholic Community Services of York Region, Centre for Information and Community Services, Job Skills and Vaughan Neighbourhood Services. The Welcome Centre offers services and supports for newcomers and immigrants.

Over the past 8 years, Erica has held various positions within Employment Services including Skills Training, Resume Writing and Critiquing, and Job Development. She and her team assist newcomers and immigrants to develop the necessary skills to be to search for employment in the Canadian labour market.

The Welcome Centre provides the following core services to newcomers and immigrants:
1. Settlement and Integration Services
2. Language Training
3. Accreditation and Qualifications Assistance
4. Employment Supports

What is the most pressing concern of new immigrants today? Newcomers and immigrants want to start working immediately when they arrive in Canada. That's why the Welcome Centre Employment staff spends time showing clients how to search for work in Canada.

According to Erica, when a candidate conducts an organized job search, she/he is more successful in finding suitable employment quickly. As recommended throughout this book, much of the work can and should be done before the individual leaves their home country. By doing their background work ahead of time, the newcomer is better prepared for the implementation of their job search when they arrive in Canada.

Erica Martin offers the following recommendations to newcomers and immigrants:

1. Utilize any international brand work experience that you might have such as previous employment with national companies such as Coca Cola and IBM. Your experience with these companies is more easily understood by potential employers.

2. If you can speak multiple languages, other than English and French, be sure to highlight that skill. Speaking more than one language is often an advantage in the Canadian labour market as more companies are doing business globally and providing goods and services domestically to a growing ethnic clientele.

3. Do your homework – be sure to have your credentials and other employment related documents translated and the originals with you. Spend some time learning all you can about Canada and its customs.

4. Include only relevant information in your resume. In Canada personal information such as age, religion etc. should not be included on a resume.

5. Apply directly to those companies that you would want to work for. If you are loyal to various global brands, then apply to companies marketing those brands.

6. Network with your local community contacts and friends. Networking can be an effective tool in landing an unadvertised job that suits your skills and experience.

7. Look at all of Canada as a potential market for your skill. Expand your search beyond your immediate location. Be open to all possibilities and you increase your chances of success.

8. Conduct information interviews. Speak to as many professionals as possible to get a sense of what's going on in your industry or profession. Information is your greatest ally so gather all the relevant information you can that will prepare you for an interview.

Advice from the experts

Yacoub Idris

Yacoub Idris joined Microskills, a Toronto-based organization in 1999. There, he puts his own talent and abilities to use with job search workshops and job development skills for clients. His main focus is helping people develop their skill base so they'll be able to find rewarding employment.

Yacoub has a background in history, African studies, and teaching and diversified these skills with English as a second language certification, so that finding employment would be an easier task. Originally, Microskills was a women's counseling centre in 1984 and grew in size to become a premier service provider in the GTA for all refugees and immigrants. Today, Microskills assists over 15,000 people each year by providing its clients with employment and language skills, along with other training such as computer training to help people find jobs.

There are now several locations in the Toronto area. Their web site can be found at: http://www.microskills.cOM.

Some of the recommendations Yacoub makes for new immigrants include:

• Do your own research before coming to Canada. The internet is a powerful tool that can help immigrants make contacts, find job opportunities, discover what skills are most in demand, and determine the approximate costs of living in all areas of Canada before deciding to move yourself and your family.

• If you are part of a regulated profession, then deal with the regulatory body to find out exactly what they need to assess your qualifications so that you can do this research in your home country before you leave.

• Upgrade all of the skills that an employer is looking for before coming to Canada. This includes language skills, communication skills, computer skills, resume writing and interviewing skills.

• Research the labour market where you plan to seek employment, so you can assess the job situation in your particular field of expertise.

• Develop relationships with family, friends, employment agencies, and social agencies. Utilize people who can help and support you because they understand the challenges you are likely to encounter and can help you overcome them.

• Maintain a positive, upbeat attitude, even when things do not appear to be going well. Remember: Every potential employer only has your resume, phone calls, emails, and a personal interview to go by in their assessment of your talents and suitability to the position. Are you positive about working for their company?

Have you conveyed a good first impression? Will you make a good fit for this organization and become a strong member of their team? If you look depressed, frustrated, or angry, you cannot expect any employer to hire you when that's the impression you're conveying.

• Be open-minded and flexible in your answers because that will show adaptability in a team environment. That's a key quality that Canadian employers value highly. If an employer senses any type of rigidity on your part, it may be enough to take you out of contention for the position.

• Be careful not to indicate a feeling that you know everything, even if you've had extensive training. Learning is a lifelong experience and we all learn throughout our careers.

• Learn how to handle rejection because rejection is a fact of life. Everyone encounters rejection at some point in their lives and most job searches are fraught with rejection – it goes with the territory. But don't take rejection personally. You may be rejected for the job for any number of reasons. But they're not rejecting you as a person. Employers are simply trying to find the best fit for their respective organizations. If you're not offered the job, simply thank them and move on. If you stick to it with positive expectations, success will eventually be yours.

• Establish relationships in your field such as professional associations, editors of industry publications, and other key contacts in your area of specialty.

• Every new immigrant should try to develop and nurture associations in your community, profession, church, mosque, etc. Say 'hello' to your neighbours. Every human being you meet could be a valuable contact, with the potential to provide you with key information like job leads.

• Canada will need many immigrants with skilled trades over the coming years. If you're part of a skilled trade, be sure to keep your apprenticeship or trade papers up to date. Continue working to improve your language skills as you do your research.

• Build a relationship with a Canadian employment agency that will be seeking targeted job matches for you and keeping you updated on opportunities in your field and location of choice.

• Be sure to follow up with each of your contacts and stay focused on finding the job you want.

• It may seem like it's a lot of work. But keep in mind that your efforts in the end will mean that you will avoid having to take any job just to make ends meet. The upfront work you do before you leave your home country is the best insurance against disappointment when you arrive in Canada.

• Don't be afraid to enter into a conversation because every point of contact has the potential to provide information on jobs, costs, places to save money, and so on. Communicate with other people at every opportunity. In effect, what you're doing is building your own network and tapping into new sources of information.

• Never underestimate your skills. You know what you're capable of and it's up to you to market yourself to potential employers. Be confident in your own skills and abilities.

• Make yourself marketable in diversified fields. Expand your horizons. Many skills are interchangeable and can be applied in a multitude of ways. Be open to any opportunity where you can utilize your skills.

• Make yourself visible at events and functions in your field of interest. Build your network of contacts and industry insiders.

• Volunteer for projects in your field of interest, your community, your church, temple, or mosque. Networking is important. Many jobs are never advertised, but are filled through interpersonal contact only.

Develop a relationship with people at various agencies. These people understand your situation because many of them have been through it themselves and often they get a charge out of helping you move forward in your life. You'll find that a lot of these people are dedicated to their work and committed to serving others. They want to help you and see you develop. Start building and nurturing these relationships today.

Even if things get frustrating, try to maintain the right attitude. You know what you want and you're moving toward it. Most of the obstacles in your way are mere speed-bumps, not roadblocks. Keep moving forward with positive expectations. Maintain an upbeat attitude and convey a level of self confidence. That's what employers want to see.

Ontario Settlement Information
www.settlement.org/site/REGIONS/home.asp

Peel Multicultural Council is an umbrella organization working with 150 agencies, institutions, and multicultural groups in Peel region which includes Mississauga and Brampton.
www.peelmc.com

Canadian Newcomer Magazine
222 Parkview Hill Cres.
Toronto, On M4B 1R8
Single Issue subscriptions:
email: subscribe@cnmag.ca otherwise copies are available at many immigrant serving agencies
www.cnmag.ca feedback@cmmag.ca

The Chang School-Ryerson University
Over 1200 courses offered
Toronto,On 416-979-5035
www.ryerson.ca/cenewcomer

Skills for Change
791 St. Clair Avenue West
Toronto, On M6C 1B8
416-658-3101   www.skillsforchange.org

South Asian Services Directory
www.action.wev.ca/home/cassa/agencies.shtml
Hamilton Centre for Civic Inclusion (HCCI)
HCCI is a community based civic resource centre. HCCI develops and shares training and education resources along with being a support mechanism for newcomer immigrant and refugee communities of diverse ethnic groups.

LIUNA Station, Lower Concourse
360 James ST. N.
Hamilton, On L8L 1H5
905-667-7502   www.hcci.ca info@hcci.ca

For a list of all of the agencies helping Newcomers to Canada (excluding Quebec which is in French and English at www.immigration-quebec.gouv.qc.ca0 refer to the following web site created by the Canadian Foundation for Economic Education (CFEE) www.cfeedayplanner.com/en/org.php?a=all

Key Immigrant Serving Organizations in the GTA (Greater Toronto Area)
ACCES (Accessible Community Counseling & Employment Services)
Suite 250, 2100 Ellesmere Road
Scarborough, On M1H 3B7
$16-431-5326   www.accestrain.com

African Training and Employment Centre
Suite 110, 1440 Bathurst Street
Toronto, On M5R 3J3
416-653-2274

Arab Community Centre of Toronto
555 Burnhamthorpe Road, Suite #209
Etobicoke, On M9C 2Y3
416-231-7746   www.arabtoronto.com

Bloor Information and Life Skills Centre
#314-672 Dupont Street
Toronto, On M6G 1Z6
416-531-4613

Brampton Multicultural Community Centre
Suite 107, 150 Central Park drive
Brampton, On L6T 2T9
905-790-8482   www.bmcentre.org

Brampton Neighbourhood Resource Centre
Unit 24, 50 Kennedy Road South
Brampton, On L6W 3R7
905-452-1262   www.bnrc.org

Catholic Cross-Cultural Services-Metro Region
55 Town Centre Ct. Suite 401
Scarborough, On M1P 4X4
416-757-7010

Catholic Cross-Cultural Services-Peel Region
10 Gillingham Dr. Suite 211
Brampton, On L6X5A5
905-457-7740

Catholic Cross-Cultural Services
1200 Markham Rd, Suite 503
Toronto, On M1H 3C3
416-289-6766

Catholic Cross-Cultural Services
90 Dundas St West, Suite 204
Mississauga, On L5B 2T5
905-273-4140

The **CENTRE** Skills Development and Training (The Centre has 6 modern professional locations in the GTA (Greater Toronto Area)

Burlington
The Bay Area Learning Centre
860 Harrington Court,
Burlington, On
905-333-3499

Georgetown - Georgetown Employment Partners Centre
184 Guelph Street,
Georgetown, On
905-702-7311

Malton (North East Mississauga) - The Centre for Skills Development and Training
3233 Brandon Gate Drive, Unit 9
Mississauga, On
905-405-8118

Milton Employment Partners Centre
Southview Plaza
550 Ontario Street South, Suite 203
Milton, On L9T 5E4
905-693-8458

Mississauga
The Centre for Skills Development and Training
33 City Centre Drive, Suite 201
Mississauga, On L56 2N5
905-276-6336

Oakville
The Centre for Skills Development and Training
465 Morden Road, Suite 109
Oakville, On L6K 3W6
905-845-1157

CAMP - Communications, Advertising and Marketing Professionals (CAMP)
CAMP is a networking organization of internationally trained professionals in the communications, advertising, and marketing sectors, located in the Toronto region.
info@campnetworking.ca

Canadian Cooperative for Language and Cultural Studies
635 Markham Road, 2nd Floor
Toronto, On M6G 2M1
416-588-3900   www.ccics.icomm.ca

Career Bridge - Internships for Internationally Qualified Professionals
Career Bridge is an innovative internship program designed to address the problem of "No Canadian experience."
Toronto Office
416-977-EDGE (3343)   info@careerbridge.ca

Catholic Community Services of York
21 Dunlop Street
Richmond Hill, On L4C 2M6
905-770-7040   www.ccsyr.org

Centennial College
School of Engineering Technology and Applied Science
941 Progress Avenue
Toronto, On M1G 3T8
416-289-5300   www.centennialcollege.ca

Centre for Education and Training
Suite 800, Robert Speck Parkway
Mississauga, On L4Z 1H8
905-949-0049   www.tcet.com

Centre for Information and Community Services
#310, 3852 Finch Avenue East
Scarborough, On M1T 3T9
416-299-8118   www.cicscanada.com

Chinese Association of Mississauga
(Offering services such as settlement services and programs for Newcomers living in the Mississauga area)
Unit 80, 1177 Central Parkway West
Mississauga, On, L5C 4P3

Community Information Toronto/FindHelp Information Services
425 Adelaide St. W. 2nd floor
Toronto, On M5V 3C1
www.findhelp.ca

Corbrook
Corbrook is a non-profit organization dedicated to providing meaningful work for people who face barriers to employment due to disabilities and injuries.
581 Trethewey Drive
Toronto, On
416-245-5565

Dufferin-Peel Catholic District School Board - South
B.J. Fleming Catholic Adult Learning Centre
870 Queen St. West
Mississauga, On
905-891-3034

North
St. Gabriel Adult Learning Centre
3750 Brandon Gate Drive
Mississauga, On
905-362-0701

India Rainbow Community Service of Peel
3038 Hurontario St. Suite 206, Mississauga, On
905-275-2369
9446 McLaughlin Road, Unit 1, Brampton, On
905-454-2598

MicroSkills Development Centre
Community Programs and Services provide access to information and resources so that newcomers to Canada can achieve full participation in community life.
1 Vulcan Street
Etobicoke, On M9W 1L3
416-247-7181   www.microskills.ca

COSTI - Head Office
(COSTI offers services in the following categories and are listed in the GTA area. Children and Youth, Employment, Family and Mental Health, Housing, Language Training, Seniors, Settlement/Immigration, Skills Training, Vocational Rehabilitation, Women's Issues)
1710 Dufferin Street
Toronto, On M6E 3P2
416-658-1600   www.costi.org

COSTI - Brampton and Caledon Employment Centre
10 Gillingham Drive
Suite 300
Brampton, On L6X 5A5

COSTI - Caledonia Centre
Also Centre for Internationally Trained Professionals and Tradespeople
700 Caledonia Road
Toronto, On
416-789-7925

Corvetti - Education Centre
760 College Street
Toronto, On M6G 1C4

COSTI - Dufferin Mall Employment Centre
900 Dufferin Street, Suite 206
Toronto, On M6H 4A9
416-588-2240

COSTI - Concord/Vaughan/North Toronto
7800 Jane St
Concord, On L4K 4R6
905-669-5627   vaughan@costi.org   www.costi.org
COSTI - Markham Employment Resource Centre
4961 Highway 7
Markham, On
905-567-0482

COSTI - Language, Employment & Skills Training Services, Richmond Hill
129 Church St South
Richmond Hill, On L4C 1W4
905-884-5235

COSTI - Employment Group Sessions
900 Dufferin Street, Suite 1
Toronto, On M6H 4A9
416-588-2240

COSTI - Employment Services for Internationally Trained Professionals
2150 Meadowvale Blvd. Unit 2
Mississauga, On L5N 5S3
905-567-0482

COSTI - Job Search Workshop
1710 Dufferin Street
Toronto, On M6E 3P2
416-658-7499
COSTI - Language & Skills Training Services
8515 McCowan Road
Markham, On L3P 5E4
905-472-4688

COSTI - North York Centre
Sheridan Mall
1700 Wilson Ave. Suite 114
Toronto, On M3L 1B2
416-244-0480
COSTI - Scarborough Centre
55 Town Centre Suite 521
Scarborough, On M1P 4X4
416-296-9393

Culturelink
Suite 300, 160 Springhurst Avenue
Toronto, On M6K 1C2
416-588-6288   www.culturelink.net

Durham Region- Pickering, Ajax, Whitby, Oshawa
Language Instruction for Newcomers to Canada
1-866-550-5462   www.durhamLINC.ca

Employment Centre for International Professionals - Seneca College
3660 Midland Avenue, 2nd Floor
Scarborough, On M1V 4V3
416-299-6625 x264

Goodwill Job Shop Program
2425 Eglinton Avenue East, Suite 300
Scarborough, On M1K 5G8
416-285-8876

Humber Institute of Technology & Advanced Learning
Centre for Internationally Trained Professionals
1620 Albion Road, 2nd Floor,
Etobicoke, On M9V 4B4
416-745-0281

Intercultural Neighbourhood Social Services
Suite 200M, 3050 Confederation Parkway
Mississauga, On M2R 3V3
905-273-4884

Jewish Immigrant Aid Services of Canada
Suite 306, 4580 Dufferin Street
Toronto, On M3H 5Y2
416-630-9051   www.jias.org

Job Start
2930 Lakeshore Boulevard West
Etobicoke, On M8V 1J4
416-231-2295   www.jobstart-cawl.org

JVS of Greater Toronto, 74 Tycos Drive
Toronto, On M6B 1V9
416-661-3010   www.jvstoronto.org

Korean Community Services
5734 Yonge St. 2nd Floor
North York, On M2M 4E7

Learning Enrichment Foundation
116 Industry Street
Toronto, On M6M 4L8
416-769-0830   www.lefca.org

Markus Garvey Centre for Leadership and Education
160 Rivaldo Road
Toronto, On
416-740-4557   www.mgcle.com

Muslim Community Services (MCS)
150 Central Park Dr. Ste. 304
Brampton, ON L6T 2T9
905-790-1910   www.muslimcommunity.org/

Mississauga Community Connections
33 City Centre Drive, #280
Hurontario and Robert Speck
905-896-2233   www.connectionsemployment.ca

Mississauga Employment Services for Internationally Trained Professionals & Tradespeople
2150 Meadowvale Blvd. Unit 2
Mississauga, On
905-567-0482

Newcomer Information Centre - Mississauga
2 Robert Speck Parkway Suite 800
Mississauga, On L4Z 1H8
905-279-0024 x1266

Newcomer Information Centre - Brampton East Suite
263 Queen Street East Unit 14
Brampton On L6W 4K6
905-595-0722 x4000

Newcomer Information Centre - Brampton South Side
7700 Hurontario Street Suite 300
Brampton, On L6Y 4M3
905-457-4747 x3013

Newcomer Services for Youth
3424 Weston Road
Toronto, On M9M 2W1
416-395-2045

Newcomer Services for Youth
4383 Kingston Road
Toronto, On M1E 2N2
416-396-5323

Newcomer Magazine and Settlement Guide for Toronto and Southern Ontario
1450 O'Connor Dr. Bldg 2, STE 105C
Toronto, On M4B 2T8
www.cnmag.ca

Northwood Neighbourhood Services
2625 Weston Rd. Building D, 2nd Floor, Unit27
Toronto, On M9N 3V8
416-748-0788   www.northw.ca

Ontario Works in Peel - Brampton
21 Coventry Road
Brampton, On L6T 4V7
906-793-9200 x8203

Ontario Works in Peel - Mississauga
6715 Millcreek Drive, Unit 4
Mississauga, On L5N 5V2
905-793-9200 x8427

Ontario Works in Peel - Mississauga- Peel Youth Village
99 Acorn Place
Mississauga, On L4Z 4E2
905-791-5576 x6

Peel Adult Learning Centre
Immigration Settlement and Adaptation Program (ISAP)
165 Dundas Street West, Suite 202
Mississauga, On L5B 2N6

Polycultural Immigrant & Community Services - Etobicoke
3363 Bloor St W
Etobicoke,On M8X 1G2
416-233-5141

Polycultural Immigrant & Community Services - Toronto
15 Roncesvalles Avenue, Suite 202
Toronto, On M6R 2K2
416-533-9471

Polycultural Immigrant & Community Services - Mississauga
2225 Erin Mills Parkway
Mississauga, On L5K 1T9
905-403-8860

Polycultural Immigrant & Community Services
3174 Eglinton Avenue East
Scarborough, On M1J 2H5
416-261-4901

Proconnect
20 Crown Steel drive, Unit 15
Markham, On L3R 9X9
905-948-0572

Toronto Chinese Community Services Association
Suite 301, 310 Spadina Avenue
Toronto, On M5T 2E8
416-977-4026   www.tccsa.on.ca

Working Skills Centre
350 Queen's Quay West Suite 204
Toronto, On
416-703-7770

Vietnamese Community Centre of Mississauga
1023 Greaves Avenue
Mississauga, On L5E 1W3
905-275-9143

Welcome Centre Immigration Service
(The Welcome centre will provide settlement and employment support services and language training, accreditation and qualification assistance)
9100 Jane Street (Rutherford and Jane)

Vaughan
Funded by Citizenship and Immigration Canada
www.WelcomeCentre.ca

Woodgreen Community Services
Employment Resource Centre 1080 Queen St. E. **Toronto** 416-462-3110
Immigrant Services 815 Danforth Ave **Toronto** 416-462-3110
Youth Job Centre, 989 Danforth Ave. **Toronto** 416-462-3110
East York Employment Resource Centre, 1450 O'Connor Drive, Building 1, Unit 4, 416-615-1515
Immigrant Services,1491 Danforth Avenue, **Toronto**, On, 416-645-6000
Neighbourhood Services, 69 Pape Avenue, **Toronto**, On. , 416-469-5211
Youth Job Centre, 989 Danforth Avenue, **Toronto,** On., M4J 1M1
www.woodgreen.org

World Education Services
Validates credentials and academic equivalents
45 Charles Street East, Suite 700
Toronto ON M4Y 1S2
416-972-0070   www.wes.org/ca

YWCA - Skills Development Centre
3090 Kingston Road Suite 300
Toronto, On M1M 1P2
416-261-0114

YMCA North York Newcomer Centre
4580 Dufferin St. 2nd Floor
North York, On M3H 5Y2
416-630-0330 x189

YMCA Scarborough Newcomer centre
10 Milner business court Suite 600
Scarborough On M1B 3C6
416-609-0218 x 242
YMCA North-East Scarborough - Employment Resource Centre
5635 Finch Avenue East
Scarborough ON M1B 5K9
416-335-5490

YMCA Etobicoke Employment resource Center
1530 Albion Road Unit 83
Toronto, On M9V 1B4
416-741-8714 x218

YMCA Korean Community services
721 Bloor St West Unit 303
Toronto, On M6G 1L5
416-538-9412

YMCA - North York Newcomer Centre
4580 Dufferin St. 2nd Floor
North York, ON M3H 5Y2
416-630-0330 x189
647-288-0249
YMCA Toronto Newcomer Centre
42 Charles St. E 3rd Floor
Toronto, On M4Y 1T4
416-928-6690

Settlement Guide to Southern Ontario
A Directory of Basic Settlement Services
A Guide to ESL Services(English as a Second Language)
A Guide to Employment Services
A Guide to Employment Assessment

Fast Track to Technology Occupations Programs for the Internationally-Trained Individual:
www.sheridaninstitute.ca/ftto

Toronto District School Board- Transition to Employment
Toronto Central 416-395-8783
Toronto South   416-396-2301
Toronto North   416-395-5104

For online and telephone access to Toronto-area information including articles, job searches, careers, education and training, toolkits for resume writing, employment counseling, job fairs, workshops and information sessions, click the links below. Included is a data base of social service agencies within the city of Toronto, to help you with all of your needs as a new arrival.
www.poss.ca   www.211Toronto.ca
Toronto directory of community, social, health & government agencies:
www.21/toronto.ca

Possibilities: Toronto's Online Employment Resource Centre:
www.poss.ca/features/

TRIEC - Toronto Region Immigrant Employment Council
(This council is working to better integrate skilled immigrants into the labour market. By partnering with employers, community organizations, and other groups TRIEC has been able to help many skilled immigrants)
Phone: 416-944-1946 Web site: www.hireimmigrants.ca

Recently newly inducted Canadian citizens in the GTA (Greater Toronto Area) have received a free year long family pass to six of Toronto's major cultural institutions. This package is called the Cultural Access Pass.
The pass is designed to let new Canadian citizens and their families visit cultural

institutions in the Toronto area. The institutions included are: Art Gallery of Ontario, Gardiner Museum, MacMichel Canadian Art Collection, Ontario Science Centre, Royal Ontario Museum and the Textile museum of Canada.

More information is available at your citizenship ceremony and from the institutions. The plan is to incorporate similar passes in other cities across Canada.

Be sure to obtain a copy of "A Newcomer's Guide to Services in Peel, Halton and Dufferin" -- Phone Toll Free-1-800-431-7774 or visit their website: www.phdtrain.com Peel (Mississauga and Brampton) Halton (Oakville, Burlington, Milton) and Dufferin (Orangeville)

Housing Services – Toronto
Catholic Cross-Cultural Services
90 Dundas Street West, Suite 204,
Mississauga,On
905-273-4140   www.ccspeel.org

Chinese Association of Mississauga - Golden Square Centre 1177
Central Pkwy W Unit 80-81
Mississauga, On
905-275-8558   cam@ipoline.com

India Rainbow Community Services of Peel
3038 Hurontario Street Suite 206
Mississauga, On L5B 3B9
905-275-2369   ircs@indiarainbow.org

Polycultural Immigrant and Community Services - Sheridan Mall
2225 Erin Mills Pkwy 2nd Floor
Mississauga, On
905-403-8860

African Community Services of Peel
20 Nelson Street West, Lower Level, Suite 102
Brampton, On L6X 2M5
905-460-9514

Halton Multicultural Council
905-842-2486 x221   www.halton-multicultural.org

Muslim Community Centre- Brampton - Civic Centre
150 Central Park Dr., 3rd Floor
Brampton, On
905-790-8482   info@muslimcommunity.org

Community Services Dufferin Orangeville
229 Broadway
Orangeville, On
519-941-6991

Employment Agency - Greater Toronto Area

There are different methods of finding employment in the Toronto area such as Workopolis, Newspaper Ads, word of mouth, and Employment agencies.

Topnotch Employment Services Inc. has been placing people in the Greater Toronto Area in positions ranging from management to administrative to clerical and general labour for over 15 years.

The Topnotch goal is to make employment opportunities equally accessible through the continuous promotion of employment diversity at all levels of society. In order to achieve this goal, Topnotch has undertaken a dedicated exercise in establishing key relationships with corporate Canada and all levels of government, where we have demonstrated that diversity in employment is a benefit to all.

Topnotch Group of Companies plays a leading role in continuously promoting the values and richness of our diverse multicultural society through its established employment service.

With over 15 years of service to the community we have acquired the knowledge, expertise and professionalism to assist you with your job search. Our service to you is free of any cost.

Call us: 416-741-2770
Fax your resume: 416-741-0069
Email your resume: sandy@topnotchempoyment.com
Visit us in person: 2365 Finch Ave. W. Suite 206 & 207
(Southwest corner of Finch and Weston Rd.)
Visit our web site: www.topnotchemployment.com

Web Sites

www.ips.iwin.ca – Inventory of programs and service
http://peel.cioc.ca- Peel Community Information Database
www.hipinfo.info-Halton-Community Services Database for Halton

Alberta Organizations serving Immigrants and New Canadians

Agape Language Centre
16 Bermuda Drive Northwest
Calgary, AB T3K 1H7
403-516-1846

ASSIST Community Services
9653 105-A Avenue
Edmonton, AB T5H 0M3
780-429-3111   www.assistcsc.org

Calgary Immigrant Aid Society
1200 910-7 Avenue Southwest
Calgary, AB T2P 3N8
403-265-1120   www.calgaryimmigrantaid.ca

Calgary Immigrant Educational Society
1723 40th Street E.
Calgary, AB T2A 4Z6
403-263-4414   www.learning-resource.com/fundinglist.php

Calgary Mennonite Centre for Newcomers
#125, 920 - 36 Street N.E.
Calgary, AB T2A 6L8

Centre for Newcomers
125, 920 - 36 Street N.E.
Calgary, AB T2A 6L8
403-569-3325   www.cmcn.ab.ca

Changing Together
#3rd floor, 10010-105 St
Edmonton, AB T5J 1C4
780-421-0175   www.changingtogether.com

Edmonton Catholic Schools, ESL Centre
10210-115 Avenue
Edmonton, AB T5G 0L8
780-989-3025   www.ecsd.net

Edmonton Immigrant Service Association (EISA)
Suite 201, 10720-113 Street
Edmonton, AB T5H 3H8
780-474-8445   www.eisa-edmonton.org

Edmonton Mennonite Centre for Newcomers
#101m 10010-107A Avenue
Edmonton, AB T5H 4H8
780-423-9685   www.emcn.ab.ca

Indo-Canadian Women's Centre
335 Tower 2, Millbourne mall
38th Avenue
Edmonton, AB T6K 3L2
780-462-6924

YMCA Calgary
101-3rd Street S.W.
Calgary, AB T2P 4G6
403-237-9622   www.Calgary.ymca.ca

Settlement Services - British Columbia

British Columbia offers a welcoming environment to people of all origins and ensures that the programs are successful by providing funding. Some resource agencies in the Vancouver area are listed below. A complete list of all British Columbia agencies is on the web site:
 www.ag.gov.bc.ca/immigration/sam/agencies.htm

The immigrant population in British Columbia was 515,835 in 1991. By 2001, it had risen to 791,620. Commonly spoken languages in BC other than English include: Cantonese, Mandarin and Punjabi.

60% of immigrants who were born in Asia have settled in British Columbia. The top 3 occupations for male immigrants in BC in 2001 were: sales and service, professional occupations in natural and applied science, and transportation equipment operators. The top three female occupations at the same time were: clerical, sales and service, and retail sales.

Vancouver is the most livable city in the world, with Toronto ranking fifth -- according to a survey conducted by the Economist Intelligence Unit. Some of the larger cities in the world did not make the list because of higher congestion, costs and crime rates.

Vancouver has consistently ranked number one in the survey since 2004. Toronto has scored a top six placement every year since 2004. The Economist's selection criteria included such things as transportation and communications, and low crime rates and incidences of terrorism.

Career Bridge is an innovative internship program designed to address the problem of "No Canadian experience."
Career Bridge - Vancouver Office
604-601-8521   infovancouver@careerbridge.ca

Collingwood Neighbourhood House Society
5288 Joyce Street
Vancouver, BC V5R 6C9
604-435-0323

Immigrant Services Society of British Columbia (ISS-Drake Street Location)
530 Drake Street
Vancouver, BC V6B 2H2
604-684-7498

Immigrant Services Society of British Columbia (ISS- Terminal Avenue location)
#501-333 Terminal Avenue
Vancouver, BC V6A 2L7
604-694-2561
Jewish Family Service Agency of Vancouver
305-1985 West Broadway
Vancouver, BC V6J 4Y3
604-254-5401

Kiwassa Neighbourhood Services Association
2425 Oxford Street
Vancouver, BC V5K 1M7
604-879-7104

Little Mountain Neighbourhood House
3981 Main Street
Vancouver, BC V5V 3P3
604-254-9626

M.O.S.A.I.C. Multi-Lingual Orientation Service Association for Immigrant Communities
2nd Floor, 1720 Grant Street
Vancouver, BC V5L 2Y7
604-254-9626

Multicultural Helping House Society
4802 Fraser Street
Vancouver, BC
604-879-3277

Pacific Immigrant Resources Society
#205- 2929 Commercial Drive
Vancouver, BC V5N 4C8
604-298-5888

Progressive Intercultural Community Services Society
200- 8161 Main Street
Vancouver, BC V5X 3L2
604-324-7733

South Vancouver Neighbourhood House
6470 Victoria drive
Vancouver, BC V5P 3X7
604-324-6212

Storefront Orientation Services
96 East Broadway, Suite #212
Vancouver, BC V5T 4N9
604-255-1881

Success (Head Office)(United Chinese Community Enrichment Services Society)
28 West Pender Street
Vancouver, BC V6B 1R6
604-408-7255

Success (Fraser Service Centre)
5834 Fraser Street
Vancouver, BC V5W 2Z5
604-324-1900

Success (Granville Street Mandarin Service Centre)
203- 8268 Granville Street
Vancouver, BC V6P 4A4

Most newcomers to Canada are initially attracted to the three biggest cities- Toronto, Montreal and Vancouver. The two biggest English speaking cities -- Toronto and Vancouver -- may have lost some of their lustre due to higher living costs than other medium-sized Canadian cities.

It is projected that many Canadians and immigrants in the coming years will choose the medium-sized cities in which to settle including Halifax, London, Windsor, Sudbury, Winnipeg, Saskatoon, Regina, Calgary, Edmonton and Victoria and Quebec City for French speaking immigrants..

All of the mid-size cities have diverse multi-ethnic populations and range in total population size from approximately 100,000 to one million people. Visit the web sites of each province and territory to see what these communities have to offer. To locate specific web sites for each region, visit: www.canada.gc.ca/other gov/prov_e.html

Settlement Services - Quebec
The following web sites provide information for immigrants needing assistance in the province of Quebec.
www.immigration-quebec.gouv.qc.ca
www.cic.gc.ca/french or english
www.akccanada.com
www.immigration-quebec.gouv.qc.ca/en/partners/services-offered.html

Immigrants requesting information or planning to settle in the province of Quebec should realize that very soon in the process their information will be provided to them in the French language because that is the working language in the province. Although it would be beneficial for you to be bilingual in French and English the immigrant candidate will find that French is principally used and much of the information that they receive will be in French on the web sites.

The following information is for specific immigrant serving organizations in Montreal and Quebec City.

Montreal, Quebec

Montreal Sud-Quest
Centre d'education et de development intercultural (CED)
3429, Rue Notre-Dame Quest, 1er etage
Montreal, Quebec H4C 1P3
514-522-8188   info@cedi.ca

Montreal Verdun - CASA-CAFI (Centre d'aide aux familles immigrantes)
4741, rue De Verdun,
Montreal, Quebec H4G 1M9
514-844-3340   casacafi@msn.com

Montreal Ville-Marie - AMPE-CITI clef pour integration au travail des immigrants
1595, rue Saint-Hubert, bureau 300,
Montreal, Quebec H2L 3Z2
514-987-1759   yann.hairaud@ampecil.ca

Montreal Villeray - CLAM(Carrefour de liason et d'aide multi-ethnique)
7290, rue Hutchison, 2e etage
Montreal, Quebec H3N 1Z1
514-271-8207   clam@bellnet.ca

Montreal Westmount - Centre social d'aide aux immigrants
4285, boulevard De Maisonneuve Quest,
Montreal, Quest
Montreal, Quebec H3Z 1K7
514-932-2963   mgobas.casai@bellnet.ca

Montreal Ahuntsic-Cartierville - Carrefour d'aide aux nouveaux arrivants
10780, rue Laverdure
Montreal, Quebec H3L 2L9
514-382-0735   infocana@can-montreal.org

Montreal Anjou - Carrefour solidarite-Anjou
8330, avenue Chenier, sale 11
Anjou, Quebec H1K 2B6
514-355-4417   camefoursolidarite@qc.aira.com

Montreal- Cote-des-Neiges-Notre-Dame-de-Grace
Centre multi-ethnique de Notre-Dame-de-Grace
6525, avenue Somerlaed, bureau 3
Montreal, Quebec H4V 1S7
514-486-7465   aymanaskar@cmendg.com

Montreal LaSalle
Centre P.R.I.S.M.E (Promotion, reference, information et services multi-ethniques)
414, rue Lafleur, bureau 1.10, 2e etage
Montreal, Quebec H8R 3H6
514-364-0939   pavoned@centreprisme.net

Montreal Mercier-Hochelaga-Maisonneuve - Accueil liason pour arrivants (ALPA)
1490, Avenue de LaSalle
Montreal, Quebec H1V 2J5
514-255-3900   alpaong@total.net

Montreal Plateau-Mont-Royal - Centre d'action socio-communautaire de Montreal
32, Boulevard Saint-Joseph Ouest
Montreal, Quebec H2T 2P3
514-842-8045   amrodrigues.cascm@bellnet.ca

Montreal Rosemont-L Petit-Patrie - Programme regional d'integration
CARI BLE
7030, Rue Saint-Denis,
Montreal, Quebec H4L 3M8
514-748-2007   carist@cari.qc.ca

Montreal St. Laurent - Programme d'accompagnement des nouveaux arrivants
CARI St-Laurent
1179 Boulevard Decarie, bureau 10
Montreal, Quebec H4L 3M8
carisi@cari.qc.ca

Montreal- Saint-Leonard - Programme d'accompagnement des nouveaux arrivants
5960, Rue Jean-Talon Est, bureau 110
Montreal, Quebec H1S 1M2
514-723-4939   aiem@qc.aira.com

Quebec City, Quebec
Centre Multiethnique de Quebec Inc
369, Rue de la Couronne 3e etage
Quebec, Quebec G1K 6E9
418-687-9771   cmq@wenet.ca

SOIIT Quebec - Service d'orientation it d'integration des immigrants au travail de Quebec
275, Rue du Parvis, bureau 300,
Quebec, Quebec G1K 6G7
418-648-0822   b-p.toure@soiit.qc.ca

Following is a list of language agencies that can be of help if you are considering immigrating to Quebec:

YMCA of Greater Montreal International Language School
1440 Stanley Street, 5th Floor
Montreal, Quebec H3A 1P7

International Language Schools of Canada
1134 Ste. Catherine, West
Montreal, Quebec H3B 1H4

Halifax, Nova Scotia
Metropolitan Immigrant Settlement Association - Chebucto Place
7105 Chebucto Road, Suite 201
Halifax, Nova Scotia B3L 4W8
902-423-3607   www.misa.ns.ca

Halifax Immigrant Learning Centre
Suite 201, 7105 Chebucto Road
Halifax, NS B3L 4W8
902-443-2937

Halifax Regional School Board- Adult ESL
Room 116A, 1929 Robie Street
Halifax, NS B3H 3G1
902-421-7779   www.hrsb.ns.ca/ESL

YMCA of Greater Halifax/Dartmouth- YMCE Centre for Immigrant Programs
65 Main Avenue
Halifax, NS B3M 1A4
902-457-9622   www.ymcahrm.ns.ca/contact.html

Ottawa, Ontario
YMCA-YWCA Language Assessment and Referral Centre
240 Catherine Street, Suite 308
Ottawa, On K2P 2G8
613-238-5462   www.ymcaywca.ca/Larc2

YMCA/YWCA Ottawa Carleton
4th Floor, 180 Argyle Avenue
Ottawa, On K2P 1B7
613-238-5462   www.educom.on.ca/ymca-ywca/
Caldwell Family Resource Centre
Unit 22, 1100 Medford Street
Ottawa, On K1Z 8L5
613-724-6052

London, Ontario
Cross-Cultural Learners Centre
505 Dundas Street East, 2nd floor
London, On N6B 1W4
519-432-1133

Thames Valley District School Board - Wheable Centre for Adult Education
70 Jacqueline Street
London, On N5Z 3P7
519-452-8770   www.tvdsb.on.ca

YMCA/YWCA London
382 Waterloo Street
London, On N6B 2N8
519-667-3306   www.londony.ca

Windsor, Ontario
English Testing Centre
1410 Quellette Avenue
Windsor, On N8X 5B2
519-253-2724
Windsor Women Working with Immigrant Women
135 Erie Street East
Windsor, On N9A 3W9
519-973-5588

Women's Enterprise Skills Training of Windsor
Suite 201, 647 Quellette Avenue
Windsor, On N9A 4J4
519-256-6621   www.westofwindsor.com

YMCA Windsor
500 Victoria Ave
Windsor, On N9A 4M8
519-256-7330   www.windsor.essex.ymca.ca

Sudbury, Ontario
Sudbury Multicultural and Folk Arts Association
196 Van Horne St
Sudbury, On P3E 1E5
705-674-0795   www.sudburymulticultural.org   www.mysudbury.ca/immigration

Winnipeg, Manitoba
Manitoba Department of Labour Immigration
5th floor- 213 Notre-Dame Avenue
Winnipeg, Manitoba R3B 1N3
204-945-6300   www.gov.mb.ca/labour/immigrate/
www.gov.mb.ca/labour/immigrate/settlement/firstweeks.html

Saskatoon, Saskatchewan
Citizenship and Immigration Canada
410-22nd Street East, Room 660
Saskatoon, Sk S7K 5T6
306-975-4619

Saskatoon Open Door Society
311-4th Avenue North
Saskatoon, Sk S7K 2L8
306-653-4464   www.sods.sk.ca

Global Gathering Place
#307, 506-25th Street East
Saskatoon, Sk S7K 4A7
306-665-0268   www.members.shaw.ca/goodsheep/ggp.html

Saskathewan Institute of Applied Science and Technology (STAST)- Kelsey Campus
P.O. Box 1520
Saskatoon, Sk S7K 3R5
306-933-8385   www.siast.sk.ca/kelsey

Saskatchewan Intercultural Association
 1702-20th Street, West
Saskatoon, Sk S7M 0Z9

Regina, Saskatchewan
The Assessment Centre - Canada Immigration Centre
1871 Hamilton Street
Regina, Saskatchewan S4P 2B9
306-780-7786

Regina Open Door Society
1855 Smith Street
Regina, Saskatchewan S4P 2N5
306-352-3500   www.accesscomm.ca?nonprofits/reg.open.dr

University of Regina
Language Institute Building, Room 211
3737 Wascana Parkway
Regina, Sk S4S 0A2
306-585-4585   www.uregina.ca/langinst/

Wilma Reitler
1871 Hamilton Street c/o CIC Regina
Regina, Sk S4P 2B9
306-780-7786   www.wirc.ca

Saskatchewan Institute of Applied Science and Technology (SIAST) - Wascana Campus
P.O. Box 556, 4500 Wascana Parkway
Regina, Sk S4P 3A3
306-798-1354   www.siast.sk.ca/wascana

Victoria, British Columbia
Intercultural Association of Greater Victoria
930 Balmoral Road
Victoria, BC V8T 1A8
250-388-4728   www.icavictoria.org
For labour market and housing information on many communities right across Canada, you can visit: www.directioncanada.gc.ca

Various Print Publications Containing Helpful Information For Immigrants
Newcomer Magazine and Settlement Guide
www.cnmag.ca

Canadian Immigrant
625 Church Street
Toronto Ontario M4Y 2G1
416-596-4393   www.canadianimmigrant.ca

Get relatives to send you copies of each magazine to your home country.

Immigrating to the East Coast Provinces
Prince Edward Island
The official government web site for Prince Edward Island can be found here:
http://www.gov.pe.ca/

Holland College
Montgomery Hall - Main Admissions Office
First floor, 305 Kent Street
Charlottetown, PE C1A 4Z1
902-629-4217   www.hollandc.pe.ca

PEI Association for Newcomers to Canada
P.O. Box 2846, 25 University Avenue
Charlottetown, PE C1A 8C4
902-628-6009   www.peianc.com

Nova Scotia
Employment Opportunities are available through the following web sites:
Civilian Careers with the Canadian Navy at: http://wwww.jobs.gc.ca
Government of Nova Scotia Executive Recruitment - email: PSC-Job-Apps@gov.ns.ca
        Opportunities Nova Scotia features ninety-five employers from across the province participated in phase 1 of the project. Over 2,300 were posted indicating that Nova Scotia has jobs to offer.
www.opportunitiesns.ca

Halifax, Nova Scotia
Metropolitan Immigrant Settlement Association - Chebucto Place
7105 Chebucto Road, Suite 201
Halifax, Nova Scotia B3L 4W8
902-423-3607   www.misa.ns.ca

Halifax Immigrant Learning Centre
Suite 201, 7105 Chebucto Road
Halifax, NS B3L 4W8
902-443-2937

Halifax Regional School board- Adult ESL
Room 116A, 1929 Robie Street
Halifax, NS B3H 3G1
902-421-7779   www.hrsb.ns.ca/ESL

YMCA of Greater Halifax/Dartmouth- YMCE Centre for Immigrant Programs
65 Main Avenue
Halifax, NS B3M 1A4
902-457-9622   www.ymcahrm.ns.ca/contact.html

New Brunswick
Multicultural Association of Fredericton
123 York Street, 2nd Floor
Fredericton NB E3B 3N6
506-457-4038   www.mcaf.nb.ca

Multicultural Association of the Greater Moncton Area (MAGMA)
Suite 2, 1299A Mountain Road
Moncton, NB E1C 2T9
506-858-9659 www.multiculturalassociation-moncton.com

University of New Brunswick
P.O. Box 4400
Fredericton, New Brunswick E3B 5A3

Newfoundland and Labrador
The provincial government web site is: www.newfoundlandlabrador.com
The main web site for new Canadians in Newfoundland and Labrador is:
Association for New Canadians (Newfoundland)
P.O. Box 2031, Station C
St. John's NL A1C 5R6
709-722-9680 www.anc-nf.cc

Web Sites - Manitoba
The two main web pages for prospective immigrants seeking Manitoba-based information and resources are:
www.gov.mb.ca/labour/immigrate/index.html
www.gov.mb.ca/labour/immigrate/settlement/firstweeks.html

These sites are all-inclusive one operated by the Manitoba government. It provides the immigrant with a great deal of information on documents, programs, English language training, and settlement help. It also lists a Provincial Nominee Program for business investors. Manitoba also has a comprehensive program for starting a new business.

The main web address for business in the Province of Manitoba is:
www.gov.mb.ca/business

Manitoba has a system in place to help match the immigrant to a potential employer. Included is key information for the immigrant's family, including any students who may be in the family.

Newcomers to Manitoba are also provided with settlement services if they so desire them. There is also an entry program for new immigrants that offers them English-language training.

In addition, new immigrants are provided information on employment, doing daily tasks, special services available to all newcomers, Canadian law, health information, and computer access for research. It's everything you need to find employment and to help you and your family settle into your new life in Canada. The main web site also contains guidance for conducting an effective job search, plus a directory of all businesses in Manitoba.

You can send an email for more information on this program to: ep_director@mts.net

The Province of Manitoba has done an excellent job designing programs for immigrants and providing them with a one-stop information source on its government-run site.

Web Sites - Saskatchewan
The following web sites provide information on job openings, a resume bank, specialized training and more within the province of Saskatchewan.
www.saskjobs.ca
www.healthcareerinsask.ca
www.aee.gov.sk.ca
www.aee.gov.sk.ca/jsfs

The following web sites offer advice, information and guidance to immigrant businesspeople, investors, and entrepreneurs interested in developing business enterprises in the province of Saskatchewan:
www.ir.gov.sk.ca
www.rd.gov.sk.ca
www.cbsc.org/sask
www.bizpal.gov.sk.ca
www.saskbiz.ca

Other important web sites for Saskatchewan are:
Global Gathering Place
#307, 506-25th Street East
Saskatoon, SK S7K 4A7
306-665-0268 www.members.shaw.ca/goodshep/ggp.html

Regina Open Door Society
1855 Smith Street
Regina, SK S4P 2N5
306-933-8385   www.rods.sk.ca

Saskatoon Open Door Society
247 1ˢᵗ Avenue North
Saskatoon, SK S7K 1X2
306-653-4464   www.sods.sk.ca

Saskatchewan Institute of Applied Science and Technology (SIAST)
Kelsey Campus
P.O. Box 1520
Saskatoon, SK S7K 3R5
306-933-8385   www.siast.sk.ca/kelsey

One of the best web sites for help in immigrating to Canada is the government web site for Canadian Citizenship and Immigration- http://cic.gc.ca/

It's a site doesn't have a lot of personality, but it does provide a tremendous amount of detailed information on the process of immigrating to Canada. Such topics as: Visiting Canada, Working Temporarily in Canada, Studying in Canada, Immigrating to Canada, The Refugee System, About Immigration, Living in Canada and Citizenship are covered.

The web site deals with the information that is necessary to you to come and/or visit, live and work in Canada. Information found there is specific and government-related. It will not get you a job in Canada or highlight any problems that you might have because that is not the function of the site. It also provides you with a list of agencies that can help you with various challenges that could come up.

The various YMCA's and YWCA's that are located in every community have links to social agencies. Helping immigrants is part of their mandate.

Ask at various agencies as to where you may be able to get your education and qualifications assessed for free or at a very reasonable cost.

Another way that visible minorities are voicing their concerns is through their ability to vote. Canada does have a process of voter registration that is based on enumeration of residences and citizenship.

The government has the responsibility for the registration of voters, and the individual is not responsible for that function so there isn't a chance of missing or excluding anyone. So in essence, the right to vote is available to everyone who meets the requirements.

Voters have in the past been able to lobby for multicultural interests and this is one method whereby the individual expresses his or her feelings on issues.

An inventory of Programs and Services by City is available at: www.ipds.iwin.ca

Canada's Association for the Fifty Plus (CARP)

CARP is a Canadian organization that represents the issues and concerns of those Canadians over the age of 50. The organization publishes a monthly magazine covering a variety of topics such as travel, health, legislation, careers, etc.

Membership in CARP also entitles the holder to discounts on health care costs, home and auto insurance, hotel and travel costs, plus an assortment of products including cell phones and car rentals. You can get more info on CARP at:info@50plus.com

Chapter Seventeen
Multiculturalism

Canada is a nation that ranks among the very best in its quality of life. A key factor in the Canadian quality of life is the diversity and culture of our people. Canadians continue to learn from the rich history of our First Nations and the history of the English and French who first colonized Canada.

Canada is a young society, one that is still being developed by immigration from all over the world. We are a country consisting of diverse people, culture, language and religions from around the world. Immigrants have been attracted to the 3 major cities of Toronto, Montreal and Vancouver or their greater metropolitan areas for these basic reasons:

1. The cities are home to their friends and family. Friends and family help the newcomer get settled in their new country giving them such things as shelter, financial and moral support and networks for jobs and cultural and religious associations.
2. The 3 major cities are centres of commerce and employment.
3. The 3 major cities are centres of culture and religion for the different ethnic groups.

Since Canada is a young country the multicultural growth in the smaller cities of Victoria, Edmonton, Calgary, Regina, Saskatoon, Winnipeg, Quebec City, Ottawa, Moncton and Halifax has just started to grow. We have tried to make these smaller Canadian cities attractive to the new immigrant because of the rising job opportunities there. Other positive factors include lower housing costs in some cases and easier access to vacation property and parkland.

Canadians are not obliged to cut their ancestral ties to their home countries in order to become integrated into their new country. In fact, the incorporation of these new immigrants along with their second and third generation children, form the fabric of a new Canada which is richer for their presence. These new Canadians are more culturally inclusive and understand the value of diversity both inside and outside of their ethnic group.

Vancouver

Vancouver has an ethnically diverse population. In 2006, 39.6% of Vancouver's population was classified as foreign-born or visible minorities. Vancouver is quite ethnically diverse with recent immigrants from the People's Republic of China at 26%, India 12% and the Philippines 11%.

During the period from 2001 to 2006, Vancouver became home to 151,695 new Canadian immigrants. The majority of immigrants were from eastern Asian, Southeast Asia and Southern Asia. The Chinese are by far the largest visible ethnic group in the city. There are also many cultural neighbourhoods such as Chinatown, Punjabi market, Little Italy, Greektown and Japantown. Other significant ethnic groups in Vancouver are Punjabi, Vietnamese, Filipino, Korean, Cambodian and Japanese.

Montreal

The Montreal region has a cosmopolitan feel and a diversified culture. More than 120 cultural communities are represented in Montreal.

Seventy per cent of individuals born abroad and residing in Quebec live in the Montreal region. These immigrants account for 28% of the total population of the region. From 2000 to 2004 immigrants who were granted permanent status and who settled in Montreal came from Asia 31% and Africa 28.7% and Europe 22.5%.

France has been the top source country of immigrants to Quebec. The countries of birth of the Quebec immigrant population are different from those of immigrants to Canada in general, with 5 of the ten top countries of very recent immigrants being: France, Morocco, Algeria, Romania and Haiti. Many of these immigrants are French speaking or have historical connections to France and its language.

Toronto

Visible minorities represent 43% of the population in the Greater Toronto Area. This percentage consists of:

South Asian	13.5%	(Includes India, Bangledesh, Pakistan, and Sri Lanka)
Chinese	9.6%	
Black	6.9%	
Filipino	3.4%	
SE Asia	1.4%	
Latin American	2.0%	
West Asian	1.5%	
Arab	1.1%	
Korean	1.1%	
Japanese	0.4%	

46.9% of Toronto's current population is made up of visible minorities. The surrounding areas including Markham at 65.4%, Brampton at 57.03%, Mississauga at 49%, and Richmond Hill at 45.7%, have among the highest percentages of visible minorities in Canada.

Vishnu Mandir Hindu Temple, Richmond Hill, Ontario

Vishnu Mandir

The Vishnu Mandir stands out as a beacon in its educational drive to promote and sustain the Hindu religious and socio-cultural heritage and values in Canada. In the earlier days of immigration to Canada, there existed no temples and devotees resorted to worship in school auditoriums. It was against this background that a conscious decision was taken by devotees to collectively embark on the construction of the first architecturally structured Hindu Temple in Canada. The realization of the Vishnu Mandir, a 30,000 square feet Temple is a living testimony to the efforts of the collective will and conviction of devotees. The Hindu Community is proud to erect on the grounds of the Vishnu Mandir, a 20-foot Bronze statue of Mahatma Gandhi.

From its early formation to date, the Vishnu Mandir has made tremendous strides in the interest of the Hindu communities in Canada, as well as the Canadian society as a whole. It has established the Montessori School, Sangeet Academy, Lakshmi Sabha, Youth Program and the Museum of Hindu Civilization and the Peace of Wall, all of which have contributed immensely not only to the education of the Hindu communities, but other members of the community especially from the academic field.

In its continuing quest to serve the communities, the Vishnu Mandir has commenced the construction of a home for seniors, which is referred to as the Anand Bhavan, Home of Bliss. A name and icon synonymous with the development of the Vishnu Mandir is the indomitable and indefatigable Pandit Budhendranauth Doobay. Pandit Doobay is a medical surgeon by profession and is the founding father of the Vishnu Mandir.

Ja'ffari Islamic Centre, Thornhill, Ontario

The Ja'ffari Islamic Centre, at 7340 Bayview Ave in Thornhill, Ontario is an Islamic Shia Ithna Asheri Jamaat with 5,000 members primarily, but not exclusively, of Shia Muslims of Indian origin from east Africa with a deep and rich history of worship, congregation and community service.

Cham Shan Buddhist Temple, Thornhill, Ontario

The Cham Shan Buddhist Temple is a large temple in the Chinese tradition. The Temple conducts regular services for the Chinese liturgical year. Languages spoken are Cantonese, Mandarin and English.

Ontario Khalsa Darbar Sikh, Mississauga, Ontario

The Mississauga area Gurudwara Sikh Temple Ontario Khalsa Darbar is located at 7080 Dixie Road in Mississauga. Special days celebrated are Bandhi Chhor, Vaisakhi, New Year, and Nagar Kirtan. Some of the events have had up to 100,000 people.

St. Lawrence Martyr Catholic Church, Scarborough, Ontario

St. Lawrence Roman Catholic Church located at 2210 Lawrence Avenue East in Scarborough is named after St. Lawrence who is one of the most venerated martyrs of the Roman Catholic Church. He is known for his service to others. St. Lawrence Roman Catholic Church has a long tradition of welcoming new Canadians and has a school nearby.

Other than the Christian religions the large religious groups in Canada are:
Muslim
Jewish
Buddhist
Hindu
Sikh

Religious Events
Outside ofthe Christian events at Christmas and Easter the following Hindu and Muslim religious events are held in various communities across the country: Hindu- Diwali, Raksha Bandhan. Muslim- Hajj,Eid-ul-Adha,Eid-ul-Fitr

Diversity of Expression in Canada

Canadian Heritage, which is a government agency, has developed a number of strategic objectives in order to encourage the individuals to develop works that reflect Canada's cultural mosaic.

Community centres and schools in many parts of the country offer courses in the language of Canada's numerous cultural communities, including Arabic, German, Arabic Hebrew, Hindi, and Vietnamese. The Canada Council For the Arts, provincial arts councils and regional and municipal governments support artists from diverse cultural backgrounds. Other Canadian institutions provide funding and support for artistic expression from diverse cultures. Diversity is also represented by the National Film Board of Canada which provides opportunities for the various communities in Canada to tell their stories.

Some of the bigger multicultural events in Canada are:

The Caribana Festival, which is held in Toronto in July and August draws hundreds of thousands (an estimated 1,000,000 attended in 2008) of people who participate in the cultural aspects of Caribbean music, cuisine, revelry, as well as visual and performing arts.

Chinese New Year celebrations held in Chinese communities each year.

The Toronto Dragon Boat Race Festival is held in June and combines the sporting event with a celebration of Chinese cultural and heritage. Other Chinese celebrations that are held in the major Chinese areas of Toronto, Mississauga, Markham, and Vancouver include:

Chinese New Year
Lantern Festival
Mid-Autumn Festival

Chapter Eighteen
Tourism in Canada

Canada is a world-class tourist destination. Best known for its large, majestic landscapes, distinctive geographic regions and its raw, natural beauty, Canada has become a popular destination for travelers the world over.

Scenic highlights of Canada include the Rocky Mountains, Niagara Falls, and the Bay of Fundy among many others. A trip through the Rocky Mountains by car or train provides numerous panoramic views of breathtaking beauty. Niagara Falls, with its dramatic 52 metre (170 foot) drop is a must see for anyone within visiting distance. And walking along the ocean floor in the Bay of Fundy at low tide is an experience you won't soon forget.

There are interesting things to see and experience, no matter what province in Canada you happen to be visiting.

Among some of the more popular destinations in Canada are the major cities of: Toronto, Montreal, Quebec City, Ottawa, Calgary, Edmonton and Vancouver. Within those cities there are numerous sights worth seeing. A major attraction for large numbers of tourists is the many multicultural events held in the major cities.

Canada is the second largest country in the world (by land mass), so there is a lot to do and see both inside and outside of the main cities.

Following are a few of the highlights in each of the main regions and cities:

Vancouver and Vancouver Island Tourism

City of Vancouver

• Museum of Anthropology at University of British Columbia featuring artifacts from Canada's West Coast Aboriginals
• Robson Street- all kinds of shopping
• Chinatown
• Granville Island - restaurants, local produce market, shops and a brewery
• Vancouver Island
• Pacific Rim National Park
• Long Beach coastline and beach
• Victoria
• Butchart Gardens
• Whistler
• Skiing
• Sightseeing and Shopping
• Mountain scenery
• Golf and fishing

Canadian Rockies

City of Calgary

Edmonton in the Fall

- Two major cities of Calgary and Edmonton
- Rocky Mountains and tourist areas of Banff and Jasper
- Calgary Stampede - a once a year summer event involving the traditional western type
- entertainment of bull riding, wagon races, calf roping, etc.
- Royal Tyrrell Museum of Paleontology in Drumheller -- housing the largest collection of dinosaur fossils in the world

Saskatchewan Tourism

- Two major cities of Regina and Saskatoon
- Home to one of the most significant and widely recognized symbols of Canadian history -- the Royal Canadian Mounted Police
- Lots of golf and lakes for swimming and fishing

Manitoba Tourism

- Home to many lakes and rivers with over 14.5% of the land covered by lakes
- These lakes and rivers offer many opportunities for outdoor recreation with hunting, fishing, boating, and some fine beaches too
- Assiniboine Park and Zoo
- Folkorama Festival
- Winnipeg Jazz Festival

Ontario Tourism

Sites of interest in Toronto

City of Toronto

- CN Tower

- Canadian National Exhibition and Ontario Place
- Ontario Science Centre
- Hockey Hall of Fame
- Bata Shoe Museum
- Toronto Zoo
- Royal Ontario Museum
- Art Gallery of Ontario
- St. Lawrence Market

Festivals in Toronto
- Caribana
- Chinese New Year
- Gay Pride

Niagara Region

Niagara Falls

- Niagara Falls
- Wineries and Wine Tours
- Ice wines
- Historic town of Niagara on the Lake
- Shaw Festival
- Ontario's fruit growing region with roadside fruit stands

Stratford
- Stratford Shakespearean Festival and Costume Warehouse
- Shopping
- World-class restaurants
- Close to the beaches of Lake Huron

Kitchener, Waterloo and St. Jacobs
- Open air markets
- German food and Mennonite culture
- Annual Oktoberfest Celebration

Ottawa (Our nation's capital)

City of Ottawa

- Parliament Hill
- National Art Gallery
- Canadian Aviation Museum
- Canadian Museum of Civilization
- Royal Canadian Mint
- Rideau Canal

Kingston
- Fort Henry
- Kingstown Old Town
- Upper Canada Village – a historic village showing life in the 1800's
- Thousand Islands
- Boldt Castle

Quebec Tourism (French-speaking province)
Montreal
- Old Montreal
- Shopping and Fashion
- Restaurants
- Museum of Fine Arts
- Laurentian Mountains, north of Montreal

Quebec City

Old Quebec City

- Old Quebec City
- Quebec Aquarium
- Plains of Abraham - historic site
- Chateau Frontenac
- Quebec Winter Carnival

New Brunswick Tourism
- Magnetic Hill
- Tidal Bore showing the power and the East Coast tides
- Hopewell Rocks
- Fundy National Park
- Whale Watching in the Bay of Fundy
- Fresh Fish and Seafood

Prince Edward Island Tourism
- Home of Anne of Green Gables and its author Lucy Maude Montgomery
- Fresh lobster suppers
- Seaside villages
- Charlottetown - home of Canadian Confederation
- Beaches of Cavendish, plus a multitude of other beaches such as Basin Head and its singing sands
- Confederation Bridge connecting PEI with the mainland

Newfoundland and Labrador Tourism
- Spectacular Icebergs and fjords
- St. John's – oldest English-founded city in North America, with its sights, pubs, east coast entertainment, and fresh fish and seafood
- Whale watching
- National Parks and Wildlife
- Mooseburgers

Nova Scotia Tourism

Peggy's Cove

- Cape Breton Highlands
- Historic Fortress Louisbourg

Halifax, the provincial capital, features shopping, fish and seafood restaurants, Citadel Fortress, Maritime Museum of the Atlantic Canada with a display on the Titanic. plus a world-class military Tattoo
- Lunenburg village - craft shops and restaurants, along with lobster tours and the historic sailboat the Bluenose
- Peggy's Cove
- Many quaint seaside villages and beaches

Northwest Territories Tourism
- Northern Lights
- Great fishing and hunting
- Wood Buffalo National Park
- Gold rush town of Dawson City
- Wilderness adventure tours
- Ice castles
- Dog sled races

Toronto as a Multicultural World Centre

Toronto is heralded as one of the most multicultural cities in the world. It is ranked by *Places Rated Almanac* as the safest of all among large metropolitan areas in North America. Diversity of race, religion and lifestyle help define Toronto and set it apart from other world class cities. Because Toronto is a relatively young city, it doesn't have the rich history of other leading cities, but it has become a welcoming point for people of all origins and cultures.

More than 100 languages and dialects are spoken in Toronto. On average, the city of Toronto welcomes over 69,000 international immigrants each year, plus more than 10,000 foreign students who choose to study there. .

About half of Toronto's population consists of immigrants, while another 22% are 2nd generation immigrants, with at least one parent born outside of Canada. That's nearly three quarters of the entire population of Toronto who are either first or second generation immigrants.

At present, Toronto has 79 distinctive ethnic publications and is considered a world centre for multiculturalism.

Toronto is host to numerous cultural, religious and entertainment events including several music and food festivals. One of the top cultural events in Toronto each year is the Caribana Festival. It's a week-long celebration of Carribean culture, music and food -- culminating in a huge, colorful parade that attracts over a million visitors each year from all over the world. Also celebrated in Toronto are the Chinese New Year, as well as various Hindu, Sikh, Muslim and other cultural and religious events.

Toronto also has various ethnic areas in the city; each with a focus on the specific foods and culture of a particular ethnic community. These neighbourhood communities include Chinatown, Little India, Greektown, and Little Italy. There is also a multitude of Thai, Carribean, Indian, and Vietnamese restaurants and specialty shops in various locations across Toronto.

In order to get a total picture of all of the events on Toronto's cultural calendar, check out the following web sites:

www.toronto.ca/quality_of_life/diversity.htm
www.toronto.ca/visitors/index.htm
www.torontotourism.com

The Top Ten Places to Visit and Things To See in Canada

1. Vancouver Island - Victoria, Butchart Gardens, Long Beach, Tolfino Whale Watching and Hot Springs

2. City of Vancouver (host of the 2010 Olympic Winter Games) -- Granville Island, Gastown, UBC Museum of Anthropology, Robson Street, Grouse Mountain, the drive to Whistler, shopping, Chinese, Asian Foods

3. Rocky Mountains, Alberta – the drive between Jasper and Banff and the Lake Louise area with its impressive scenery

4. Lake Superior drive – from Sault Ste. Marie to Thunder Bay

5. Toronto -- Canada's great Multicultural centre, Niagara Falls, Niagara-on-the-lake, Kitchener and St. Jacobs, Stratford and the beaches of Lake Huron

6. Ottawa - the capital city of Canada

7. Montreal and Quebec City, plus the drive to the Laurentian Mountains

8. Northwest Territories – Untouched natural beauty, Fishing, Hunting, Dog Sleds, Ice Castles, Wild Game, and the Northern Lights

9. Maritime provinces of PEI, Nova Scotia and New Brunswick -- Beautiful sea-coast drive, quaint villages, wonderful fish and seafood, impressive ocean views, numerous beaches and the Cape Breton Highlands

10. St. John's Newfoundland

External Links to Canadian Tourism
Canadian Tourism Commission
Tourism British Columbia(BC)
Tourism Vancouver (BC)
Tourism Victoria (BC)
Travel Alberta (AB)
Banff Lake Louise Tourism (AB)
Edmonton Tourism (AB)
Tourism Calgary (AB)
Travel Manitoba (MB)
Destination Winnipeg (MB)
Tourism Toronto (ON)
Tourism Montreal (QC)
Tourism Yukon (YT)
Nunavut Tourism
Travel Canada's Northwest Territories

Travel Distances	*Kilometres*
St. John's Newfoundland to Halifax Nova Scotia	1503
St. John's Newfoundland to Montreal, Quebec	2602
St. John's Newfoundland to Toronto, Ontario	3141
Charlottetown PEI to Halifax NS	280
Charlottetown PEI to Fredricton NB	373
Charlottetown PEI to Montreal Quebec	1199
Charlottetown PEI to Toronto Ontario	1738

Halifax NS to Fredricton NB	415
Halifax NS to Montreal Quebec	1249
Halifax NS to Toronto, Ontario	1788
Fredricton NB to Montreal Quebec	834
Fredricton NB to Toronto, Ontario	1373
Quebec City Quebec to Montreal Quebec	270
Montreal Quebec to Toronto Ontario	539
Montreal Quebec to Ottawa Ontario	190
Toronto Ontario to Ottawa Ontario	399
Toronto to Winnipeg Manitoba	2099
Toronto to Vancouver British Columbia	4412
Winnipeg Manitoba to Regina Saskatchewan	571
Regina Saskatchewan to Edmonton Alberta	785
Regina Saskatchewan to Calgary Alberta	764
Edmonton Alberta to Calgary Alberta	299
Edmonton Alberta to Vancouver British Columbia	1164
Edmonton Alberta to Whitehorse Yukon	2086
Edmonton Alberta to Yellowknife NWT	2052
Vancouver British Columbia to Victoria British Columbia	105
Vancouver British Columbia to St. John's Newfoundland	7323

Some sample travel distances between Canadian major cities. Note the final figure that shows the distance between Vancouver British Columbia and St. John's Newfoundland which is the total distance across the country and it gives the New Canadian an idea how large Canada is.

Chapter Nineteen
Common Problems and Suggested Solutions
For the Immigrant Candidate, Business and Government

Problem: Trying To Land A Job in Canada in Advance Can Be Difficult.

For Immigrant Candidates: Preparation is the key. It's a mantra that's been repeated throughout this book for a reason. Preparation is something that is solely your responsibility. No one else can do the essential background work for you. It's up to you to research market demand in the various areas of Canada and to identify employment opportunities that are a suitable match to your skills, training, and experience.

Canada is an expanding nation with a growing economy. But not all areas are equally rich in employment opportunities. Be willing to look beyond the traditional employment strongholds of Toronto and Vancouver and explore available positions in mid-size cities and smaller communities where growth rates are strongest.

It's also important to begin your search early. Don't wait until you arrive to launch your search for a suitable job. Start exploring and establishing contact with potential employers and agencies online, from your home country. Let people know what you do and the kind of work you desire in Canada. A proactive approach from the start is the best way to overcome the difficulty many immigrants experience when looking for a job.

For Businesses in Canada: Recognize the value skilled immigrants can bring to your organization. Many immigrants are highly-skilled, hard-working, independent types who are capable of taking on projects and seeing them through to completion. Of particular value to many Canadian companies who have added new immigrants to their workforces are the unique experiences immigrants bring to the table. They've seen life, business, and client relations from a different viewpoint and it's this experience that leads to original thinking, problem solving and business breakthroughs in many cases.

Not accepting immigrants because they lack "Canadian experience" just doesn't make sense in many instances. We're part of a competitive global marketplace where the various

247

economies of the world have become integrated. Today, international experience should be valued as much or more than doing the same kind of work in Canada alone.

For The Government: As a nation, we are dependent on immigrants and the varied skills, knowledge and experience they bring to Canada. Immigrants make a significant contribution not just to the economy, but culturally, artistically, and socially too.

All indications are that the economy as a whole will be even more dependent upon immigration to meet the demand for skills and expertise in the future. So it only makes sense to modify the system to make it more efficient and more reflective of the real needs of businesses today.

Problem: The Realities of Coming To Canada As An Immigrant Can Be Very Different From The Fantasy

For Immigrant Candidates: It's important to do your own research. Sure, you can and should consider the opinions and comments of others. But be very careful of any immigration advisor who paints a picture of utopia and suggests that it all can be yours by simply coming to Canada.

My principal purpose in writing this book is to provide you, the prospective immigrant to Canada, with an objective view. It's my intention to provide you with enough information and varied opinions for you to make your own decision. Use this book as a resource to help you decide. But whatever you decide, it's important that you make your decision based on solid information, not on the slick words of someone who stands to profit by selling you a dream. Claim responsibility for your life's decisions and conduct your own due diligence before taking a giant leap and settling in a new country.

For Businesses In Canada: There's no doubt that international recruiting creates a much larger talent pool for Canadian businesses to tap in order to overcome their own labour shortages. At the same time, accessing international labour markets opens channels of communication between employers and prospective employees. It's this direct role of business that leads to an accurate exchange. Not only will potential employees learn about job descriptions and requirements firsthand, they'll also get a better feel for Canada and what it would be like living and working there.

For The Government: Perhaps it's time for Canada to take a more active role in promoting this country on an international scale as a great place to live, work, and play.

There's no doubt that Canada has a lot to offer immigrants who choose to make our country their new home. If Canada had more of a presence in the immigrant marketplace and was more vocal in conveying to outsiders what Canada is all about, there would be less opportunity for manipulation and misinformation spread about by others seeking to take advantage of lesser-informed immigrants.

Canada has real opportunity to become a world leader over the next 2-3 decades. But we have to realize that we're in a competitive arena, seeking human talent, along with every other developed and developing nation on the planet. We need both skilled and unskilled workers in order to continue to grow economically and their degree of contribution is largely dependent on Canada's ability to attract, inspire and train people.

The country of Canada has a lot to offer. But it's no longer the promised land of 'milk and honey' for immigrants that it once was. To continue to thrive and be one of the world's great nations, we must become a country where opportunities and encouragement are abundant. Some of our New Canadians have not been treated well or dealt with respect and dignity and may have feelings of dissatisfaction. We cannot have dissatisfied New Canadians communicating their bad impressions like unhappy customers and must treat them as extremely valuable assets of our country and find jobs in their field which is why they came here.

Problem: Jobs In My Field Seem To Be In Short Supply In The Area Of Canada That I Want to Relocate To

For Immigrant Candidates: It's best to understand the current job market, as well as any trends affecting the market before you arrive in Canada. Once again, conducting your own research is of paramount importance. You need to be aware of Canada's regional economies and the job prospects within the areas you prefer to settle.

Most immigrants choose the major cities of Toronto, Vancouver, or Montreal to be close to family, friends and an established ethnic community in which they feel a sense of connection and comfort. But the winds of economic change have come and the big urban centres may no longer be the best places to find a job.

To increase your chances of finding suitable employment within a reasonable period of time, look towards the many mid-size cities in various locations across the country. None of these can offer the same degree of diversity that Toronto can, but most cities of all sizes have notable immigrant populations who have established roots there.

For Canadian Businesses: Consider the entire world your potential marketplace for locating and recruiting quality people to your organization. Look beyond the local market and widen your search on a global scale. Other countries and organizations have already begun doing so. Consider recruiting staff the way colleges and universities in the U.S. recruit athletes.

Attracting the best talent means communicating your staffing requirements wherever quality candidates are likely to hear your message. Since so many immigrants lean towards the big cities, part of your recruiting strategy could include advertising there and then "selling" candidates on the community that your business is a part of.

For the Government: Look at the realities of Canada's workforce today. Compared to 20 or 30 years ago, Canada's workforce of today is significantly different. And it's a trend that will continue to define the economic performance of our nation over the next 15 to 20 years. The trend I'm referring to is the increasing proportion of new immigrants joining the workforce, and our dependence on these people to sustain our economy and propel it forward.

Most vacancies in the labour force over the next 15 to 20 years will be filled by immigrants. Canada's population is aging. More "baby-boomers" will retire earlier, even if employment is offered to them, as many seek to pursue other interests in their later years. Secondly, our birthrate is declining so we cannot even replace retiring workers internally, let alone supply workers to fuel economic growth. Essentially, this leaves us with one option; attract more immigrants to the workforce.

Immigrants are essential to the quality of life we've come to enjoy in Canada. And as we seek to continually grow, we'll need more skilled and capable immigrants than ever before. If we cannot attract quality talent from abroad, we're in serious trouble. But we cannot afford to sit back and wait. We need a more aggressive and active approach. We need to view human talent as a valuable asset and the key to our future the way our rich natural resources have served us in the past and continue to serve us today.

Problem: It's Difficult For Foreign-Trained Doctors To Practice in Canada Due To The Additional Time and Expense of Certification.

For The Candidate: Recently there has been some effort to improve the flow of foreign-trained doctors coming into Canada. In fact it is a little known fact that in the last four years Ontario has approved more foreign trained doctors for licensing than domestic ones. But the process is still lengthy and expensive for immigrant doctors wanting to practice here. Control over medical certification is held by the respective Colleges of Physicians and Surgeons in each province where regulations may vary from one jurisdiction to another with no national organization assembled to assume a leadership role over the administration, testing and accreditation of immigrant doctors.

It's best to be prepared for a challenging climb with tight restrictions. There is neither a quick or easy way for foreign-trained doctors to apply their education, skills, and experience in Canada. Refer to the chapter on regulated medical professions in Canada for the requirements necessary for foreign trained doctors to practice in Canada.

For The Government: Currently there is a critical shortage of family doctors, emergency care physicians and medical specialists in numerous communities, right across the country. This is a serious issue, with no fast solution on the horizon. We need more doctors, yet there are a large number of foreign-trained practitioners who would be ready, willing and capable of stepping in and filling these important medical vacancies that Canada cannot fill with doctors who trained in Canada alone.

Clearly, the protection of patients is of utmost importance to the integrity of health care in Canada and that protection should never be compromised. But not having access to a medical doctor in some communities, makes universal health care difficult to access and ineffective in meeting the needs of Canadians living there. Surely there must be a better way.

Safeguards are crucial to the protection of the Canadian public. But are foreign-trained medical professionals any less capable of performing in a professional capacity as their Canadian-trained counterparts? Extensive testing and monitoring should be sufficient to prove one's capability to perform to strict Canadian medical standards. It seems to be a terrible waste of resources to not make this option available to both immigrant doctors and the Canadian public.

No one should be allowed to practice medicine in Canada without being able to prove their qualifications, expertise, and capability to consistently perform to established Canadian standards. But where they obtained their medical training should be of lesser importance than an ability to demonstrate a high level of knowledge, skill and experience. We also have a history in this country of placing highly qualified doctors and specialists who are foreign trained and who have for decades been providing world class treatment to all Canadians.

Problem: Some professionals who come to Canada end up working in low paying service jobs because that's all they can get.

For Immigrant Candidates: Yes, there are plenty of examples of professionals who have arrived in Canada expecting to land jobs in their area of expertise, only to find themselves accepting low paying services jobs, in order to feed and shelter themselves and their families. Canada does have an excellent track record of employing professional immigrants and those numbers have surged since the 1980's. Today, a majority of people in many different professions are actually foreign-trained immigrants.

But lately, it's been considerably more difficult for immigrant professionals to work in the fields they trained for. These changes have mostly occurred over the last decade, with the following happenings:
- Language requirements are becoming even more important in Canada
- Some jobs are drying up in the major cities, creating more intense competition amongst domestic and immigrant populations for those positions that are available

Bottom line is that immigrant candidates need to do more research before making the decision to come to Canada. Gain a realistic picture and assess the job prospects and costs of living in your chosen community, so you know exactly what you can expect when you arrive. Expecting to have an easy time finding a position in your area or expertise and then facing challenging circumstances would dampen anyone's enthusiasm. But knowing that you will face challenges and then being as prepared for those as you can be will ultimately increase your chances of getting exactly what you want.

For The Government: Couldn't the department of Citizenship and Immigration provide more accurate, up-to-date information to prospective immigrants about jobs and careers in Canada and what they are and where they are located. With the way things are now, immigrants entering this country are often badly misinformed about the realities of the Canadian job market, the economy, and the cultural make-up of the country with its regional variations.

Each immigrant candidate should conduct their own research. But why couldn't we also provide updated information on the economy, jobs, and where the best opportunities exist for today's new immigrants? It would seem that this approach would better serve everyone — the immigrant, Canadian businesses, and the country as a whole.

The Canadian economy has become increasingly dependent on immigration to maintain strong growth and the standard of living we all enjoy today. We need talented, capable people who want to contribute. And we need to treat these people as the valuable resources that they are. If we miss the mark, we risk losing them to another expanding economy that is also competing for their skills. The world has become a smaller place and Canada needs to take a more proactive role in international recruiting if it hopes to maintain its position among the great nations of the world.

Problem: The "Points System" Makes It Difficult For Many Immigrants To Qualify

For Immigrant Candidates: This system has been in place for years. Even to this day, it's the most used avenue of admission into Canada. But now with the Provincial Nomination Program in place right across the country, there's another option available. Provincial Nomination can slash the time it takes to be granted official immigrant status, while bypassing many of the difficult to overcome challenges presented by the "Points System" or Skilled Worker Program. There isn't much any individual can do about the traditional method of immigration other than to understand it and improve your skills such as language, so you can meet the requirements.

For Canadian Businesses: When recruiting staff from abroad, you would be well advised to have them opt for Provincial Nomination instead. It's the ideal system to serve immigrants and companies who've had previous contact and are a compatible match.

Since a primary concern of a growing enterprise is to find skilled talent for relevant, vacant jobs, the Provincial Nomination Program looks like it could be a viable solution for years to come. But to date, this program has only channeled approximately 10% of the immigrant volume entering Canada. Clearly its an underutilized program, one that perhaps isn't yet understood by the majority of businesses.

For The Government: I suggest that it's time for the government to take a good long look at the Skilled Workers program with respect to its overall effectiveness. Just as the makeup of our country has evolved over the years, so too have the staffing requirements of Canadian business. In order to keep the wheels turning and the economic engines running at full power, the needs of businesses change. But has Canada's immigration programs kept up with these changing times?

The Skilled Worker Program best serves a specific candidate. It may be attracting highly-educated professionals to the country -- without having the positions available for these people to effectively utilize their academic credentials and training. The current system places an emphasis on education – a fine attribute. But it doesn't serve the needs of the candidate, industry, or the country when a new arrival cannot find gainful employment in the field of specialization for which he or she is trained and experienced in.

Canada's immigration programs must become a route to a certain job -- and not just an evaluation technique to determine one's suitability for acceptance into Canada.

At present, it takes candidates 3-4 years on average to gain entry into Canada through the Skilled Workers Program. In this age of high technology, such a lengthy waiting period seems at best to be an unnecessary and unacceptable waste of human resources. A streamlined process that matches qualifications to specific jobs in demand and does so in a relatively expedient manner would better serve all parties involved. Many of the jobs on the 'Jobs Under Pressure' list and the job vacancies in each province, refer to skilled and semi-skilled labour positions, light industrial, clerical and retail. Yet the point accumulation on the Skilled Worker Program makes it very difficult for semi-skilled and retail candidates to get into the country. How can we change the Skilled Worker Program to address the actual needs of large and small business?

Another problem with the program as it exists today is the language emphasis on both

English and French, rather than one or the other. To score the maximum number of points for language, a candidate would need fluency in both official languages.

The obvious problem is that the majority of jobs in today's marketplace do not require bilingualism, but rather, proficiency in the one language spoken in the area where the job is offered. Bilingualism is really only a job requirement for a government or customer service position which many immigrants would not qualify for or be interested in those positions. For most immigrants, neither English nor French is their native language. So admittance to Canada means learning another language to the point of fluency, in order to record an acceptable score using the points system.

To ask immigrants to learn 2 new languages so that they can optimize their points on the language tests -- and to in effect penalize them for not doing so -- when the job market clearly doesn't require it, seems somewhat unfair to applicants. At minimum, the points scoring system needs to be reevaluated and adjusted. Canadians become fluent in a second language as a result of education and training in their lives. Why can't an immigrant be given the same opportunity and just have proficiency in one language?

Problem: Temporary Work Permits Are Not Avenues for Permanent Residency

For Immigrant Candidates: The Temporary Foreign Worker Program can help you in your endeavours to immigrate to Canada. It will give you the experience of coming to Canada and actually experiencing what it's like to work here. It's important however to take note of the word "temporary".

Working in Canada as a Temporary Foreign Worker is not part of the process to apply for immigration or permanent residency unless the candidate looks into a new classification called the Canadian Experience Class. It's merely a temporary work permit that allows you a limited time to work in Canada, after which you are required to return to your native country. It's a great way to experience Canada in a very real sense. You'll get to taste the experience of what it's like to live amongst the population, while getting up and going to work every day. This gives you a much more accurate depiction of life in Canada than the impression one gets as a visiting tourist. To apply for a temporary work permit from outside of Canada you need:

1. A job offer from a Canadian employer
2. A completed application
3. Other requirements related to health, financial ability, no criminal record, plus the acknowledgement that you will leave Canada at the end of your work permit
4. A Temporary Resident Visa in order to stay in Canada during the assigned period

Additionally, the employer must get a written confirmation from HRSDC (Human Resources Canada) that a foreign worker can fill the job. Some positions require the temporary worker to obtain a work permit, while others do not. Some categories of jobs have permits granted quicker than others. Even if a work permit is deemed unnecessary in your situation, other documentation will be required.

For Canadian Businesses: The federal government's Temporary Foreign Worker Program is another staffing tool available to you. It allows eligible foreign workers to work in Canada for an authorized period of time.

One key qualification is that an employer needs to demonstrate that they are unable to find suitable Canadian/permanent residents to fill the position, so that the admission of temporary workers does not have a negative impact on the Canadian labour market.

For The Government: The Temporary Foreign Worker program draws on the talents and skills of foreign workers to help fill shortages in Canada on a temporary basis, but does it serve any useful purpose to the worker, other than a paycheque while they're here?

Perhaps the experience of working here and making a contribution in Canada should be a stepping stone towards permanent residency in Canada. After all, one requirement that's often cited among many Canadian businesses seeking staff is that employees have "Canadian work experience". How are we publicizing the Canadian Experience Class as a vehicle of selling Canada as a place for permanent residency? Temporary workers meet this qualification by virtue of having been in Canada in a workplace environment over a period of time. Shouldn't that boost their qualifications for immigration to Canada? The reward of having a job for three years may not be enough to make the Temporary Worker Program successful.

Key Point Summary
Problem: Trying To Land A Job in Canada in Advance Can Be Difficult.
- Candidates should prepare well in advance of your proposed arrival is the key
- Businesses need to establish more of a presence in the international job market
- Improvements to the process would better serve everyone, including the country

Problem: The Realities of Coming To Canada As An Immigrant Can Be Very Different From The Fantasy
- Do your own research to separate facts from fabrications
- Business needs to take a more proactive role in recruiting to project a realistic picture
- The Government needs to actively market Canada for all it has to offer workers and families

Problem: Jobs In My Field Seem To Be In Short Supply In The Area Of Canada That I Want to Relocate To
- Research and establish contacts with employers and agencies to get a real sense of the job market
- Candidates primarily look to the large urban areas first, so that's where employers need to advertise available positions and then "sell" potential employees on the benefits of locating elsewhere
- The government needs to better serve and recognize the primary supply of labour growth in Canada

Problem: It's Difficult For Foreign-Trained Doctors To Practice in Canada Due To The Additional Time and Expense of Certification

- It's a frustrating, expensive and slow process for foreign-trained doctors to practice in Canada
- Improving the flow of doctors into Canada would help alleviate the shortages of medical professionals that many communities are experiencing

Problem: Many professionals who come to Canada end up working in low paying service jobs because that's all they can get.

- Some professional organizations in Canada have tightened their membership qualifications, so it's best to investigate your profession first
- The government should provide up-to-date information about the job market in Canada and related qualifications so newcomers have a realistic vision of what they can expect

Problem: The "Points System" Makes It Difficult For Many Immigrants To Qualify

- Most problems associated with Skilled Workers Program (Points System) for immigration can be overcome via the Provincial Nomination process
- Businesses wanting to expedite hiring need to direct applicants to apply through the Provincial Nomination Program
- The Skilled Worker Program is in need of a major overhaul to better meet the needs of business, immigrants and the country as a whole

Problem: Temporary Work Permits Are Not Avenues to Permanent Residency

- The Temporary Foreign Worker Program gives you the opportunity to experience Canada as part of the workforce, rather than a tourist
- Temporary Foreign Workers can help meet the immediate needs of businesses in Canada
- Work and life experience in Canada should act as a credit, giving temporary workers an advantage should they choose to apply for permanent immigrant status

Chapter Twenty

A-Z Summary -

An Action Planner For Immigration to Canada

Applications and Accuracy - Know your forms and fill them out accurately and correctly. It is very important that all documents be filled out accurately and truthfully. Any document that is not filled out correctly could hold up your application for months and completely change all of your plans. Have friends and family check your work. Ensure that you bring your documents with you from your home country and that they are translated into English.

Business Owner - A business owner can come to Canada as a visitor and research any business ventures that he or she might want to pursue in this country. The stories of frustration and disappointment do not seem as prevalent with the businessman as they are with the skilled worker who does not find a job to meet his education and qualifications. The difference between the two might be that the businessperson creates his own employment and has a job while the skilled immigrant has to find work in a competitive marketplace. The business immigrant also has a substantial net worth that he/she is bringing from their home country.

Aside from visiting Canada there are three types of business investor immigrants coming for permanent residence status:

Investors - these people must demonstrate business experience and have a minimum net worth of CDN $800,000 and be prepared to make an investment of $400,000 Canadian.

Entrepreneurs - entrepreneurs are people who will own and manage businesses in Canada which will contribute to the Canadian economy and create jobs for Canadians. An entrepreneur will demonstrate business experience and have a minimum net worth of $300,000 Canadian.

Self Employed Persons - these people must have the plan and intent of creating their own employment. They could create their own job by contributing to the artistic, cultural or athletic life in Canada. Refer to the government website:
http://www.cic.gc.ca/englishskilledasess/index.html

CIIP - CIIP is a project funded by the federal government which helps immigrants in their home country with the following information:
- Information of the Canadian labour Market occupations and the steps required for integration
- Advice and guidance to assist in planning successful entry to the Canadian labour market
- Practical assistance in identifying and contracting Canadian organizations for further assistance

Citizenship - You can apply for Canadian Citizenship if you have a permanent resident card and have been a permanent resident for three years or more. The rights of Canadian citizenship include the following: the right to vote or be a candidate for election; the right to apply for a Canadian passport and to leave and return to the country at any time; the right to live in any part of Canada that you desire. You can apply for Canadian citizenship if you meet the following conditions:
- have lived in Canada for 3 out of the last 4 years
- be at least 18 years of age
- can talk in either English or French
- have knowledge of Canada
- are not under a deportation order
- are not in a Canadian prison
- have been charged or convicted of an indictable offence

You can get an application for Canadian citizenship from a Canadian Immigration Citizenship call centre or download it from: http://www.cic.gc.ca

Documents - Ensure that you have all of the correct documents for:
Immigration to Canada
Employment in Canada
Educational and Qualification Assessment

English (and/or French)-language proficiency is very important to your future in Canada. It would be beneficial if you were developing your language skills over a period of years prior to coming to Canada. It is your vehicle of communication for application, entry, and job search. Language is one of the six selection factors for skilled workers. Your future in Canada depends on your language skills. The advancement of your employment could be delayed substantially by poor language skills. The assessment of language is broken into the following areas:

Listen	High	Moderate	Basic	No—does not meet basics
Speak	High	Moderate	Basic	No-does not meet basics
Read	High	Moderate	Basic	No-does not meet basics
Write	High	Moderate	Basic	No-does not meet basics

The best way to show your language proficiency is to take a language test that is given by an organization approved by Citizenship and Immigration Canada. The testing will be paid by you and you should submit the results with your application. Take language courses in your home country. Read English newspapers and watch English television programs. Join English speaking clubs in order to improve your conversation skills which won't be appreciated unless you develop confidence in conversation.

The English Tests are administered by:
International English Language Testing System (IELTS)
http://www.ielts.org/

Canadian International Language Proficiency Index Program (CELPIP)
www.ares.ubc.ca/CELPIP/index.html

French Tests
Test d'Evaluation de Francais (TEF)
www.franedc.org

There are a number of jobs available in Canada for bilingual people in English and French such as in Customer Service and government positions. There is a definite shortage of qualified bilingual candidates in Canada so the competition for these positions is less than most of the unilingual positions.

Friends and Family - Use the resources that your friends and family provide. This resource is extremely valuable and can include financial support, shelter in Canada, information on everything from job searches to qualification firms, references for a good lawyer or consultant if one is required, a place to stay and a guide when a person considering immigrating to Canada makes a visit. These friends and family can also make internet searches and guide you through various websites that you can personally visit when you make a vacation trip to Canada.

Government - The main government web site for immigration and citizenship is:
http://cic.gc.ca

Health Care - Canada has a universal health care system that covers all members of your family. You must apply for a health care card for each individual member including infants. Some provinces have waiting periods of three months so you must get private health care insurance for that time period. This insurance should be arranged before you leave your native country. In some communities it is hard to find a family doctor on short notice so there are multiple walk-in clinics where you can use their services on a walk-in or appointment basis and at least develop a relationship with the staff of doctors at the clinic. The best way to get a family doctor is through references of friends and family.

259

Information and Integration - You should have developed files of information on Canada and organized them in an efficient manner so that they are at your fingertips- even though you are thousands of miles away you have the same opportunity of many Canadians to learn about the country. You should have files on applications, documentation, job searches, education, personal preparedness including health insurance and social insurance, education if you have small children, town and city locations where you want to live and work, and costs.

The immigrant will help themselves into the Canadian environment by integrating into all aspects of Canadian society. The immigrant will find that his journey will be easier if an effort is made to integrate into their new society. There is no problem in retaining most of your culture but the days are gone when immigrants lived solely on their native culture in their new country and did not attempt to integrate. Immigrants may also be going to parts of Canada that do not have as large a multicultural base as the big cities and the ability to integrate and accept the communities' values will be important to the immigrant's ability to find a place in the community. This may be part of the reason that immigrants feel unwelcome at times. Any participation in your new country's society is desirable and any immigrant would expect the same if a Canadian went to their country. Professor Randall Hansen says in a Toronto Daily Star article on multiculturalism that "You're welcome in Canada. There is no inherent problem in your retaining most of your culture. But there are common values we expect you to adopt. It's acceptable and it's smart for a country to be confident in its values. It is also smart for an immigrant to be confident and comfortable in the values of the country that he or she has chosen to build their future."

Also refer to the information on this web site for news in the working environment regarding diversity: www.hireimmigrants.ca/articles

Jobs, Agencies and Jobs Under Pressure - The attainment of work in Canada really is your responsibility. You should not wait until you come to this country to begin your job search. For all intents and purposes you should have a job to go to when you arrive. Your chance of success in Canada and the happiness of yourself and your family members will be counting on your employment. Canada is not a pleasant country to live in if you do not have a job that meets your personal qualifications and goals and provides you and your family with a decent wage. Some of the processes that you should be developing when you are conducting your job search are:

1. Plan a visit to Canada before you lean towards a more permanent move. Develop a relationship with some job agencies and find out what jobs are available and where they are located. Learn as much as you can about the economic prospects of the areas that you are considering.

2. Use any web site resources that list jobs such as Human Resources Services Development Canada(HRSDC) and the Jobs Under Pressure list which shows job in demand by province

3. If you are finding that there are no jobs in Canada for your education and qualifications then maybe you should look at other avenues of employment. There are many highly-

educated people in foreign countries; people who are very intelligent and degreed and speak English fluently, but their qualifications are not in the areas required by Canadian employers or government. These individuals easily pass the skills test, but are disappointed when they arrive in Canada to find that there are not jobs open for them.

4. Use the Provincial Nominee process if you are qualified for an occupation that is in demand. That process was specifically developed to meet the shortages that are developing in the provinces. Use the temporary work permit which allows you to work in Canada in your chosen field and meanwhile gain valuable work experience, language experience and knowledge of Canada along with developing credit for the Canadian Experience Class method of admission.

5. Some companies are going directly to the host countries in search of employees with valuable talent and abilities. They are using global employee referrals and global recruitment agencies to find their candidates. Keep an eye out for these agencies and keep in touch with your friends, relatives and business associates so that you will be aware of all of your opportunities. Check out the best companies in Canada for immigrants and develop a relationship or communications link with them. You will find that they are tracking and cataloging talented immigrants from around the world.

Kits for Driver's License, Insurance and Home Insurance - Ontario has
a graduated two-step licensing process whereby the driver passes a vision and road knowledge test to receive a first level G1 license. This license has some restrictions regarding where you can drive and you are required to drive with and adult licensed driver. A G2 license can be attempted 12 months later and this license provides the rights and responsibilities of a typical everyday driver.

It is recommended that you receive driver's training because they will cover all areas noted in the handbook and the passing of a driver's education course gives you a lower insurance rate. The same companies in Canada that provide car insurance also provide home insurance. It is a good idea to protect your home and contents against damage and theft even if you are living in an apartment because in the beginning your household contents may be all that you own. The insurance company or your employer will also sell you life insurance to protect your family if anything happens to you. You should put together a set of files of information on these subjects and update them as time passes.

Lawyers and Consultants - If you feel that you don't need any help with your
immigration application, then you can download the blank application from Canada's immigration web site at: http://cic.gc.ca (Citizenship and Immigration Canada Government of Canada)

If you need help you can use a member of the Canadian Society of Immigration consultants or an immigration lawyer. Remember Consultants are not regulated in Canada and definitely have no regulations on them in your home country so you are taking your chances with someone located in your home country. Lawyers are regulated by the provincial law societies that also have a complaint mechanism. You must shop around for rates and qualifications. Ask friends and family for recommendations and references.

There are some not-for-profit groups that can provide you with free or low-fee help as a starter. You could also ask them about immigration consultant and lawyer reference and recommendations. A list is included in the Resources section.

If you do hire a consultant or lawyer you should ask about their services, fees and qualifications. You should ensure that any lawyer you're considering belongs to their respective provincial law societies. On March 10, 2009 Citizenship, Immigration and Multiculturalism Minister Jason Kenney addressed the issue of immigration fraud. An information video is available on the Citizenship and Immigration web-site. www.cic.gc

Some examples of fraud were described in the immigrant's native country where they are not regulated by Canadian law and some cases occurred in Canada. Again, buyer beware. Ensure that you get everything in writing and that you keep your original documents and get copies of all documents. If a lawyer or consultants suggest that you be untruthful on a document it is time to find another one.

In some cases complaints have been filed with the Provincial Law society and actions have been taken against the lawyer. Unlike immigration consultants who do not have a complaint mechanism the lawyers have a compensation fund that helps clients who have been cheated by a dishonest lawyer.

Money and costs - Canada is one of the lowest cost countries in the G7. However, it can be expensive for an immigrant in relation to their home country. If the immigrant has never stayed in a large metropolitan city before they might be astounded at the costs that are required for shelter, food, transportation, etc. Canada uses the Canadian dollar as the basis of their currency. For years the Canadian dollar was trading well below the American dollar in exchange, however, recently the country has had a good economic performance and the Canadian currency is above par with the US dollar.

Listed below are some sample costs of living for Ontario. Costs in Alberta and British Columbia could be slightly higher. Costs of accommodation tend to far higher in the larger cities because of supply and demand and more remote locations could be cheaper but there would be higher food costs because of transportation.
- Loaf of bread- $2.80
- Milk – 2L container- $3.99
- Minced Beef-1 kg- $8.49
- Whole Chicken-whole per kg-$6.99
- Eggs-one dozen-$3.99
- Sugar-4 kg bag-$4.99

Other costs - One litre of gasoline (petrol) currently was costing about $1.25 and it's expected to go over $2.00 a litre in the next five years. The cost of gasoline plunged downward with the world economic crisis at the end of 2008 and was at 85 cents starting out 2009 but energy prices were slowly creeping up as supplies leveled out and the world economy and demand for oil began to move back to pre-recession levels.

Accommodation costs - You will find that accommodation will form the largest major cost that you will incur. A couple could require $1200 to $1700 a month in rent while a single person could spend $800 to $1200 a month depending upon the type of accommodation.

A note of caution - Alberta is experiencing the highest growth rate in Canada which could be up to three times higher than the other provinces. Although there are good paying jobs available in large numbers the cost of living is accelerating at a quick pace and can be a shock to a newly arrived immigrant.

Nominee - The methodology of applying for Provincial Nomination is listed below:
1. Obtain a Certificate of Provincial Nomination-each province has different nomination procedures which are available on the link to the web-site listed below
www.cic.gc.ca/english/immigrate/provincial/apply-how.asp
If the province successfully nominates you will receive a certificate of provincial nomination and a copy of that certificate will be automatically be sent to the visa office by the province.

2. Obtain, print and complete the application kit.

3. Submit your application to the correct visa office in your home country

4. Obtain the instructions for the visa office on such items as medical examinations, criminal and security checks.

5. Calculate your fees

6. Check and submit your application.

Medical, Security and other requirements - Under all classifications of permanent residency you and your family must pass a medical examination and security and criminal checks. You can find more information on these subjects in the Quick find section of the web-site.

An example of how quick the Provincial Nominee Program is was provided in a Toronto Daily Star article (October 29, 2007) on fast tracking for Radiologists. Demetris Patsios had taken nine months to get a temporary work permit and it would have taken approximately three more years to get landed immigrant status through the skilled worker program. Demetris was able to get nominated through the Provincal Nomination Program and had his immigration application approved in 10 days. The program allows the province to screen applicants for final approval by the Federal government and greatly speeds up the processing times.

Opportunities - You should do all of your employment searching in Canada before you enter the country looking for permanent residency. Visit the country and get help from family and friends in your job search. You should develop relationships with reputable employment agencies. You should have your qualifications reviewed for Canadian equivalency before you come to Canada and have potential employers review your qualifications and education before you make your entry for permanent residency. You should know about and take advantage of any programs which help you get Canadian experience.

Planning - Is a very important discipline for the immigrant and needs to be active at every stage of the process. The various plans could involve:

Plan a visit to Canada - It would be extremely valuable for you and your family to plan a visit to Canada before considering applying as an immigrant. The purpose of the visit would be:
  • View and experience various areas of the country
  • Experience the neighbourhoods, costs of accommodation friends and family, cultural associations
  • Experience the Canadian climate and social scene
  • Review all of costs of living such as fuel, transportation, food
  • Review employment opportunities with local employment agencies
  • Review social agencies and immigration assistance

Plan a job search - According to the Canadian Labour and business Centre, 2002 Viewpoints Survey the major obstacles in hiring foreign-trained workers was:
  • cultural differences
  • too difficult to recruit abroad
  • lack of Canadian experience
  • difficulty in assessing foreign credentials
  • language difficulties

The first item of cultural difference should be resolved over time as society becomes more diversified and used to differences and appreciates those differences as positive influences in the workplace. Companies are not being asked to recruit abroad as much as immigrants are asked to do their job search in Canada. The Provincial nominee program helps companies find the proper candidates in their home countries.

Lack of Canadian experience can be rectified by working temporarily in Canada before coming over for permanent status. If you cannot work temporarily then do research on the job that you want to do and find out how it can related to Canadian experience by using firms specializing in that service.

The same goes for foreign credentials. Use firms that can provide you with the information on finding the correct assessment of credentials.

The area of language should be resolved before leaving your home country so that you can communicate with your employers. Canada is not an easy country to live in if you do not know either of the official languages. You should be upgrading your English language skills in the years prior to moving to Canada and you should be testing those skills against the requirements of the immigration points system.

You can overcome many of these challenges by: maintaining your own cultural identity but also integrating into Canadian society, doing as much research in your host country before coming to Canada, having your credentials and education verified before coming to Canada and having an agent of reference in your host country, having a professional resume, being able to conduct a job interview by practicing with friends, family, teachers; and practicing your English and testing yourself. (Plan for entry into Canada- refer to the section – "Your First Day in Canada")

Plan to apply as an immigrant through one of the various routs -- skilled worker, foreign worker, provincial nomination, Canadian Experience Class or student. The government has a mechanism where you can find out how many points you qualify for by doing an on-line self assessment. The web site for this practice assessment is:

http://www.cic.gc.gc.ca/english/skilled/assess/index.html

Qualifications - As has been mentioned on frequent occasions in this book that the skilled worker assessment of education and work experience is only used for the calculation of points on the assessment. These points do not give you a job in Canada and you most likely will have to have your qualifications and education reviewed in Canada. The Canadian Information Centre for International Credentials web site at: www.cicic.ca has information on academic and occupational credentials for all of Canada. The centre does not provide equivalencies but it does give advice and refers immigrants to people who can help them.

Canadian Information Centre for International Credentials
95 St. Clair Avenue West, Suite 1106
Toronto, Ontario M4V 1N6
T: 416-962-9725 F: 416-962-9725
info@cicic.ca   www.cicic.ca

World Education Services will provide you with an evaluation of your education versus a provincial institution of learning. The contact email and web site are:
icesinfo@ola.bc.ca   www.ola.bc.ca/ices

Each province has a regulatory body that oversees the various professions such as medical doctors, nurses, accountants, engineers, etc. You should contact the regulatory body if you want to have your qualifications reviewed.

References - You should have references from your native country for your work experience and education. These references should be able to provide detailed information on your experience and education. A written reference is satisfactory as long as there is personal contact information. You should also have references such as those given by people who are in a religious order, a lawyer, professionals, bankers, investment holders.

Skilled Immigrant Permanent Status - A skilled worker is a person who has the skill, qualifications, education, and experience that is desired by Canada in order to immigrate here. The individual needs to apply and fill out a skills assessment and is scored on their entries. The individual is also applying for permanent Canadian residency. Be aware that the skills

assessment does not give you a job in Canada. You must go through the appropriate assessment agencies, schools, licensing bodies, employers, etc. in order to obtain employment. The six selection factors in the skilled worker program are: education, work experience, language proficiency in English or French, age, arranged employment in Canada, adaptability including spouse's education and family relationships. The skilled immigrant must score over 70 to pass the assessment. Remember that this score does not entitle you to a job in Canada. The sole purpose of the assessment is to qualify you for immigration to Canada. You need to validate your education and qualifications with agencies, educational institutions, licensing bodies and employers before they are accepted in Canada.

Taxes - Canada has a relatively high level of taxation and is higher than the U.S., but not as high as the Scandanavian countries. With this relatively high level of taxes you get a universal health care system and a relatively moderate cost of university education based against many countries in the world. Grade and high school are free unless you want your child to attend private school. Taxes are federal, provincial, and municipal. Federal and provincial sales taxes and hidden luxury taxes are placed on alcohol, cigarettes and gasoline. Each province has a sales tax which is paid when you purchase goods and services. Sales tax consists of a 6% federal tax and an 8% provincial tax. Don't forget this tax when you are making a purchase on anything but food (prepared fast food is taxed) because it amounts to a substantial amount of money particularly on large consumer items like furniture, appliances and cars. Alberta is the only province that does not have a provincial sales tax. On top of your taxes you will be required to pay Canada Pension Plan and Employment Insurance which provides you with a small pension upon retirement and protects you with a salary for a period of time if you become unemployed.

Some cities have excellent public transportation systems which are partially funded by taxpayers but there will always be a charge for the rider. It is highly recommended that the new immigrant use public transit because of the high cost of buying a car, insurance, gas and parking that would have to be absorbed.

A requirement is that every new immigrant brings in $10168 Canadian if he/she is single and $18,895 for a family of four. This sum is to provide for new immigrants and their families for the initial six month period in Canada. Many Canadians would look at that figure and say to double it, particularly if the immigrant had to search for and find a job in his/her chosen field. Many immigrants have run out of money during their job search and had to take a job well below their stature in life and became very frustrated and saddened by their experience in Canada. The guideline levels are in line with the defined Canadian poverty level lines for singles and a family of four which look at $19,261 for a single person and $36,247 for a family of four in 2002 figures. We may be leading immigrants to think that they have adequate funds to support themselves and their families for a long period of time while the adults search for jobs. If the individual or family did not have family support they would be in financial trouble in a short period of time if they could not find work. We think that the financial guidelines should be reviewed with the goal of providing income for a single person or family for one year in Canada without employment and be well above the poverty line guidelines.

Whether this starts to reduce the number of people who qualify for immigration may be a factor, but we need to bear in mind the responsibility that we have as a nation to ensure that new immigrants are not driven into financial problems in their first few years in Canada.

Unwelcome - You may at times feel unwelcome in Canada. This feeling may be totally opposite to the impressions that you were given in your home country by the Canadian Consulate or Embassy. Some of these feelings may present themselves to you by the border agents when entering Canada. This unwelcome feeling could continue as you deal with various government agencies upon your arrival in Canada. The unwelcome feeling could again appear in you community or neighbourhood.

It can seem as though the only friendly place that you feel comfortable is your own community in a large city like Toronto. This is why immigrants are moving in large numbers to areas where they can join their relatives and friends.

The problem with immigrant growth in urban centres is that the supply of jobs is being challenged by the domestic and immigrant population and there may eventually be a scarcity of jobs in the urban areas. Canada's high degree of multiculturalism in its urban areas have made it more welcoming for the immigrant from a cultural standpoint but the job prospects may not be as good as some cities in western Canada.

The multicultural population in some parts of Canada is not as deep as it is in the major urban centres of Toronto and Vancouver. New Canadians may feel somewhat isolated until more immigrants make the choice of moving to Western Canada. Multiculturalism stimulates understanding and promotes the living together of many diversified peoples wherever it exists in the country. As far as government services are concerned, we will be seeing more and more different cultures holding positions in government and immigration and this will change unwelcome to welcome.

Some Canadians may not fully understand the full contribution that immigrants are making to this country in terms of cultural and economic stimulus. Also in poor economic times some Canadians may look on immigration as a complicating factor. Every-one has to come together to realize that attracting skilled and hard-working immigrants is the only way that Canada will compete globally and support its standard of living.

Visit - it is extremely important that you visit Canada before you choose to settle here as a permanent resident. On this trip you can enjoy the beauty, attractions, multicultural life of Canada along with doing a lot of research and planning on your trip. This research done both at home and during your visit will spare you from any unpleasant surprises and give you a realistic picture of what to expect if you decide to come to Canada. Have friends and relatives give advice on costs, location, job opportunities, agencies and services, qualification measurement, etc so that all of this work is done before you leave your home country.

World Wide Web - You have as much information available to you as a person living in Canada with the help of the worldwide web. This book has given you many of the web sites containing valuable information that will help you. Use this information to create a plan for immigrating to Canada that will include proper documentation, advice, financial resources, a cost of living and an occupation that fits your skills and talent. Conduct your own research before you arrive in Canada as an immigrant. You will find that it's a job in itself but it will make life much easier once you arrive.

X symbolizes the right to vote - An X is the normal method of marking a ballot

in Canada for all three levels of government and any referendums that occur. The right to vote is only available to Canadian citizens. The right to vote for your candidate and platform will become a powerful tool for all immigrants as they qualify for permanent residency. There are no exclusionary tactics practiced in this country on who can vote once you get citizenship and you are also allowed to place your name for nomination at various levels of government if you pass the party's requirement. As immigrants gain in number and power there will be changes to how they are treated coming into the country and living in Canada because their voice of diverse experience will influence and shape the Canadian perspective of the future.

Yes - Canada needs your skills and experience and culture to grow our country. If we do not

treat you with the respect and dignity that you deserve then we as a nation lose out in the competitive world economy. Our government needs to look at how we treat our immigrants and start changing our ways and not wait for the multicultural community to voice their complaints. We need to look at our border entry points and government services and treat the immigrant like a customer rather than a security risk. We can protect our borders while at the same time strengthening our nation to become the best country in the world for everyone.

Zero Problems - if you use the A to Z planner we would hope that you encounter zero

problems in your goal of immigrating successfully and happily to Canada.

Chapter Twenty-One
Conclusion

It's been my observation through 30+ years in Canada -- as a citizen and business owner – that unfortunately many immigrants land here with the wrong perception. Too many newcomers arrive ill-equipped, misinformed, and unprepared. As a result, they often flounder.

If they choose to stay in Canada, many new immigrants end up living far below their capabilities, in a field unrelated to their training. And if they return to their home country, they do so with shattered dreams, empty pockets and bitter memories of the experience.

But this kind of outcome need not occur at all. It's completely unnecessary and totally avoidable.

The certain way of avoiding this pitfall is getting access to information, or more specifically, *accurate information*. With the right information at hand, the candidate should have a realistic picture, rather than an incorrect perception of life in Canada.

Every potential immigrant needs to be:
    A. Aware of the challenges, obstacles and limitations -- as well as the possibilities in Canada.
    B. Sufficiently armed with the tools and information to overcome any bump on the immigration path.

That's been my dominant intention throughout these pages. I want to help familiarize, inform, educate, and guide potential and new immigrants to help minimize the struggles and ease their transition to life in Canada.

Before coming to Canada, there are certain things you need to know and specific actions you need to take in order to give yourself and your family the best opportunity. Once here, you need to get established and adapt to your new surroundings.

Ultimately the value of your immigration experience will be based on two keys:

1. Your ability to find gainful employment utilizing your skills and...

2. Your ability to adapt and integrate into Canadian society, while retaining the cultural roots that are important to you.

You've already taken an important step by reading this book. What you hold in your hands is critically important reading for every individual considering Canada as a long-term destination. It's a valuable preparatory tool. Reading, comprehending, and taking action on the information presented here will give every potential immigrant a significant advantage. The insights and knowledge gained will better prepare and position you to obtain the results you intend.

What Every Candidate Should Do

There are several key action steps every serious candidate should take. These include:

• Learning or improving one's English language skills

• Having your education and qualifications documentation certified and translated to English

• Researching opportunities, industries and regions and learning about the Canadian economy-much of this work can be done before you come to Canada

• Ensuring that there are jobs available in the area where you are looking to settle in the field that you have chosen

• Planning a course of action

• Visiting Canada to gain first-hand experience of life here

• Contacting potential employers, placement agencies and social service agencies who offer help to new immigrants before you leave your home country and during your initial arrival in Canada

• For the business investor reading the business chapter and using the information to better guide your business opportunities in Canada

Above all else, it's important to maintain a positive, enthusiastic attitude. If one lead fails to produce a positive outcome, simply move onto to another. Don't let frustration get the best of you. Persistence always pays dividends.

Immigrants have long played a key role in Canada's growth, development and standard of living. But the key is that immigrants will be even more vital over the next couple of decades as the domestic population ages and the birth rate declines. Canada needs immigrants and for those with serious intentions of moving to Canada they should position themselves to respond to this need. In addition, the emergence of developing nations and the global marketplace makes it a much more competitive environment for worldwide human resources.

Your best bet is to be adequately informed so you can make knowledgeable decisions. Know the rules, requirements, and procedures -- and follow them. Research, prepare and plan your course of action. Do that and you've significantly improved your odds.

What Businesses Could Do

Businesses need to look beyond any perceived negatives in hiring immigrants such as a lack of Canadian experience, or speaking with a foreign accent. In an increasingly competitive global market for human talent, international experience is an asset. An inside knowledge of specific customs and native language could prove invaluable to a growing business looking to penetrate ethnic communities within Canada, as well as international markets.

But it requires businesses to be more flexible and open to the possibilities that emerge as a result. Given the opportunity, capable talent shines irrespective of origin. All that's required is more long-term, strategic thinking on the part of the business community and the flexibility to look beyond traditional horizons as the answer to the growing demand for skilled people.

Utilize the skills and international experience and increase the value of your human resource assets through training. English language training could prove to be a valuable addition offered by growing organizations.

What Canada Can Do

It's important for Canada and Canadians to recognize these trends. It's a much different world today than it was 30 years ago. Canada needs to acknowledge these global shifts and make the changes that will keep this country strong and competitive. Why not be on the leading edge, rather than the tail end?

It's my opinion that changes in Canada's immigration policy and procedures are inevitable. Change will be necessary in order to keep pace. But this kind of fundamental change doesn't happen overnight. Typically it's an evolutionary process that takes years to come to fruition. An example would be the changes to immigration policy meant to provide Canada with the skilled immigrants that it needs to grow and prosper but a points system that does not focus on trade skills and skills required by small business. The points system also rewards bilingualism when many jobs under pressure do not require that ability.

By assuming the role of international recruiting, Human Resources Canada could be taking a more direct and proactive approach to matching the labour market needs of Canadian businesses with the skills and experience of those who want to come here.

In the area of business investment an article in the Toronto Daily Star titled, " Visa rules costing Canada billions", says that a Conference Board of Canada study found that some of our current visa rules could inhibit investment in Canada. A solution offered by the Conference Board included a 10 year multiple-entry visa that could be transferred to a new passport. The United States has a similar program. In an answer to the suggestion of the Conference Board Citizenship and Immigration Canada says that they are reducing wait times for visas and offers multiple entry visas.

Ultimately we all have to ask ourselves if we are doing enough to reduce the backlog of immigrant applications and speed up business investor visas. Doesn't our future as a country depend on our world class response to these issues? Are we just continuing in our old traditional approach and watch the rest of the world move past us? We first need to recognize that there are problems with our immigration policy before we can fix them. Perhaps what comes out of reading this book is that we can and must do better for all of those immigrants who want to work in this country and businessmen who want to invest in Canada.

271

What Does It All Mean To You?

Canada is a wonderful country. It's a nation that's capable of providing you and your family with comfort, opportunity, peace, freedom, and plenty of wide-open spaces.

In order for things to work out positively what you need is an accurate, up-to-date, realistic picture of Canada today. And you need to hear it from someone who has been in your shoes -- so you can make the right decision for you. It's been my intention through these pages to deliver that information to you as objectively as possible.

When I think of Canada and all it has to offer, I'm reminded of a valuable 'life lesson' I first heard a number of years ago. I'm paraphrasing, but the gist of the message is clear in the following statement: *"The universe feeds every bird on the planet, but it never delivers the food to the nest.* The opportunity in Canada is yours -- seize it.

But what you need to know is that opportunities are not always obvious and seldom are they presented on a silver platter. In reality, your results are essentially up to you. Recognize the choices and opportunities available. Then strategize and implement your well-researched plan to take advantage of those opportunities for new immigrants to Canada.

What you get out of the entire process of applying as an immigrant and coming to Canada is largely based on your attitude, knowledge, and how much effort you're willing to put into it. Nothing in life worth pursuing comes without some effort. You can't just show up in Canada and expect to find utopia here. It doesn't work that way, regardless of what others might have told you. But armed with the truth, you are now able to distinguish fact from fantasy.

It has been an interesting journey from where we began on page one to where we are now at the book's conclusion. In that time, there have been changes to some of the information shared, particularly on the economy.

As this book goes to press, Canada, like other countries is experiencing the effects of the global recession. While it's encouraging to note that international experts have collectively declared Canada as one of the strongest G20 nations financially, the worldwide economic challenges continue to affect many people and industries in Canada.

In the interests of providing accurate and current information for my readers, I wanted to reference these two changes that are important enough to significantly impact new Canadians and potential immigrants:

1. With the global economic slowdown, there are massive job cuts throughout the entire Canadian manufacturing and resource industries. Canadian automotive manufacturing has been particularly affected. I do not expect any significant recovery until the world economy -- and the economy of the United States in particular -- starts to recover. The impact on the North American automotive market may be long-term in nature because of excess capacity and the growing need to produce more energy-efficient vehicles.

2. Some groups are lobbying the government to reduce the number of immigrants entering Canada in reaction to this economic slowdown and rising unemployment. However, the fact remains that it takes up to four years to gain entry to Canada and many of the skills required by Canada are long term in nature. Indications are that the recovery will be in place within a three year horizon. Immigration will have a positive effect on any long-term

recovery because it provides the necessary skills and people to drive Canada's economic growth into the future.

Apart from being a very time consuming project, every aspect of research that went into the completion of this book was a challenging experience. It took more than a year of intense research and focus to present the facts as clearly as possible. It is my hope that the effort has been a worthwhile endeavor for prospective immigrants to Canada over the coming years.

I cannot overemphasize the motivating force behind the writing of this book. It has been my innermost urge to present the information from a factual and critical perspective. My intention is to make individuals and families from any country who may be considering immigrating to Canada, to be fully armed with relevant and accurate information to help them make an informed decision. It's my hope you have found the contents of this book to be as informative and helpful as intended.

My singular, most important recommendation to prospective immigrants is that if you have the opportunity to visit Canada, you should do so. This will enable you to make an assessment based on your own personal experience and circumstances. In the event you are unable to visit Canada prior to deciding to immigrate, I strongly recommend that you conduct your own due diligence and arrive at an informed decision. Too many immigrants have been unprepared, shocked at the reality of their actual experience upon arriving in Canada.

You now have a solid background and understanding of what is involved in immigrating to Canada. You've learned what it takes, where the best opportunities exist today, and how to give yourself the best possible shot at suitable employment, happiness, comfort and a successful future in Canada.

Whatever you decide, you can rest assured that your decision will be based on a foundation of accurate and objective information.

May you find whatever it is in life that you're looking for.

Sincerely,

Terry Sawh

Bibliography and References

Toward 2025 Assessing Ontario's long-term Outlook, Ministry of Finance, Province of Ontario

Securing Tomorrow's Prosperity –Alberta Government, Summer 2005

Immigration and small Business Ideas to better Respond to Canada's Skills and labour shortage, Canadian Federation of Independent Business

Guberman, Garson, Bush- Immigration lawyers

Canadavisa.com

Campbell, Cohon –Canadian Immigration lawyers

Provincial Outlook Long-Term Economic Forecast 2007 The Conference Board of Canada

Regional Occupations under Pressure List Government of Canada Web-site

TD Bank Financial Group TD Economics Regional Economic Forecast

Canada's new Government Announces new measures to help Ontario Employers interested in hiring foreign workers- Government of Canada web-site

The Oil Price Mirage- Pierre Lemieux

Immigration to Canada and finding Employment by Tariq Nadeem

Toronto Star

GTA Economy lagging rest of country, study shows, Tuesday, July 17th 2007

Ontario to hand pick overseas workers, July 17th 2007

Three part series Lost in Immigration June 2007

Invest in Canada-government of Canada Web-site

Toronto Daily Star, Monday, October 29th, 2007, Radiologist rides fast track to Job

The Foundation for Learning, Ontario Government Web-site

Foreign worker program HRSDC

www.hireimmigrants.ca-a website containing valuable information for employers and immigrants

Alberta, Canada A Wealth of Opportunity ministry of Alberta Economic Development

Immigrant settlement and Orientation Resources Toronto Public Library

Ontario government web site, Ministry of Labour, Occupational Health and Safety Act

Alberta government web-site, Employment, Immigration and Industry, Occupational Health and Safety Act 2006

Immigrants need not Apply, Canada barring highly skilled immigrants from practicing professions and trades, by Andrew Brouwer, The Maytree Foundation

Citizenship and Immigration Canada Facts and Figures basis of graph material

Ontario's growth limited by rising dollar, National Post, Aug. 2, 2007

More Americans heading north, Toronto Daily Star, August 6th , 2007

Ontario Driver Licensing web-site: www.mto.gov.on.ca

Trade and Commerce Magazine, volume 102, Number 2, Summer 2007

Toronto Daily Star, Lawyer blamed for client's woes, Monday, August 13, 2007

www.people for education

www.pulsehr.com

www.paceimmigration.com

www.newstartintoronto.com

www.camsc.ca

Immigration Trends 2006 Multiculturalism and Immigration Branch, B.C. Government

www.ag.gov.bc.ca/immigration

www.peopleforeducation.com

National Post, Friday, August 24th, 2007, Mid-size matters, The Five most liveable cities.

www.hireimmigratns.ca

www.paceimmigration.com/canadian/jobs

www.hireimmigrants.ca

The Toronto Daily Star, Monday, September 10, 2007, Province fast-tracks hiring abroad

The Globe and mail, Tuesday, September 11th, Newcomers have a hard time finding work in Quebec.

www.canadianbusiness.com

msn.careerbuilder.com

www.immigranttoolbox.ca

www.hireimmigrants.ca

www.toronto.ca/toront-facts/diversity.htm

The Toronto Daily Star, Thursday, September 20th, 2007, Tough to fit in, award winner says

Profit, Your Guide to Business Success, October 2007,Canada's Emerging Growth Companies 2007

www.drmichaelpilon.com/mdshortage.htm

www.hireimmigrants.ca/articles/bornInChina.htm

multiculturalism policy falling behind the times, Toronto Daily Star, May 29th, 2007

Immigrants need not apply, Andrew Brouwer, The Maytree Foundation

Reference to Page 111 in the Index

Diversity in Canada, Canadian Heritage, Jacques Paquette, director General, Multiculturalism and Human Rights Branch, Canadian Heritage

www.poss.ca

Immigrants Work, HR Professional, October/November 2007

Toronto Daily Star, October 30th, 2007, Work Permit regulations prove costly for Canada

The Globe and Mail, Wednesday, October 31, 2007, Flaherty targets lowest tax rate in G7

The Toronto Daily Star, Wednesday, November 7th, 2007, Mining Industry faces shortage of Skilled Staff

The Toronto Daily Star, Friday, October 26th, 2007, We're Canadian and we're Muslim

www.rockportinstitute.com/resumes.html

www.Job-Interview.net

www.cvtips.com/job_interview.html

www.entercanada.ca/blog/2007/07/continuing-problems-with-immigration.html

A Newcomer's Guide to Services in Peel, Halton and Dufferin

www.credentials.gc.ca Government of Canada Foreign Credentials Referral Services

Toronto Daily Star, Wednesday, December 5th, Census of New Immigrants

Ottawa Citizen, Tuesday, February 6, 2007, Canada's Major cities Need Special Attention"

The Globe and Mail, Wednesday, Dec.12, 2007" Cities in global competition for Talent

Toronto Daily Star, Temporary Workers Seek Holiday Pay, Tuesday, December 18,2007

Canadian Immigrant web-site, thecanadianimmigrant.com

www.ontarioimmigration.ca/English

www.canada.com/topics

www.workersactioncentre.com

Toronto Daily Star, Saturday, January 26, 2008, "Smaller is better for Immigrants"

www.en.wikipedia.org/wiki/Canadian_immigration_and_refugee_law

www.canada-law.com/familyclass.htm

Toronto Daily Star, Monday, February 11th, 2008, "Immigration wait-time surge angers Liberals" Page A 4

National Post, "Canada's 50 Best Managed Companies" Tuesday, February, 12, 2008

www.triec.ca/index

www.hrsdc.gc.ca/en/employment/ei/index.shtml

www.tdcanadatrust.com/rsp/introrsp.jsp

www.canadaonline.about.com/cs/retirementfinance/g/rpp.htm

www.tdcanadatrust.com/rsp/rsp_faq.jsp

www.retireplan.about.com/cs/retirement/aa_defined_a5.htm

www.forums.canadianbusiness.com

www.tdcanadatrust.com/resp/edu_planning.jsp

www.cra-arc.gc.ca/tax/individuals/topics/rrsp/hbp/menu-e.html

www.calgarytransit.com/html/fares.html

www.edmonton.ca/portal/server/

www.city.vancouver.bc.ca/residents.htm

www.gotransit.com

www.mississauga.ca/portal/residents/publictransit

www.toronto.ca/ttc/index.htm

www.microskills.ca/contact.html

www.credentials.gc.ca

www.ogov.newswire.ca/ontario

www.cfsontario.ca/english/general.php

www.is2007.ca/IS/press.php?art=2007winnerprofiles

www.hireimmigrants.ca/articles/FirmsDoomediftheyfailtotapdiversetalentppl.htm

Toronto Star, Thursday, February 21st, 2008, Best Employers for New Canadians

The National Post, Saturday, March 1, 2008 " After Hours Canada's 50 Best Managed Companies"

National Post, Thursday, February 14th, 2008, " Jobless rate highest fro African immigrants, by Charles Lewis.

The Toronto Sun, Call of the West, March 9th, 2008

The Toronto Sun, Lack of workers hurting Ontario's small business, March 9, 2008

www.newswire.ca/en/releases/mmnr/cmhc20051215/

www.akcanada.com

Macleans Magazine, Volume 121 Number 14, April 14, 2008, 'Good for Canada'? We certainly hope so.

National Post, Thursday, April 3, 2008, Integration a challenge, professor says

Toronto Daily Star, Thursday, April 3, 2008, Visible minorities gaining

www.ohrc.on.ca

National Post, Invited into Inner Circle, Wednesday, April, 9th, 2008

www.torontopolice.on.ca/publicinformation

www.culture.ca

www.immigration-quebec.gouv.qc.ca

www.akcanada.com/lic_vancouver.cfm

www.culture.ca

www.pch.gc.ca

Toronto Daily Star, Lost in Migration, Sunday, May 11th,2008.

Canadian Newcomer Magazine- March/April 2008

Toronto Daily Star, Monday, May 12, 2008, "Aussies fix immigrant woes"

The Globe and Mail, Monday May 19th, 2008, "Ottawa looks to Mexico to ease labour crunch"

Toronto Daily Star, Foreign-trained doctors to get a break in Ontario" Saturday, June 7th, 2008

Nation building through immigration: workforce skills comes out on top, Nik Nanos, Nanos Policy Options, June 2008

hireimmigrants.ca, e-tips 105, Evaluating New Canadians requires new tactics

Toronto daily Star, "Employers calling immigration shots, critics maintain" Wednesday, August 13th, 2008

Toronto Daily Star, Licensing offer draws few takers, Thursday, August 14th, 2008

www.tiec.ca/index

The Globe and Mail, "Immigrants bypassing Toronto to follow money west, study finds" Thursday, Sept. 2008

Macleans, October 13th 2008, Diversity or Death

Hireimmigrants.ca, a TRIEC Program, Promising Practices and Tips for Integrating Skilled Immigrants Into the Workplace

Public Policy Forum, Bringing employers Into the Immigration Debate: Survey and Roundtable (2004) Sandra Lopes, Research Associate and Yves Poisson, Director of Special Projects

msn.careerbuilder.com, 7 things you should never do in a job search

www.sbinfocanada.about.com

www.canadaone.com

The Toronto daily Star, Saturday, October 18th, 2008 GTA's Top 75 Employers

Hireimmigrants.ca, Workshop: Creating Metrics, What gets measured gets managed

The Toronto Daily Star, Saturday, October 25th, 2008 economy will need more immigrants

www.graybridgemalkam.com, Newsletter on integrating non-traditional talent into your organization

CEP Newswires, Mon., Nov. 3rd. 2008, Conference Board sees Gloomy Year Ahead for Canadian Economy, Geoff Matthews

The Globe and Mail, Wednesday, January 14th, 2009, The 50 Best Employers to Work For, Wallace Immen

www.successbc.ca/eng/component/option.com_contact

www.reach.ca

www.flsc.ca/en/about/contact.asp

Toronto Daily Star, Foreign-trained lawyers hold their breath for help, Thursday January 25th 2009 by Paul Dalby

Globe and mail, Monday, January 26th, 2009 report on Diversity

www.loonlounge.com

www.hireimmigrants.ca, Resource Room- Success Stories- Mount Sinai Hospital

www.msn.careerbuilder.com/jobseeker/careerbytes/quiz

www.msn.careerbuilder.com/Article/MSN

Chapter Twenty Three
Definitions

Business Immigrants
There are three classes of Business Immigrant to Canada

1. Investors-must show that they have business experience, a net worth of Canadian $800,000 and be prepared to make an investment of Canadian $400,000.

2. Entrepreneurs- these business immigrants will own and manage a business in Canada. They must have business experience a net worth that is above Canadian $300,000.

3. Self-employed persons- these people must be able to create their own job. They are also expected to enhance the cultural, artistic or athletic attributes of Canadians. Web site info: www.enterprisetoronto.com

Businessmen
-a businessperson visits Canada to meet with other business people. A temporary resident visa may be required depending upon your home country. Businesspeople may be better off stating that they are in Canada to conduct business meetings with associates rather than stating that they are here to conduct business which may leave the border people enquiring about taking work from resident Canadians.

Canadian Citizenship
-people who are permanent residents and have been living in Canada for three years or more can apply for Canadian citizenship. An application needs to be filled out plus a test on your knowledge of Canada and finally an oath ceremony.

CIC- Citizenship and Immigration Canada

-This government department is the main regulating agency and information centre for people immigrating to Canada. Information on forms, definitions and guidance is available on their website:

www.cic.gc.ca

Driver's License

-a Provincial Driver's License is required to drive on the Province's roads. There may be some reciprocal agreements that allow you to drive a car if you have a driver's license in your own country for a period of time such as a year but after you must pass through the Province's licensing program. Refer to driver's license and the government web-site

:www.mto.gov.on.ca

Family Class Immigration

-this type of immigration is aimed at reuniting families in Canadian homes and would consist of bringing family members from a home country to be with relatives in Canada

Foreign workers

-the federal government's Temporary foreign Worker Program allows foreign workers who are eligible to work in Canada for a specific period of time if employers can prove that there are no suitable people to do the work who are permanent residents of Canada. Employers form all types of commerce can find foreign workers who have the skills that business requires to meet shortages in the labour market. These workers are not trying for permanent residency but in most cases return to their home country. A Labour Market Opinion(LMO) is usually required and requested by the employer before the foreign worker is allowed to file a work permit.

Health Insurance

- in Ontario-OHIP-Immigrants who are permanent residents and their families receive universal health care. That is free medical treatment. Some provinces stipulate a three month waiting period so the immigrant would have to get health care coverage for them and their families during that period. Foreign students and not classed as permanent residents and need to provide their own private health care.

HRSDC

-Human Resources Development Canada- a government body that performs such functions as Labour Market Opinions (LMO's). This government department helps develop the labour force and people policies of all of the workers in Canada.

IELTS Test

-International English Language Testing System web site: http://www.ielts.org
This test tests your English language ability for assessment on the points system

Immigration Consultant

-an immigration consultant may be in your home country or may reside in Canada. In your home country an immigration consultant is not regulated by any body in Canada and is an independent businessman who wants to earn money by helping you immigrate to Canada. His or her advice may or may not be with your best interests in mind. Beware of any consultant that promises you a job in Canada or a fast track immigration because they know some-one at the Canadian embassy or consulate.

Immigration consultants in Canada may or may not be members of the Canadian Society of Immigration Consultants. Of the 6,000 consultants in Canada only about 1600 are members of the Canadian Society of Immigration Consultants which is not a regulatory nor disciplinary body.

Immigration Lawyer

-an immigration lawyer is a lawyer who gives advice to clients on immigration matters. All lawyers in Canada are regulated by their respective bar associations and are licensed by them. Lawyers could be disbarred for giving their clients fraudulent information. The client also has the recourse of filing a complaint against their lawyer through the provincial association. These may be two good reasons why the selection of an immigration lawyer is superior to an immigration consultant who are not regulated in Canada. Whatever you do you should get information on your lawyer or consultant, ensure their qualifications and get references through family and friends.

Intra Company transfer of professionals

-Companies wishing to transfer individuals to Canada from foreign operations use this process of moving these professionals around the world. If a company wants to move a foreigner to a Canadian operation the company usually has to go through the labour market opinion route and they have to show that they have advertised in Canada for a suitable candidate. If they are successful in having their foreign candidate picked the individual would get a work permit and a temporary resident visa to stay and work in Canada for a specific period of time

Labour Market Opinion(LMO)

-an opinion given by Human Resources Development Canada on whether a candidate is taking a job away from a Canadian or that there is a legitimate need for an immigrant to have a specific job that cannot be filled by a Canadian. The company requesting the foreign applicant must show that they have advertised in Canada for a qualified Canadian to fill the vacancy.

NAFTA

-the North American Free Trade Agreement- Chapter 16 of the agreement between Canada, the United States and Mexico allows for the temporary entry of businesspeople to each of these countries. These conditions merge together with the rules that control the movement of goods and services between the three countries. Any experience at the border crossing between the United States and Canada might give a businessman the impression that there isn't any agreement on the free movement of businesspeople between the companies. If you declare that you are going to either country to conduct business then be prepare for a list of questions to answer. Ensure that you do not give the impression that you are entering the workforce of the country being visited or that you are receiving pay in the country that you are visiting. Anyone wishing to reside and work in one of the three countries has to go through the appropriate work permit process.

National Occupation Classification List (NOC)- a classification list that identifies the kind of work that you did in your home country versus jobs in Canada. It allows you to use titles and gives you points on the skilled worker program if your experience matches a particular job and duties in Canada.

Permanent Resident Card
-this card is given to people who have completed the Canadian immigration process and have obtained permanent resident status but are not yet Canadian citizens.

Permanent Resident Visa- it is a document that allows a person to live and work in Canada and gives the holder a Permanent Resident card to carry as identification   A person who is a Permanent Resident may apply for Canadian Citizenship after residing in Canada for over 3 year

Occupational Health and Safety Act and WHMIS
-each province has an act to protect workers and have them work in safe conditions and be informed about their workplace. The act also shows how and Joint Health and Safety Committed is composed and the responsibilities of the Committee members. WHMIS stands for Workplace Health Material Information Sheets which are information sheets on all chemicals stored and used in the employees' workplace. A file is maintained so that employees and supervisors can determine the correct handling, storage and clean-up of any chemical.

Provincial Nominee Program
-persons who immigrate to Canada have the skills and experience necessary to contribute to the national and provincial economies of Canada. They are ready to live in Canada and establish themselves as permanent residents of Canada. The Ontario Provincial Nominee program is new in 2007 and is employer driven in that employers are the driving force in the program and are looking for people with the skills that they need. The employer is pre-screened by the Provincial government, the position is approved, and the employer provides the nominee with and application package. The province sends suitable names to the Federal government and final approval is issued after final security and health clearance. The appropriate web-site is www.ontarioimmigration.ca.

.Refugee Status- Refugees and people needing protection are those people who fear that if they return to their home country they will be persecuted or put at risk. Canada provides refugee status to thousands of people in keeping with its history of treating people in need. Groups and individuals can sponsor refugees from abroad who pas the qualifications to come to Canada. You can seek protection as a refugee as a Convention refugee or as a person in need

of protection by applying with-in Canada at a CIC office or at an entry point. A Convention refugee cannot return to their home country because of fear of race, religion, political opinion, nationality or membership in a specific social group. A person in need of protection would be a person who may be submitted to torture, injury or death if they return home. Refugees seeking status because of what they consider to be economic circumstances in their home country do not have success under this category because it does not fit the requirements and would apply to millions of people wanting to come to Canada. Ensure that you have all documentation required if you plan on applying for refugee status.

Regional Occupations Under Pressure List
-the Federal Government has started to produce a list of jobs in demand in the provinces of Alberta, British Columbia and Ontario in order to try to address the problem of skilled labour shortages in the respective provinces. The appropriate web-site for this information is; www.immigration.ca/jobs-underpressure.asp

Social Insurance Number(SIN)
-a social insurance number is issued by the Federal Government and is required to work in Canada. It tracks each person's taxes and contributions to various programs such as: Canada Pension and Unemployment Insurance. .

Skilled Worker- is a person who applies through the Skilled Worker Program for permanent residency in Canada

Study Permits
-study permits are special permits issued to foreign students specifying their school of acceptance and the time period of their studies

Temporary Resident Visa
- (TRV's)- visitors to Canada including some tourists depending on their source country, students, and workers, may need a TRV from Citizenship and Immigration Canada in order to enter the country.

Tourists
-an individual coming to Canada as a visitor- a temporary resident visa may be required depending upon your home country.

Work Permits
- a work permit allows a person to live and work in Canada for a limited period of time. The type of work that the individual can perform is also regulated by the work permit. The individual must leave the country at the time of expiration or make all of the necessary arrangements to have their stay extended.

Index

A

O

P

Q

qualifications and credentials, 265
Quebec
   economic growth patterns, 74
   health care, 156
   housing prices, 182
   immigration offices, 29–30
   language skills, 12, 218
   multiculturalism, 11
   permanent French speaking residents, 56
   settlement services, 215–218
   tourism, 240–242

R

racism, 17
real estate, 181–183. *See also* housing
recession, 272. *See also* economics
recreation, 17, 172–174. *See also* tourism
recreation occupations, 84, 85
recruiting immigrant employees, 247–248, 249, 252, 271
references for work and education, 265
refugees, 41
Regina, 220–221
Registered Education Savings Plan (RESP), 181
regulated professions, 87–97
religion, 119, 229–232
renting property, 182–183
researching the possibilities, 248
resident visas, 27–28. *See also* temporary worker visas and work permits
resumes, 23–24, 102–103, 107, 108–112
Retirement Savings Plans (RSP), 177, 179–181
Roman Catholics, 231
routes to immigration, 30–31
Royal College of Dental Surgeons of Ontario, 93–94

S

salary, 158, 160
sales and service occupations, 84
Saskatchewan
   agriculture, 53
   economic growth patterns, 10, 69, 71
   International Medical Graduate program, 89
   job growth, 9

visas, 27–28, 188. *See also* temporary worker visas and work permits
Vishnu Mandir, 229
visiting Canada, 101, 264, 267
voting, 163, 268

W

wages, 158, 160
wait times, 8–9, 42
Warda, George, 93
Waterloo, 240
weather conditions, 16–17
"Welcome to Canada - What You Should Know," 154
Western ESL Services, 191
Western provinces, 67, 69
Williams, Laura K., 130
wills, 185
Windsor, 219
Winnipeg, 71, 72, 220
winterizing cars, 17
work hours, 157
Workers' Action Centre, 159–161
workers' compensation, 135–136, 159
workers' rights, 159–161
Working in Canada Tool, 30–31, 101–102
workplace health and safety, 156–157, 159–161
Workplace Support Services Office, 189
World Education Services - Canada, 113–114, 146, 265
worldwide web, 267–268
wrongful dismissal, 131–132

Y

YMCA, 189, 190, 208–209, 213, 218–219
Young Drivers of Canada, 168
The Yukon, 75

About the Author:

Terry Sawh

Terry Sawh is the President and Owner of the Topnotch Group of Companies. Terry arrived in Canada 30 years ago from Guyana with $24 dollars in his pocket and a tremendous amount of enthusiasm and hope for a better future.

Terry has built Topnotch Employment Services Inc. from a small agency to a large employment and recruiting firm comprised of three divisions: Executive Staffing which places people in office positions of clerical, administrative, financial and accounting, customer service, IT and managerial. The Topnotch division handles general labour and light industrial along with fork-lift operator positions. The PRIMEtime+ division helps people over the age of 50 find employment and provides outplacement services for people affected by job re-structuring.

Terry is a certified supplier of CAMSC (Canadian Aboriginal Minority Suppliers' Council) which helps minority-owned and aboriginal Canadian businesses form relationships with large and medium- sized Canadian companies. Terry has been the Chairman for the Supply Committee of CAMSC since 2008. Terry is also a Certified Sales Professional (CSP).

Terry's work over the years on behalf of immigrants has placed him in competition for TRIEC's Immigrant Success Awards. Terry has recently been awarded to be one of the "Top 25 Immigrants in Canada" by Canadian Immigrant Magazine.

Terry's mission in life is to help members of minorities find employment and realize their dreams just as he was able to do. This goal was the reason why Terry wrote this book. Terry is active in business associations, local charities, service clubs and the Guyanese community. Terry resides with his wife, Hera, and his two children in Toronto.

Guy Tremblay
Researcher/Writer

Guy Tremblay is a Business Development Consultant with Topnotch Employment Services Inc. Guy initially started with Topnotch by developing the marketing programs for PRIMEtime+. PRIMEtime+ is a division of Topnotch specializing in finding work for people over 50 or helping in the outplacement of people affected by job re-structuring.

Guy was assigned by Terry Sawh to do the research, initial writing and lay-out of the book. Guy has over 30 years of experience in Physical Distribution and Inventory with ICI Paints Canada and the Glidden Paint Company of Canada. Guy has a B.A. in Economics from Laurentian University in Sudbury.